MONOGRAPHS OF THE
SOCIETY FOR RESEARCH IN
CHILD DEVELOPMENT

*Serial No. 230, Vol. 57, No. 6, 1992*

# DEVELOPMENT OF INFANTS WITH DISABILITIES AND THEIR FAMILIES: IMPLICATIONS FOR THEORY AND SERVICE DELIVERY

*Jack P. Shonkoff*
*Penny Hauser-Cram*
*Marty Wyngaarden Krauss*
*Carole Christofk Upshur*

**WITH COMMENTARY BY**
*Arnold J. Sameroff*

MONOGRAPHS OF THE SOCIETY FOR RESEARCH IN CHILD DEVELOPMENT
*Serial No. 230, Vol. 57, No. 6, 1992*

# CONTENTS

# ABSTRACT

SHONKOFF, JACK P.; HAUSER-CRAM, PENNY; KRAUSS, MARTY WYNGAARDEN; and UPSHUR, CAROLE CHRISTOFK. Development of Infants with Disabilities and Their Families: Implications for Theory and Service Delivery. With Commentary by ARNOLD J. SAMEROFF. *Monographs of the Society for Research in Child Development*, 1992, **57**(6, Serial No. 230).

This *Monograph* presents the results of a nonexperimental, longitudinal investigation of developmental change in 190 infants and their families after 1 year of early intervention services. The Early Intervention Collaborative Study (EICS), conducted in association with 29 community-based programs in Massachusetts and New Hampshire, was designed to assess correlates of adaptation in young children with disabilities and their families over time, to inform social policy by analyzing the influences of family ecology and formal services on child and family outcomes, and to generate conceptual models to guide further investigation.

The study sample (mean age at entry = 10.6 months) includes 54 children with Down syndrome, 77 with motor impairment, and 59 with developmental delays of uncertain etiology. Data were collected during two home visits (within 6 weeks of program entry and 12 months later) and included formal child assessments, observations of mother-child interaction, maternal interviews, and questionnaires completed independently by both parents as well as monthly service data collected from service providers.

Child and family functioning varied considerably. Developmental change in the children (psychomotor abilities, adaptive behavior, spontaneous play, and child-mother interaction skills) was influenced to some extent by gestational age and health characteristics, but the strongest predictor of change was the relative severity of the child's psychomotor impairment at study entry. Families demonstrated generally positive and stable adaptation (in terms of the effect of rearing a child with disabilities on the family, parenting stress, and social support), despite persistent challenges with respect to mother-child interaction and differences in reported stress between mothers and fathers. Documentation of services revealed that early intervention is a complex and multidimensional experience that spans multiple public and private systems. Vulnerable and resilient subgroups within the sample were identified, and different correlates of adaptive change were demonstrated. Results of data analyses suggest new perspectives on the study of early childhood disability. The implications of the findings for developmental theory and social policy are discussed.

# I. INTRODUCTION

Twenty-five years ago, young children with developmental disabilities generally faced a shortened life span and either inadequate custodial care or an isolated, home-bound existence. Beginning with the establishment of high-risk follow-up programs and early childhood demonstration projects in the late 1960s, and culminating in the enactment of the Education for All Handicapped Children Act Amendments of 1986 (Public Law [PL] 99-457), infants and toddlers with special needs and their families have gained increasing social and political visibility (Shonkoff & Meisels, 1990; Zigler & Berman, 1983). Under the provisions of the renamed Individuals with Disabilities Education Act (IDEA), special education for eligible children is now an entitlement beginning at 3 years of age, new federal incentives are available to encourage states to develop family-centered, community-based services for infants—even newborns—with disabilities, and greater collaboration between the health and the education sectors has become a policy mandate (Garwood, Fewell, & Neisworth, 1988; Hauser-Cram, Upshur, Krauss, & Shonkoff, 1988; Meisels, 1989; Smith & Strain, 1988). With this increase in public commitment, the press for accountability in the service arena has intensified, and the need for a revitalized research agenda has become increasingly clear (Krauss & Hauser-Cram, 1992).

Much has been written about the methodological and conceptual shortcomings of research on the development of children with disabilities and on the effects of early intervention services (Meisels, 1985; Shonkoff, Hauser-Cram, Krauss, & Upshur, 1988; Woodhead, 1988). The study presented in this *Monograph* was designed to address six specific inadequacies in the existing knowledge base. First, investigations of developmental change in children with disabilities have focused largely on differences in IQ or developmental quotients while neglecting other domains of competence and behavior that may be more valid ecologically and linked more closely to specific service objectives. Second, previous studies of participants in early intervention programs have focused primarily on developmental change in children, with little attention directed to the adaptive characteristics of their families

1

and virtually none to potential interactions between these two domains. Third, most research on children with disabilities and their families has focused on modal population characteristics (i.e., "the average child with Down syndrome" or "the typical parent of a handicapped child"), with relatively little empirical examination of differences among distinctive subgroups within and across these heterogeneous populations.

Fourth, research on children with disabilities has traditionally emphasized the identification of risk factors that predict poor outcome, with less attention directed to the elucidation of variables that predict positive adaptation for both children and their families. Fifth, most studies of service recipients have been cross sectional or have extended over relatively short time intervals, thereby providing limited empirical data that address questions about the stability of subgroup differences and the continuity of developmental adaptation over time. Sixth, much of the research on the efficacy of intervention has been conducted on demonstration projects or experimental models, yielding limited data on the effects of broad-based, publicly supported service systems.

The Early Intervention Collaborative Study (EICS) was established in 1985 to address three interrelated goals: (1) to enhance our understanding of variations in the development of young children with disabilities and in the adaptation of their families over time; (2) to contribute to the knowledge base that informs social policy by analyzing the mediating influences of family ecology and early intervention services on selected child and family outcomes; and (3) to generate conceptual models of child and family development to guide future research on children with special needs. Theoretically, the design of the study has been influenced by the transactional model of human development (Sameroff & Chandler, 1975), an ecological model of child and family functioning (Bronfenbrenner, 1979), and the concepts of vulnerability and resilience (Garmezy & Rutter, 1983; Werner & Smith, 1982). Thus, the development of competence in young children with disabilities and the adaptation of their families are viewed as multidimensional processes that are influenced by both intrinsic and extrinsic factors related to the child and to the ecology of the family. The overall purpose, scope, and methods of the study have been guided by a commitment to both basic developmental research and policy-relevant investigation and by a belief in the essential interrelatedness of child and family development for atypical as well as for normally developing populations.

The first phase of this ongoing longitudinal study, which is the focus of this *Monograph,* investigated the development of 190 infants and toddlers with disabilities and their families during their initial year of participation in an early intervention program. Two areas of inquiry were addressed. First, we tested the relations among a set of child and family status variables, mediators, and changes in child and family outcomes over the 12-month

TABLE 1

INDEPENDENT, MEDIATING, AND OUTCOME VARIABLES

| Independent Variables | Mediating Variables | Outcome Variables |
|---|---|---|
| *Child demographic and health characteristics* | *Child temperament, family ecology* | *Child competence* |
| | Quality of home environment | Mental age |
| Age | Family adaptability | Spontaneous play |
| Type of disability | Family cohesion | Adaptive behavior |
| Severity of psychomotor impairment | Maternal locus of control | *Mother-child interaction* |
| Gender | *Early intervention services* | |
| Prematurity status | Service intensity | Mother contribution |
| Presence or absence of cardiac problem | Staffing structure | Child contribution |
| | Service location | *Social support* |
| Presence or absence of seizure disorder | Service format | Network size |
| | *Services other than early intervention program* | Helpfulness |
| *Family demographic characteristics* | Child-oriented support | *Family adaptation* |
| Maternal education | Child-oriented therapy | Parenting stress |
| Maternal marital status | Family-oriented support | Effects on family |
| Maternal employment status | | |
| Maternal health status | | |

study period. Second, we analyzed the extent to which specific types and characteristics of early intervention services contributed to the explained variance in child and family outcomes. The justification for the selection of the study variables (listed in Table 1) was derived from consultation with our professional and parent advisory boards, in conjunction with a multidimensional literature review (presented in Chap. II). Although each variable domain has been the subject of previous investigation, the existing knowledge base on early developmental dysfunction is not sufficient to inform the construction of a comprehensive conceptual model of child and family adaptation. Indeed, our knowledge concerning the mechanisms that mediate differences in child development and family adaptation, particularly in the context of biologically based disability, is still limited. Thus, this first phase of our study should be viewed as an empirical investigation of a series of policy-relevant research questions and hypotheses, not as the systematic testing of a fully integrated developmental model. Ultimately, as discussed in the final chapter, our intention is to see the findings presented in this *Monograph* contribute to the construction of such a model, which can then guide the design of subsequent studies of both theoretical and policy-oriented significance.

Finally, it is essential that the findings of this study—an investigation of young children and families who are enrolled in community-based early intervention programs—be considered within a social policy context. All 29 participating programs shared a common service orientation that reflected the philosophy of the federal law (PL 99-457) that was enacted during the period of sample enrollment and that has guided program development nationally into the 1990s. The central thrust of that philosophy is an explicit commitment to an integration of both child- and family-oriented goals and the identification of the parent as an important vehicle for influencing children's development. Service providers whose professional training may have been largely child focused were charged to identify the provision of family support as a vital program objective. Each program offered a comparable array of home- and center-based services, provided by a multidisciplinary staff that included a core of early childhood educators and physical and occupational therapists, supplemented by varied combinations of nurses, social workers, speech and language pathologists, psychologists, and paraprofessionals. The content of home visits varied from teaching parents specific therapeutic and educational techniques to working directly with the child alone or providing supportive counseling to the parent. Center-based activities were designed to provide therapeutic services and socialization experiences for the children or for children and parents together as well as to offer opportunities for both structured and informal interactions among families to promote peer support. Each program provided a variety of service options; the specific "intervention" experience was based on individualized goals determined collaboratively with each family.

The EICS demonstrates both the strengths and the limitations of a naturalistic investigation in an area with important policy implications. The most significant confounding variables (e.g., variations in age of enrollment; large, nonrandom differences in service plans and experiences; and unmeasured qualitative variations in service provider–service recipient relationships) reflect the essential characteristics of early intervention services in the United States in the 1990s. In fact, the controlled provision of a tightly defined service model over an extended period of time would bear little resemblance to the functioning of contemporary programs (and would be in violation of the parental prerogatives mandated by the law). Thus, many of the most formidable analytic challenges in this study are inevitable consequences of current policy decisions and implementation practices in this rapidly evolving area of human service.

In summary, the fundamental research problems currently facing the field of early childhood intervention are both theoretical and pragmatic. On a conceptual level, many important questions remain unanswered about the range of variation in adaptive patterns demonstrated by children with disabilities and their families as well as about developmental continuities and discontinuities and the stability of individual differences throughout the early childhood period. From the practical perspective of service delivery, designing individualized intervention strategies for a diverse population of children and families and measuring their effect over time are critical if policy objectives are to be translated into effective programs. The central challenge confronting policymakers, service providers, and academic investigators is the need to integrate basic developmental and policy-related research in order to respond to these complex issues.

## II. REVIEW OF THE LITERATURE

Three bodies of literature have contributed to the design of this investigation. The first and second address evolving conceptualizations of child competence and family adaptation to the challenges of rearing a child with a disability. The third focuses on assessment of the effects of early intervention services on infants and toddlers with special needs and their families. This chapter provides a brief overview of selected empirical and theoretical contributions that have been influential in shaping our work.[1]

### CONCEPTUALIZATION OF COMPETENCE IN CHILDREN

The search for a meaningful conceptual framework to guide the study of emerging skills in young children with disabilities has challenged scholars of human development for generations. In an attempt to move beyond the traditional focus on intelligence (as defined by performance on a standardized test), many theorists and investigators have explored such concepts as "adaptive behavior" and "social competence" as promising assessment alternatives. Despite their appeal, however, these "simple" concepts have proved to be deceptively complex, have eluded precise definition, and, consequently, have been difficult to measure (Anderson & Messick, 1974).

In a seminal paper on effectance motivation, White (1959) defined competence as "an organism's capacity to interact effectively with its environment" (p. 298). Waters and Sroufe (1983) characterized the competent individual as "one who is able to make use of environmental and personal resources to achieve a good developmental outcome" (p. 81). Zigler and Trickett (1978) recommended a simplified and pragmatic approach to the measurement of social competence that focused on two major domains: "the success of the human being in meeting societal expectancies" and "self-

---

[1] For interested readers, references to review articles that reflect the scope of inquiry in each of these areas of study more fully are included among the citations.

actualization or personal development" (p. 795). They suggested that the construction of a social competence index be designed to measure four variables: physical health and well-being, formal cognitive ability, school achievement, and motivational/emotional variables.

As the demands for assessment of adaptive behavior and social competence have intensified over the past decade, the absence of conceptual clarity in this domain of child development has persisted (Dodge, Pettit, McClaskey, & Brown, 1986). Although consensus does not exist about the elements that compose the construct of competence in infants and toddlers, three aspects of behavior (in addition to cognitive abilities) are emphasized in most discussions: (1) meeting societal expectations regarding daily routines; (2) spontaneous interest in learning; and (3) developing interpersonal relationships. Recent reviews of the range of options that are available for evaluating the performance of young children underscore the complexity of this challenge for special populations (Barnard & Kelly, 1990; Cicchetti & Wagner, 1990; McCune, Kalmanson, Fleck, Glazewski, & Sillari, 1990).

*Meeting societal expectations (adaptive behavior).*—As a construct, adaptive behavior generally includes aspects of functioning that indicate the degree to which individuals meet standards of personal independence and social responsibility (Grossman, 1983). For young children, such demands often require skills related to mobility, independence in dressing, eating, and toileting, and communication. Although children with disabilities generally demonstrate poorer adaptive skills in comparison to their peers (Slate, 1983), certain subgroups tend to perform at higher levels than others. Children with learning disabilities, for example, tend to have higher adaptive scores than children with mental retardation, and children with Down syndrome tend to have higher scores than those with other forms of mental retardation (Harrison, 1987). Very few studies have concentrated exclusively on the adaptive behavior of infants and toddlers with disabilities.

*Spontaneous interest in learning (play).*—Piaget (1952) emphasized the importance of children's self-initiated activity in guiding their learning about the world of objects and, ultimately, in affecting their cognitive development. Because it is a central medium through which children master their environment, play is one of the best indices of a child's spontaneous interest in learning (Rubin, Fein, & Vandenberg, 1983). In contrast to standardized assessment procedures in which an examiner attempts to elicit specific responses to discrete tasks, an evaluation of unstructured play relies heavily on children's self-directed activity.

Garwood (1982) outlined the general sequence of children's interactions with toys as progressing from exploration (tentative interaction with objects or events to determine their nature and safety), through play (non-goal-oriented experimental activity), to application (goal-oriented behavior). Belsky and Most (1981) developed a more elaborate taxonomy that charts

7

the development of exploratory behaviors in the early years from primitive, indiscriminate mouthing to complex, symbolic play.

Children with developmental delays appear to demonstrate a progression of play similar to that seen in nondelayed children (Beeghly & Cicchetti, 1987; Cunningham, Glenn, Wilkinson, & Sloper, 1985). Differences have been found, however, in the amount and variety of symbolic activity that occurs spontaneously. In a study of preschool children with Down syndrome, Hill and McCune-Nicolich (1981) found a low level of combining pretense acts in comparison to that found for nondisabled children matched for mental age. Riguet, Taylor, Benaroya, and Kline (1981) reported that young children with Down syndrome tended to elaborate the same idea repeatedly and displayed fewer different substitute symbolic uses than nondisabled children. Beckman and Kohl (1987) also found less functional and less pretense play among a group of children with developmental delays in comparison to other children in their classroom. In their research on spontaneous play behaviors, Krakow and Kopp (1982, 1983) found that children with Down syndrome focused their attention almost exclusively on toys to the exclusion of other aspects of the environment, whereas children with developmental delays engaged in more unoccupied and socially oriented activity to the relative exclusion of attention to toys. These findings suggest that children with disabilities may differ among themselves and from normally developing children in the qualitative as well as the quantitative aspects of their play.

*Interpersonal relationships (child-parent interaction).*—Vygotsky (1978, 1986) stressed the critical importance of social context as an influence on children's cognitive development. For infants and very young children, the central aspect of that context is their interaction with their caregivers (Rogoff, Malkin, & Gilbride, 1984). The literature on child-parent interaction is extensive and documents the multiple and complex ways in which reciprocal causes and effects of behavior unfold (Ainsworth & Bell, 1974; Clarke-Stewart, 1973; Comfort, 1988; Osofsky & Connors, 1979). Highly responsive infants may promote enhanced attention from their parents (Olson, Bates, & Bayles, 1984), whereas less socially responsive infants may precipitate stress or undermine parental well-being (Gunn & Berry, 1985). Research on children with developmental disabilities indicates that they tend to be less ready for interaction and less responsive to their caregivers (Stoneman, Brody, & Abbott, 1983). Compared to their nondisabled peers, children with disabilities tend to display diminished affect (Cicchetti & Sroufe, 1976) and reduced spontaneous social behaviors (MacTurk, Hunter, McCarthy, Vietze, & McQuiston, 1985). Abnormalities in muscle tone, variations in state control, and impairments in information processing often make their cues more difficult for parents to decipher (Brooks-Gunn &

Lewis, 1982; Buckhalt, Rutherford, & Goldberg, 1978; Eheart, 1982; Goldman & Johnson-Martin, 1987; Jones, 1977, 1980; Maurer & Sherrod, 1987).

Parents' contributions to their interactions with their children present a complementary perspective on this crucial area of research interest. It has been suggested that optimal child development occurs when parents provide experiences that are appropriate for their youngster's level of competence (Stern, 1974) and when certain aspects of maternal style are present, especially the dimensions of warmth and affection, sensitivity to the child's state and interests, and contingent responsiveness (Beckwith, 1990; Bee et al., 1982; Belsky, Goode, & Most, 1980). A substantial body of empirical data on the interactions between parents (usually mothers) and their infants with developmental delays or disabilities indicates that these parents tend to be more directive and to take more of a "manager" role in play with their children than do parents of nondisabled youngsters (Brooks-Gunn & Lewis, 1982; Buckhalt et al., 1978; Buium, Rynders, & Turnure, 1974; Cunningham, Rueler, Blackwell, & Deck, 1981; Eheart, 1982; Kogan, Wimberger, & Bobbitt, 1969; Mahoney, 1983; Marshall, Hegrenes, & Goldstein, 1973; Terdal, Jackson, & Garner, 1976).

## CONCEPTUALIZATION OF FAMILY ADAPTATION

Reviews of research conducted prior to the early 1980s on family adaptation to the challenges of rearing a child with disabilities have noted a primary focus on mothers rather than on families and a general reliance on a simplistic deficit or pathological model of adaptation (Byrne & Cunningham, 1985; Crnic, Friedrich, & Greenberg, 1983; Farber & Rowitz, 1986; Krauss, 1986). Such research assumed that rearing a child with a disability was inherently stressful and that affected families were a homogeneous group. In contrast to hypothesized normal family developmental patterns, families with a disabled child were found to experience (a) higher levels of marital disintegration (Farber, 1960); (b) elevated levels of marital dissatisfaction (Friedrich & Friedrich, 1981); (c) greater role tension and psychological dysfunction among siblings (Farber, 1960; Gath, 1973; Grossman, 1972); (d) chronic and dysfunctional stress, particularly among mothers (Cummings, Bayley, & Rie, 1966; Holroyd, 1974; Holt, 1958; Tew & Laurence, 1975) but also among fathers (Cummings, 1976); (e) restricted social mobility (Farber, 1960, 1968, 1970) and social relationships (Davis & MacKay, 1973; McAllister, Butler, & Lei, 1973); and (f) poor mother-child relationships (Beckman, 1983; Cunningham et al., 1981; Kogan et al., 1969; Vietze, Abernathy, Ashe, & Faulstich, 1978).

Farber and Rowitz (1986) argued that these early studies served a useful purpose in focusing attention on the enormous difficulties experienced by families who received little or no public services to support their caregiving efforts. However, in view of the substantial strides that have been made in publicly supported early intervention systems, educational inclusion policies, and family support programs over the past decade (Krauss, 1986), studies reported prior to the early 1980s must be assessed as investigations of a substantially different cohort of families in comparison to research conducted within the context of current service initiatives. Indeed, there is growing evidence that many families of children with disabilities demonstrate generally positive adaptation (Bristol, 1987; Noh, Dumas, Wolf, & Fisman, 1989; Singer & Farkas, 1989) and that variability in parenting stress and family functioning is comparable to that found in the general population (Frey, Greenberg, & Fewell, 1989; Gowen, Johnson-Martin, Goldman, & Appelbaum, 1989).

In addition to significant changes in available service options, there has been a concomitant refinement in the theoretical approaches taken by researchers to the study of family adaptation to chronic stress. Contemporary conceptual models of family adaptation incorporate advances from the fields of (a) family sociology, which has focused on describing enduring dimensions of family life that can be observed in all families (Epstein, Bishop, & Baldwin, 1982; Moos & Moos, 1976; Olson, Russell, & Sprenkle, 1983); (b) family systems theory, which approaches families as complex organizations in which inputs and outputs affect all members (Ackerman, 1958; Minuchin, 1974; Walsh, 1980); and (c) family life-cycle theory, which posits that families have a fairly predictable life cycle governing their growth, development, and functioning (Carter & McGoldrick, 1980; Duvall, 1962). Common to most contemporary theoretical frameworks of family adaptation is the perspective that families, as a system, have to change in response to normative transitions and unpredictable events while preserving their integrity and organizational coherence (Krauss & Jacobs, 1990; Melito, 1985; Shonkoff, Jarman, & Kohlenberg, 1987). Within this context, successful negotiation of the opposing tendencies of change and stability characterizes positive family functioning (Ackerman, 1958).

Several models of family adaptation have been formulated since the early 1980s. They include the Double ABCX Model of Adjustment and Adaptation (McCubbin & Patterson, 1983), the Stress-Adaptation Model (Farran, Metzger, & Sparling, 1986), and the Model of Stress, Coping, and Family Ecology (Crnic et al., 1983). While the three models differ in their emphases, they converge in their identification of determinants of adaptation, including characteristics of the stressful event, available internal and external resources, the family's attribution of meaning to the event, and interactions among the various ecological contexts in which the family operates.

Because of their direct relevance to the goals of many early intervention programs, four indices of family adaptation were selected for review. One index, the dyadic interaction between mother and child, was discussed earlier in this chapter. The other three (parenting stress, effects on the family of rearing a child with disabilities, and social support) are described below. As a group, these four constructs represent both theoretically and programmatically salient aspects of family functioning that are expected to exhibit change over time. Finally, the literature on the adaptive patterns of fathers of children with disabilities is reviewed in order to examine a broader perspective on the concept of family context.

*Parenting stress.*—Stress associated with the parenting role has been the outcome of "choice" in much research over the last three decades on families of children (and especially young children) with disabilities (Beckman, 1991; Crnic et al., 1983; Cummings, 1976; Cummings et al., 1966; Friedrich, 1979). Its appeal is grounded in the literature on family stress theory, which posits that stress (manifested as depression, social isolation, role restrictions, marital discord, etc.) is a signal of disequilibrium in personal or family functioning that may result from difficulty in coping with either normative or nonnormative events (Hill, 1949; Pearlin & Schooler, 1978). As a marker variable, stress has been found to differentiate families of children with different types of disabilities (Holroyd & McArthur, 1976), levels of severity of disability (Beckman, 1983), available social support (Dean & Lin, 1977), and strategies for coping with a provoking situation (Friedrich, Wilturner, & Cohen, 1985).

There is increasing evidence, however, that parenting stress is not invariably elevated in families of young children with disabilities as compared to families of young children without disabilities (Frey et al., 1989; Gowen et al., 1989). Interest has now turned to identifying social and psychological processes that account for variations in parenting stress and other indices of family functioning among parents of children with disabilities (Landesman, Jaccard, & Gunderson, 1991). Most of the research, however, is cross sectional in design, and the development of longitudinal data sets that chart modulations of parenting stress across the early childhood period is rare. Consequently, there is little empirical research on the role of specific service interventions or on particular child or parent characteristics that are associated with changes in parenting stress over time.

*Effects on the family of rearing a child with disabilities.*—Whereas most of the research over the past three decades has focused on a mother's point of view, there is widespread consensus that the effects of rearing a child with disabilities or delays are not limited to mothers (Crnic et al., 1983). Family systems theories have emphasized that novel demands on any member of a family have reverberating effects on other members and on the family as an organizational unit (Walsh, 1980). For families of children

11

with disabilities, common tasks such as locating baby-sitters may present unexpected difficulties. The disproportionate allocation of parental time for a child with a disability may cause strain for both parents and other children. Finding family activities that are enjoyable and appropriate for all members may be especially difficult if the child with a disability has unusual caregiving requirements. Thus, the family conceptualized as a social and organizational unit is seen to be experiencing an array of effects, including changes in social and occupational mobility (Farber, 1970; Watson & Midlarsky, 1979) and effects on both intra- and extrafamilial relationships (McAllister et al., 1973; Turnbull, Summers, & Brotherson, 1986).

Concurrent with an interest in the family-level effects of specific childhood impairments, there is a growing appreciation of the potential similarity of effects across families caring for a diverse range of chronically dependent members. Studies using comparable measures have been conducted with families of children with a variety of chronic illnesses (Stein & Riessman, 1980), rheumatic diseases (McCormick, Stemmler, & Athreya, 1986), and a range of disabilities that prompt referral to early intervention programs (McLinden-Mott & Braeger, 1988). In general, the severity of the child's disability or medical problems was found to be a significant correlate of higher (more negative) family-level effects.

*Social support.*—Garbarino (1983) defined social support networks as a "set of interconnected relationships among a group of people that provides enduring patterns of nurturance and provides contingent reinforcement for efforts to cope with life on a day-to-day basis" (p. 5). As noted by Bronfenbrenner, Moen, and Garbarino (1984), the most proximal network for families includes individuals and/or agencies with whom contact is maintained in the course of meeting family needs. Particularly for families with a member with a disability, the affective and instrumental support provided by intimate and extended family members, professionals, and community agencies can be extensive.

Social support networks are hypothesized to buffer individuals from the potentially depleting effects (physically and emotionally) of normative and nonnormative stress (Dunst, Trivette, & Cross, 1986; Koeske & Koeske, 1990). Well-developed and protective support networks are often characterized by their size (e.g., larger networks contain more sources of potential support) and perceived helpfulness (e.g., their ability to provide concrete assistance and/or convey emotional and psychological support). While the measurement of social support networks varies from relatively straightforward counts and ratings of helpfulness to detailed investigations of the structural and functional relations among network members, the salience of the perceived helpfulness of the network has been demonstrated repeatedly in empirical studies (Barrera, 1981; Dunst et al., 1986).

There is an extensive literature describing the positive relation between social support and parental well-being (Beckman, 1991; Dunst & Trivette, 1990; Levitt, Weber, & Clark, 1986), diminished maternal depression and an enhanced sense of parental competence (Gowen et al., 1989), mother-child interaction (Crnic, Greenberg, Robinson, & Ragozin, 1984), and recovery from physical illness (Wortman & Conway, 1985). Social support may be differentially effective, however, as suggested by Frey, Greenberg, and Fewell (1989), who studied correlates of family adjustment, parenting stress, and psychological distress among mothers and fathers of preschoolers with disabilities and found that social support was associated only with maternal family adjustment.

Other studies have noted that the effect of stressful situations on individual and family outcomes may be strongest when social supports are inadequate, suggesting an indirect or buffering rather than a direct or main effect of social support. Koeske and Koeske (1990), for example, investigated the effects of parenting stress and social support on satisfaction with the parenting role, parental self-esteem, and psychological complaints in a sample of young mothers. They found that stress was associated with negative outcomes only for mothers with inadequate support.

Given the potentially important and positive effects of a satisfying social support network (Cohen & Syme, 1985), many early intervention programs explicitly target the enhancement of parental supports as a primary intervention goal (Dunst, Trivette, & Deal, 1988). This programmatic strategy may be particularly important given the long-noted vulnerability of parents of children with disabilities to social isolation within their extended families as well as within the community at large (Crnic, Greenberg, & Slough, 1986; Suelzle & Keenan, 1981).

*Mother-father differences.*—Although most research on family issues related to childhood disability has focused on mothers, a growing literature suggests that the adaptation of fathers may differ in some important respects (Krauss, in press). Whereas some studies have found mothers to have higher levels of parenting stress and depression (Bristol, Gallagher, & Schopler, 1988; Kazak, 1987), others have reported that fathers experience higher levels of stress associated with their child's temperament (Goldberg, Marcovitch, MacGregor, & Lojkasek, 1986; Noh et al., 1989). Gender differences with regard to the correlates of stress also have been found, with cognitive coping factors reported to have more influence on the adjustment of fathers than mothers of young children with disabilities (Frey, Fewell, & Vadasy, 1989). Notwithstanding the emergence of greater attention to fathers by the research community, similarities and differences in the adaptive patterns of both mothers and fathers of young children with disabilities remain relatively unexplored.

## EFFECTS OF EARLY INTERVENTION SERVICES ON YOUNG CHILDREN
## WITH DISABILITIES AND ON THEIR FAMILIES

Multiple reviews of the literature on early intervention efficacy have demonstrated that programs for infants and toddlers with disabilities are moderately effective in producing short-term benefits, as measured by conventional intelligence tests or traditional developmental measures (Casto & Mastropieri, 1986; Shonkoff & Hauser-Cram, 1987; Simeonsson, Cooper, & Scheiner, 1982). Knowledge in this area, however, is tempered by substantial methodological limitations that characterize much of the available research, including designs that fail to eliminate major threats to validity, insufficient descriptive data on program participants and the services they receive, reliance on a restricted range of dependent measures for children, and significant neglect of family-oriented outcome variables (Bailey & Bricker, 1984; Dunst, 1986; Dunst & Rheingrover, 1981; Farran, 1990; Guralnick, 1989; Shonkoff & Hauser-Cram, 1987; White, Mastropieri, & Casto, 1984).

Notwithstanding these caveats, the use of meta-analytic techniques to summarize empirical data on the effects of early intervention services has highlighted areas of consensus, points of continuing controversy, and potential directions for future investigation (Casto & Mastropieri, 1986; Shonkoff & Hauser-Cram, 1987; White, Mastropieri, & Casto, 1984). The conclusion that intervention programs can produce short-term gains in IQ or developmental quotient, for example, is widely supported and would, therefore, appear to be a low priority for further study. The long-term stability of developmental gains, however, has not been investigated adequately. Moreover, the growing demand for additional outcome variables that are valid ecologically and linked closely to specific service objectives for children with disabilities and their families is evident (Dunst, 1986; Shonkoff et al., 1988).

*Questions for further study.*—Specific issues on which meta-analytic reviews have either contradicted conventional clinical wisdom or failed to reach a consensus highlight important priorities for investigation (Dunst & Snyder, 1986; Strain & Smith, 1986). One example is the issue of the different effects of varying amounts of service.

White, Bush, and Casto (1985) found that, in 18 of 24 published reviews of early intervention efficacy research, earlier provision of services was reported to predict better child outcomes. In a meta-analysis of 74 studies of preschoolers with disabilities, however, Casto and Mastropieri (1986) found little data to support the notion that "earlier is better." Shonkoff and Hauser-Cram (1987) conducted a meta-analysis of data from 31 studies of children with disabilities who entered programs before 36 months of age, finding an interaction between severity of disability and age at program entry.

In the latter analysis, infants categorized as mildly impaired demonstrated significantly better outcomes if they were enrolled in programs before the age of 6 months than if services were begun at a later age; children with severe disabilities, on the other hand, appeared to show a constant level of benefit (half a standard deviation) regardless of their age at the time of program entry. Because data collection in all the studies was restricted to the time of enrollment in an early intervention program, we do not know whether *long-term* child effects differ by severity level for those who begin services at different times in early childhood. Furthermore, none of the studies looked at the effect of age at the time of program initiation on a range of important outcome variables, such as mother-child interaction or family adaptation. The fact that the timing of referral for services is influenced by the type and severity of the child's disability as well as by differences in family characteristics, however, makes age at program entry a complex variable to study.

A related quantitative aspect of early intervention programming that has received inadequate empirical investigation is the effect of service intensity (independent of age at program entry) on specific child and family outcomes. Available data suggest that longer, more intense intervention programs are associated with greater effectiveness for children with disabilities from birth through 5 years of age (Casto & Mastropieri, 1986). Few studies, however, have reported sufficient data on the actual number of service hours received by children and families to assess the effect of variation in service intensity on outcomes adequately (Shonkoff & Hauser-Cram, 1987).

Perhaps the most contentious issue raised by the published meta-analytic reviews has been the assertion by Casto and Mastropieri (1986), based on data reported from 74 studies of services for children with disabilities up through 5 years of age, that parent involvement does not influence program effects. In direct contrast, Shonkoff and Hauser-Cram (1987) analyzed data obtained from 31 studies of programs for children under 3 years of age and found that both the extent and the type of parent participation had a significant effect on child outcomes.

*The need for data on the natural history of disability.*—In order to answer specific questions about the effects of early intervention services on the development of young children with disabilities, it is necessary to know about variations in outcomes in the absence of program influences. However, reliable data on the natural history of infants and toddlers with developmental problems are virtually unavailable, in large part owing to the marked heterogeneity of the service population.

Shonkoff and Hauser-Cram (1987) analyzed data from 31 investigations and found that the majority of the intervention programs served children with a variety of disabilities. Farran (1990) reviewed 42 studies, 29 of which involved projects that served a heterogeneous population of children and 13 of which focused on programs exclusively for children with Down syndrome. Of the 29 projects that dealt with a diverse service population, the most frequently cited subgroup was composed of children with cerebral palsy (which is itself a heterogeneous category of disabilities); the next most common categorization was "general developmental delay of unknown etiology." Differences in patterns of dysfunction across and among diagnostic groupings, the considerable variability in severity of disability within subgroups, and the high prevalence of a diversity of relatively rare handicapping conditions within the early intervention population have each presented a major challenge to program evaluators. Consequently, the problem of generalization of study findings is a significant issue in the efficacy literature.

As a group whose incidence and identifiability at birth make them the best candidates for empirical studies, children with Down syndrome have been the focus of the most work in this area. Early studies of youngsters reared at home without specific intervention services provided important "normative" data on the achievement of specific developmental milestones (e.g., Carr, 1975). Most of the currently existing data on the development of children with Down syndrome, however, have been collected from children who have experienced a wide variety of services, thereby making it difficult to interpret variations in their rates or patterns of development.

Several investigators have reported steady declines in developmental progress for children with Down syndrome, yet the described patterns differ. Piper and Pless (1980) documented a persistent decline in the rate of development of their intervention sample, but followed the children only until age 15 months. Ludlow and Allen (1979) reported a similar pattern among a group that they followed up to 36 months of age, and Woods, Corney, and Pryce (1984) reported the lowest point in development between 30 and 40 months, at which time the trend was noted to reverse. In contrast, Sharav and Shlomo (1986) documented a decline in developmental attainment until 18 months of age, which then reversed until age 5 years. Hayden and Haring (1977), Clunies-Ross (1979), and Berry, Gunn, and Andrews (1984), on the other hand, recorded generally lower functioning among children with Down syndrome, but their data did not support the concept of an inevitable decline in their rate of development during the first 5 years of life.

Farran (1990) reported that the areas of development that seem to be most affected in children with Down syndrome are motor, language, and personal-social skills and noted that variation in developmental attainments among children with Down syndrome is more extreme than in normally developing youngsters. Because of the larger standard deviations and greater ranges within which various milestones are achieved, she argued that some of the difficulty encountered in plotting accurate developmental functions for children with Down syndrome is related to small samples and different developmental domains emphasized by different assessment techniques as well as to the lack of uniformity within the population.

Relatively few studies of children with Down syndrome have investigated specific predictors of variation. Some have reported better developmental outcomes for girls than boys (Piper, Gosselin, Gendron, & Mazer, 1986; Rynders & Horrobin, 1980; Sharav & Shlomo, 1986; Woods et al., 1984), but most studies have not examined gender differences. Social class influences have not been well investigated, although Sharav, Collins, and Shlomo (1985) found correlations between maternal education and child IQ in the school-age years.

In summary, the descriptive literature on the development of infants and toddlers with disabling conditions (diagnosed or nonspecific) is extremely limited. Furthermore, the relatively meager nature of the available data on natural history presents a significant impediment to the task of program evaluation.

# III. STUDY METHODS AND SAMPLE CHARACTERISTICS

## SAMPLE SELECTION

### Recruitment Sites

The study sample was recruited from 29 community-based early intervention programs (25 in Massachusetts and four in New Hampshire) that were selected on the basis of their size (each serving 50 or more children) and their geographic location (covering diverse yet accessible areas of the two states). Although the group of participating programs did not constitute a random sample, the inclusion of sites from a variety of urban, suburban, and rural areas in two state systems was designed to enhance the potential generalizability of the study findings.

### Eligibility Criteria

The ultimate reference population for the study sample is the mandated target population for early intervention services defined under Part H of PL 99-457 (i.e., developmentally delayed or disabled infants and toddlers under 36 months of age and their families). In order to define this target group more precisely, we conducted an independent analysis of client registration data collected by the Massachusetts Division of Family Health Services for all children and families enrolled in the state-supported early intervention system during the year that preceded the initiation of the study (Shonkoff, Hauser-Cram, Krauss, & Upshur, 1990). Building on the results of that analysis, eligibility criteria were defined for the study sample on the basis of the child's presenting developmental problem(s), which reflected the three most common categories of disability or delay reported for children served by the Massachusetts early intervention system in 1984: Down syndrome, motor impairment, and developmental delay (see Table 2).

TABLE 2

SAMPLE ELIGIBILITY CRITERIA FOR THREE TARGET GROUPS

| | Down Syndrome | Motor Impairment | Developmental Delay |
|---|---|---|---|
| Age at referral to early intervention services ... | Up to 12 months | Up to 24 months | Up to 24 months |
| Criteria for inclusion .... | Confirmation of diagnosis through medical record review | Evidence of abnormal muscle tone (hypotonia or hypertonia) or coordination deficit, along with delayed or deviant motor development, with or without other delays | Evidence of delays in two or more areas of development, with no established diagnosis or etiology that implies a specific prognosis |
| Criteria for exclusion .... | None | Children with spina bifida or diagnosed myopathy | Any diagnosis given before study entry that predicts mental retardation (e.g., congenital infection, inborn errors of metabolism, neurocutaneous disorders, chromosomal abnormalities other than Down syndrome, etc.) |

*Overall inclusions and exclusions.*—History of prematurity or perinatal asphyxia by itself was not considered as an etiology for developmental delay. Children were excluded if their family's primary language was not English, if they lived in foster care, if they were one of a multiple birth (where other siblings had survived), or if they had a sibling who was receiving early intervention services concurrently.

## Recruitment of Children and Families

The study sample was enrolled over a 2-year period from November 1985 to December 1987. If, at the time of initial referral to an early intervention program, available information indicated the likelihood of sample eligibility, the early intervention intake coordinator informed the parent about the existence of the study, offered a brochure that explained its general focus and design, and asked the family for permission to be contacted by a member of the research staff. If the family declined to be contacted, nonidentifying child and family demographic data were supplied to the research staff by the early intervention intake coordinator. These data were collected to assess potential demographic differences between the study sample and eligible nonparticipants. If the family expressed an interest in participating, project staff contacted the family to describe the study further and then mailed additional written material about the study and an informed consent form. Within 4–6 weeks of the initial referral, research staff visited the child and family in their home for the Time 1 (T1) data collection.

## Characteristics of the Children

Medical records for each enrolled child were reviewed by the principal investigator to confirm assignment to type of disability group. Initial developmental assessments conducted by early intervention service providers for children in the *developmental delay* and *motor impairment* groups were reviewed by research staff for final confirmation of the child's classification.

Chromosomal analyses for the 54 sample children with Down syndrome indicated that 44 had trisomy 21 and two had translocations; specific karyotype information was unavailable for eight children.

The neuromotor characteristics of the 77 children in the motor impairment subgroup revealed that children with quadriparesis (with hypertonia or fluctuating tone) and those with generalized hypotonia each constituted just over one-third of the subgroup (36.3% and 33.8%, respectively). One of seven (14.3%) children with motor impairment had diplegia, one in eight (11.7%) presented with hemiparesis, and three children (3.9%) demonstrated choreoathetosis. All the children in this subgroup had abnormal muscle tone, with 41.5% demonstrating hypertonicity, 33.8% presenting with hypotonicity, and 24.7% exhibiting fluctuating or mixed tone.

The medical records of the 59 children with developmental delays confirmed that none had a medical diagnosis that either identified a specific etiology or implied a prognosis for mental retardation at the time of enrollment in the study. Their referral and acceptance into an early intervention program was based on measured delays in at least two areas of development.

The demographic and perinatal characteristics of the sample children are summarized in Table 3. Although the mean age at study entry was 10.6 months, children with Down syndrome (who typically are referred for early intervention services shortly after birth) were significantly younger than those in the other two groups. The subgroup with Down syndrome also was distinguished by lower rates of prematurity and severe disability. ANOVA

TABLE 3

DEMOGRAPHIC AND PERINATAL DIFFERENCES AMONG SAMPLE CHILDREN
BY TYPE OF DISABILITY

| Characteristic | Down Syndrome ($N$ = 54) | Motor Impairment ($N$ = 77) | Developmental Delay ($N$ = 59) | Total Sample ($N$ = 190) |
|---|---|---|---|---|
| Age at T1 (months): | | | | |
| Mean (SD)[a] . . . . . . . . . . . . | 3.4 | 11.5 | 16.0 | 10.6 |
| | (2.0) | (4.4) | (5.8) | (6.6) |
| Range . . . . . . . . . . . . . . . . | 1.3–10.8 | 5.0–22.9 | 4.5–26.9 | 1.3–26.9 |
| Gender (% male) . . . . . . . . . . | 44.4 | 59.7 | 62.7 | 56.3 |
| Ethnic group (%): | | | | |
| White . . . . . . . . . . . . . . . . . . | 87.0 | 89.6 | 91.5 | 89.5 |
| Hispanic . . . . . . . . . . . . . . . | 5.6 | 3.9 | 3.4 | 4.2 |
| Black . . . . . . . . . . . . . . . . . . | 1.8 | 3.9 | .0 | 2.1 |
| Mixed/other . . . . . . . . . . . | 5.6 | 2.6 | 5.1 | 4.2 |
| Gestational age (weeks): | | | | |
| Mean (SD) . . . . . . . . . . . . | 38.8 | 37.9 | 37.8 | 38.1 |
| | (1.7) | (3.7) | (3.6) | (3.2) |
| Range . . . . . . . . . . . . . . . . | 31–41 | 27–42 | 27–43 | 27–43 |
| ≥ 37 weeks (%)[b] . . . . . . . . | 90.7 | 70.1 | 74.6 | 77.4 |
| Birth weight (lbs.): | | | | |
| Mean (SD) . . . . . . . . . . . . | 6.8 | 6.6 | 6.4 | 6.6 |
| | (1.1) | (1.9) | (1.9) | (1.7) |
| Range . . . . . . . . . . . . . . . . | 3.6–8.9 | 1.9–10.0 | 1.6–10.4 | 1.6–10.4 |
| Apgar score: | | | | |
| Mean at 1 min . . . . . . . . . . | 7.2 | 6.8 | 7.6 | 7.2 |
| Range . . . . . . . . . . . . . . . . | 2–9 | 1–9 | 1–10 | 1–10 |
| Mean at 5 min . . . . . . . . . . | 8.6 | 8.3 | 8.8 | 8.5 |
| Range . . . . . . . . . . . . . . . . | 6–10 | 2–10 | 6–10 | 2–10 |
| Neonatal medical care: | | | | |
| Intensive care nursery: | | | | |
| % admitted . . . . . . . . . . | 18.9 | 27.3 | 20.7 | 22.6 |
| Mean no. of days . . . . . . | 13.3 | 23.8 | 64.0 | 33 |
| Range . . . . . . . . . . . . . . | 1–67 | 1–92 | 2–288 | 1–288 |
| Special care nursery: | | | | |
| % admitted . . . . . . . . . . | 15.4 | 12.0 | 14.0 | 13.2 |
| Mean no. of days . . . . . . | 7.7 | 40.4 | 43.3 | 33 |
| Range . . . . . . . . . . . . . . | 1–20 | 1–93 | 1–288 | 1–288 |
| Adopted children ($N$) . . . . . . | 1 | 0 | 1 | 2 |
| Severity of psychomotor impairment:[c] | | | | |
| MDI ≥ 50 . . . . . . . . . . . . . | 51 | 46 | 43 | 140 |
| MDI < 50 . . . . . . . . . . . . . | 3 | 31 | 16 | 50 |

NOTE.—MDI = Mental Development Index.
[a] Age at T1, $F(1,189)$ = 118.43, $p < .001$.
[b] Full-term gestational age, $\chi^2(2, N = 190)$ = 8.08, $p < .05$.
[c] Severity of impairment, $\chi^2(2, N = 190)$ = 19.74, $p < .001$.

tests revealed no other significant demographic or perinatal differences among the three disability groups.

The degree of severity of impairment for each child was assessed at study entry through administration of the Mental Scale of the Bayley Scales of Infant Development. The mean Mental Developmental Index (MDI) for the sample was low ($M = 63.7$) and the standard deviation large (SD = 24.4) in comparison to the norms for the standardization sample. About one-quarter (26.3%) of the study children had an MDI of 49 or less, and 16.9% had a score of 27 or lower, based on extrapolation procedures (Naglieri, 1981). The mean MDI for each type of disability group varied from 70.7 (SD = 14.3) for children with Down syndrome to 67.3 (SD = 27.8) for children with developmental delays and 56.3 (SD = 25.3) for those with motor impairment.

For some analyses, sample children were divided into two groups on the basis of the severity of their impairment. Children with an MDI of less than 50 were considered to have a more severe level of impairment (in the moderate to severe range), while children with an MDI of 50 or greater were considered to have a less severe or mild level of impairment. This classification is consistent with the criteria of both the DSM-III-R (American Psychiatric Association, 1987) and the American Association on Mental Retardation (Grossman, 1983), which use standardized IQ scores to classify children and adults with developmental disabilities. It should be noted, however, that an MDI is not the same as an IQ score, that classifications of very young children who are growing and changing rapidly do not necessarily predict long-term outcomes, and that the range of abilities within each of these two groups is large. Most important, we recognize that a Bayley MDI may not be a valid measure of intellectual ability, but rather a reflection of psychomotor performance. Although this caveat is applicable to all infants and toddlers, it is especially pertinent for children with motor impairment, for whom low test scores may reflect physical difficulties in task execution and mask stronger cognitive skills. Therefore, although we recognize the problem of potential confusion with the Psychomotor Developmental Index derived from the Bayley Motor Scale (which was not administered in this study), we use the term "psychomotor impairment" in this *Monograph* to characterize the level of developmental deficit reflected in child performance on the Mental Scale.

Information on associated health conditions obtained from a comprehensive medical record review (see Table 4) indicated that the majority of the sample children were physically quite healthy. Seizure disorders, as would be expected, were significantly more frequent in infants with motor impairment, although the higher number of children in this group with evidence of strabismus was not statistically significant. Cardiac anomalies were predictably more common among children with Down syndrome.

## TABLE 4

ASSOCIATED HEALTH CONDITIONS FOR THE TOTAL SAMPLE AND BY TYPE OF DISABILITY FROM BIRTH TO T2 AS DETERMINED BY MEDICAL RECORD REVIEW

| Condition | Total Sample (N = 190) | Down Syndrome (N = 54) | Motor Impairment (N = 77) | Developmental Delay (N = 59) | Chi Square[a] |
|---|---|---|---|---|---|
| Seizure disorder | 35 | 3 | 20 | 12 | 9.2** |
| Hydrocephalus | 8 | 0 | 7 | 1 | |
| Metabolic disorder[b] | 1 | 0 | 1 | 0 | |
| Chromosomal abnormality[c] (other than Down syndrome) | 6 | 0 | 4 | 2 | 45.9*** |
| Congenital cardiac anomaly | 46 | 31 | 6 | 9 | |
| Endocardial cushion defect | 13 | 13 | 0 | 0 | |
| Tetralogy of Fallot | 3 | 1 | 1 | 1 | |
| Ventricular septal defect | 15 | 8 | 3 | 4 | |
| Atrial septal defect | 16 | 14 | 2 | 0 | |
| Coarctation of the aorta | 3 | 1 | 0 | 2 | |
| Aortic stenosis/pulmonic stenosis | 6 | 2 | 1 | 3 | |
| Patent ductus arteriosus | 7 | 6 | 1 | 0 | |
| Other | 9 | 4 | 2 | 3 | |
| Asthma | 22 | 4 | 11 | 7 | 1.5 |
| Bronchopulmonary dysplasia | 4 | 1 | 1 | 2 | |
| Strabismus | 38 | 9 | 21 | 8 | 4.7 |
| Cataract | 1 | 0 | 0 | 1 | |

[a] Only conditions with at least five expected cases per type of disability were analyzed.
[b] Propionic acidemia.
[c] 9q abnormality; 18q−; ring 18; 7q+; 6.8% mosaicism for monosomy 21; additional fragment on chromosome 21, not classified as Down syndrome.
** p < .01.
*** p < .001.

All the sample children had an identifiable source of pediatric primary care. The mean number of primary care visits during the 12-month study period was 9.4 (range = 0–37). Children with Down syndrome had more frequent well-child visits (related to their younger age), $F(1,189) = 13.18$, $p < .001$, whereas no significant differences were found among the groups in their number of problem-oriented medical visits. Similarly, $F$ tests indicated that the number and duration of hospital admissions were not significantly different among the three subgroups. About one-third (36.6%) of the sample children were hospitalized during the study period, with almost three-quarters of that group having only one inpatient admission.

## Characteristics of the Families

The demographic characteristics of the sample families are summarized in Tables 5 and 6. On enrollment in the study, most of the children were living with both parents; only one out of eight lived with their mothers only. Five children had changes in their custodial arrangements over the 12-month study period. Slightly more than one-third (35.3%) were only children. Over one-third of the families reported annual incomes over $30,000, while one-fifth earned less than $10,000 in the year prior to study enrollment. One year after initiation of the study, considerable shifts in the percentage of families in the highest and lowest income groups were found, with 43% reporting annual incomes in excess of $30,000 and 14% reporting incomes below $10,000 per year. Mean educational attainment for both mothers and fathers was relatively high (13.8 years), with approximately half the sample reporting some education beyond high school. Slightly over one-third of the mothers were working full or part time outside their homes at study entry, while 13% of the fathers were not employed full time. The employment status of mothers increased to almost half the sample during the study period, while the employment status of fathers remained about the same.

Analyses of demographic differences by type of disability group revealed few statistically significant findings. The mean maternal age at the birth of her child was slightly older for mothers of children with Down syndrome (30.0 years) than for mothers of children in the other two disability groups (27.6 and 27.8 years), $F(1,189) = 4.05$, $p < .05$. In addition, although the self-reported health status of mothers did not differ by children's disability at T1, at the end of the study period mothers of children with motor impairment reported significantly lower health status ratings than did mothers in the other two groups (a decrease from 50% to 36% reporting their health status as excellent), $\chi^2(1, N = 186) = 5.46, p < .05$.

TABLE 5

DEMOGRAPHIC CHARACTERISTICS OF SAMPLE
FAMILIES ($N$ = 190)

| Characteristic | T1 (%) | T2 (%) |
|---|---|---|
| Family composition: | | |
| Single child . . . . . . . . . . . . . . . . . . . | 35.3 | 32.1 |
| 2 children . . . . . . . . . . . . . . . . . . . . | 40.0 | 43.7 |
| 3 or more children. . . . . . . . . . . . . | 24.7 | 24.2 |
| Custodial arrangements at T1: | | |
| Child living with both parents . . . | 87.4 | 87.4 |
| Child living with mother only . . . | 12.6 | 12.1 |
| Child living with father only . . . . | .0 | .5 |
| Income: | | |
| < $10,000 . . . . . . . . . . . . . . . . . . . . | 19.4 | 14.4 |
| $10,000–19,999 . . . . . . . . . . . . . . | 19.4 | 17.6 |
| $20,000–29,999 . . . . . . . . . . . . . . | 25.7 | 25.0 |
| ≥ $30,000 . . . . . . . . . . . . . . . . . . . | 35.5 | 43.0 |
| Residence: | | |
| Massachusetts . . . . . . . . . . . . . . . . | 83.2 | 83.2 |
| New Hampshire . . . . . . . . . . . . . . | 16.8 | 16.8 |

## DATA COLLECTION PROCEDURES

All participating families received a home visit within 6 weeks of their entry into an early intervention program (T1). Each home visit, which took approximately 1½–2 hours to complete, was conducted by two members of the research staff, who remained independent of the service delivery system and blind to the study's hypotheses. One staff member administered a multidimensional, structured evaluation of the child, which included a standardized developmental assessment, a free-play observation, and a rating of mother-child interaction. The second staff member conducted an interview with the mother, which included an evaluation of the child's adaptive behavior, a review of services received (by the child and/or the family) in addition to those provided in the early intervention program, information about the child's health status, and the collection of basic sociodemographic information on the family. If the child or parent was having a "bad day," or if the child became too tired or fussy before the protocol could be completed, another visit was scheduled. Subsequently, birth records, hospital discharge summaries, and reports from primary care and consulting physicians were obtained to compile a comprehensive pediatric data base.

At the end of the T1 home visit, two identical packets of self-administered questionnaires were left to be completed independently by the child's mother and (if available) father. The questionnaires included scales on parenting stress, social support, family functioning, locus of control, and effects

TABLE 6

Demographic Characteristics of Sample Mothers
and Fathers ($N = 190$)

| Characteristic | Mothers | Fathers |
|---|---|---|
| Mean age in years at T1 (SD) . . . . . . . . . . . . | 29.1 | 31.5 |
| | (5.0) | (5.8) |
| Range in age (years) . . . . . . . . . . . . . . . . . . . | 17.5–43.3 | 17.0–53.3 |
| Age at child's birth (%): | | |
|   &lt; 20 years. . . . . . . . . . . . . . . . . . . . . . . . | 4.2 | 1.1 |
|   ≥ 35 years. . . . . . . . . . . . . . . . . . . . . . . . | 9.5 | 21.9 |
| Marital status (%): | | |
|   Married . . . . . . . . . . . . . . . . . . . . . . . . . | 81.0 | 82.0 |
|   Unmarried . . . . . . . . . . . . . . . . . . . . . . . | 11.6 | 10.1 |
|   Separated . . . . . . . . . . . . . . . . . . . . . . . | 5.8 | 4.8 |
|   Divorced . . . . . . . . . . . . . . . . . . . . . . . . | 1.1 | 3.2 |
|   Widowed . . . . . . . . . . . . . . . . . . . . . . . . | .5 | 0 |
| Education (%): | | |
|   12 years or less. . . . . . . . . . . . . . . . . . . | 47.3 | 48.9 |
|   13–16 years . . . . . . . . . . . . . . . . . . . . . . | 38.9 | 35.3 |
|   17 years or more . . . . . . . . . . . . . . . . . . | 13.8 | 15.8 |
| Mean years of education (SD) . . . . . . . . . . . | 13.8 | 13.8 |
| | (2.5) | (3.1) |
| Range in years of education. . . . . . . . . . . . . | 8–22 | 6–23 |
| Ethnic group (%): | | |
|   White. . . . . . . . . . . . . . . . . . . . . . . . . . . | 92.1 | 90.0 |
|   Hispanic . . . . . . . . . . . . . . . . . . . . . . . . | 3.7 | 4.7 |
|   Black . . . . . . . . . . . . . . . . . . . . . . . . . . | 2.1 | 3.2 |
|   Other. . . . . . . . . . . . . . . . . . . . . . . . . . . | 2.1 | 2.1 |
| Religion (%): | | |
|   Catholic. . . . . . . . . . . . . . . . . . . . . . . . . | 54.2 | 55.1 |
|   Protestant . . . . . . . . . . . . . . . . . . . . . . . | 27.9 | 22.5 |
|   Jewish . . . . . . . . . . . . . . . . . . . . . . . . . | 3.7 | 2.7 |
|   Other. . . . . . . . . . . . . . . . . . . . . . . . . . . | 9.5 | 8.5 |
|   None . . . . . . . . . . . . . . . . . . . . . . . . . . | 4.7 | 11.2 |
| Employment status (% full or part time) . . . | 36.9 | 86.8 |
| Self-reported health status (%): | | |
|   Excellent . . . . . . . . . . . . . . . . . . . . . . . . | 56.1 | 60.1 |
|   Good . . . . . . . . . . . . . . . . . . . . . . . . . . | 40.7 | 31.9 |
|   Fair . . . . . . . . . . . . . . . . . . . . . . . . . . . | 3.2 | 6.9 |
|   Poor. . . . . . . . . . . . . . . . . . . . . . . . . . . | 0 | 1.1 |

of a child with disabilities on family life. Each parent received a $10.00 reimbursement on receipt of a set of completed questionnaires. For families who had difficulty filling out the forms, a repeat home visit was scheduled to provide assistance.

After the completion of each T1 home visit, the appropriate early intervention program was notified, and standardized information on child and parent services received through the program was then collected on a monthly basis. Twelve months after the T1 assessments, a second home visit (T2) was conducted. This visit consisted of a repeat administration of the child evaluations and a detailed interview with the mother that paralleled the T1 protocol (with the addition of specific questions regarding the past year's early intervention experience). A packet of questionnaires was left for each parent to complete independently of his or her partner, which contained the same instruments completed at T1 together with several additional questionnaires on parental assessment of their early intervention experience. A $15.00 reimbursement was sent to each parent who returned a completed packet of questionnaires.

Quality control mechanisms to ensure accurate, complete, and reliable data for all study measures were developed and implemented on an ongoing basis. If missing or ambiguous answers were detected on the parent questionnaires, the respondent was contacted to obtain clarification or completion. After initial training on the observation measures was completed, reliability checks were performed throughout the period of data collection for the child's spontaneous play and the assessment of mother-child interaction by having an additional observer record data on a random sample of 26 visits. Interrater reliability of .85 or greater (based on percentage agreement) was maintained for the mother-child interaction measure and of .80 or greater (based on Finn's $r$) for the children's play scale (Finn, 1970).

## THREATS TO VALIDITY

### Known Biases in the Study Sample

Three different analyses were conducted to examine possible biases within the study sample as a result of selection effects, differential attrition, or missing data. With regard to selection effects, analyses revealed that families who were eligible for the study but who declined to participate ($N = 49$) were more likely to have a mother working full time outside the home, $\chi^2(2, N = 233) = 10.12, p < .01$, and to have a child categorized as developmentally delayed with an uncertain etiology, $\chi^2(2, N = 239) = 19.96, p < .001$. No significant differences were found in income, marital status (based on chi-square tests), or maternal education (based on $t$ tests).

Approximately 10% ($N = 23$) of the study sample was lost through attrition between the first and the second data collection points. These families were disproportionately in the lowest income category, $\chi^2(3, N = 207) = 21.36, p < .001$, and headed by a single parent, $\chi^2(1, N = 213) = 3.89, p < .05$. Withdrawal from the study was explained by several factors, most commonly as a result of family relocation within or outside the state or the death of the study child.

Finally, analyses were conducted to investigate differences between those families for whom data collection was complete ($N = 152$) and those who did not return all the self-administered questionnaires. Sample mothers with complete data had higher levels of education ($M = 14.0$ years vs. $M = 12.7$ years, $t[188] = 2.93$, $p < .01$) and reported higher family cohesion ($M = 66.0$ vs. $M = 62.1$, $t[176] = 2.02$, $p < .05$) than sample mothers without complete data. Statistical analyses revealed no other differences among other child or family status variables, in any of the outcome measures, or in the patterns of service received by the two groups.

In summary, the study sample did not differ in significant ways from those who were eligible but chose not to participate. Furthermore, missing data from the self-administered questionnaires did not appear to reflect a systematic pattern related to the child outcomes or to the representativeness of any other key variables. Attrition, however, was not random, as the final sample comprised a slightly more socioeconomically advantaged group of families than the original.

### Absence of a Control Group

Perhaps the most formidable methodological challenge in the design of early intervention efficacy research is whether to create a "no treatment" control group. There are three primary reasons for the absence of a control group in this investigation. First, all children under 3 years of age with disabilities or delays in development are eligible for enrollment in early intervention programs in Massachusetts and New Hampshire. Consequently, children and families who choose not to participate in early intervention programs are likely to differ in important characteristics (e.g., child's level of impairment, family organization, etc.) from participating families, thereby yielding problematic selection effects. Second, it would be ethically untenable and logistically impossible to retain a control group for study purposes over an extended period of time without providing services. Third, the purpose of this study is to investigate within-group predictors of child and family development during the first year of early intervention services, not to address the question of whether developmental outcomes differ between children who receive services and those who do not. Nevertheless, it is important to acknowledge that, because the groups are not based on random assignment, the study is vulnerable to several threats to validity, particularly with respect to history and testing practice effects.

### History and Testing Effects

History would prove to be a significant threat if sample children and families received other services that could account for differences in outcomes in addition to those provided through their early intervention program. This threat was minimized, however, by the collection and analysis of data on other services received by families. Testing practice effects represent another potential threat to the study's validity, a threat that was minimized by the 12-month hiatus between test administrations. Furthermore, two of our core measures involved minimally structured observations (the assessment of mother-child interaction and the evaluation of spontaneous play) and, therefore, do not lend themselves to practice effects.

## INSTRUMENTS

Five general methods for collecting data were used in this study: structured interviews with the mother; completion of standardized questionnaires by both the mother and the father independently; direct child assessment and observation in the home; structured data collection from early intervention service providers; and a systematic review of birth records, primary and consultant physician medical records, and hospitalization discharge summaries for each study child.

The instruments used in this study are described briefly below. Where applicable, the Cronbach's reliability coefficient for the instrument as derived from the T1 maternal scores for the study sample is reported. The independent, mediating, and dependent variables derived from these instruments and other data are described in Table 7.

### Child Measures

*Bayley Scales of Infant Development (Bayley, 1969).*—The Mental Scale, a 163-item scale, assesses object relations, perceptual-motor skills, memory, learning, problem-solving ability, and early communication through a series of tasks presented to the child by an examiner. The second and third components, the Motor Scale and the Infant Behavior Record, were not administered for this study. The Bayley Scales have not been standardized on a population of children with disabilities, and interpretation of scores is particularly problematic for children with motor impairments. Nevertheless, they are the most frequently used infant assessment instrument, and the scores are useful for comparison with normal samples. The Mental Scale yields a raw score that can be converted to a standard score, the Mental Developmental Index (MDI), or a mental age equivalence score. The standard score, adjusted for gestational age for children born prematurely, was used to define two groups by level of severity of psychomotor impairment.

*EICS Observation Scale of Children's Spontaneous Play.*—This scale was adapted from a scale of spontaneous play, developed originally by Belsky

## TABLE 7

| Variable | Measure |
|---|---|
| A. Child demographic and health characteristics: | |
| 1. Age | Parent report |
| 2. Gender | Parent report |
| 3. Prematurity | Medical records |
| 4. Cardiac problem | Medical records |
| 5. Seizure problem | Medical records |
| 6. Type of disability | Medical records |
| 7. Severity of psychomotor impairment | T1 standard score (MDI) on the Mental Scale of the *Bayley Scales of Infant Development* |
| B. Family demographic characteristics: | |
| 1. Maternal education | Maternal report |
| 2. Maternal marital status | Maternal report |
| 3. Maternal employment status | Maternal report |
| 4. Maternal health status | Maternal report |
| C. Child temperament | Sum of adaptability, demandingness, and mood subscales of *Parenting Stress Index* |
| D. Family ecology: | |
| 1. Quality of the home environment | Total score on *HOME* |
| 2. Family adaptability | Score on 14 items from the *FACES II* scale |
| 3. Family cohesion | Score on 16 items from the *FACES II* scale |
| 4. Maternal locus of control | Scores on the *Child Improvement Locus of Control Scales* |
| E. Early intervention services: | |
| 1. Service intensity for total services, home visits, center-based individual services, child groups, parent groups | *Monthly Service Records,* indicating hours for each type of service and discipline of provider |
| 2. Staffing structure (unidisciplinary vs. multidisciplinary) | '' |
| 3. Service location (home, center, mixed) | '' |
| 4. Service format (individual, group, mixed) | '' |
| F. Services other than early intervention program: | |
| 1. Child therapy (physical therapy, occupational therapy, speech/language therapy) | Parent report of receipt of services and hours of service |
| 2. Child support services (visiting nurse, case management) | '' |
| 3. Family support services (counseling, case management, visiting nurse, respite care, homemaker) | '' |

TABLE 7 (*Continued*)

| Variable | Measure |
|---|---|
| G. Child competence: | |
| 1. Mental age...................... | Age equivalent of raw score on the Mental Scale of the *Bayley Scales of Infant Development* |
| 2. Spontaneous play .................. | Mean level of play on 14-step *EICS Play Scale* |
| 3. Adaptive behavior................. | Age equivalent of total raw score on *Vineland Adaptive Behavior Scales* |
| 4. Child-mother interaction ............ | Score on child subscales of *Nursing Child Assessment Teaching Scale* |
| H. Family adaptation: | |
| 1. Mother-child interaction ............ | Score on parent subscales of *Nursing Child Assessment Teaching Scale* |
| 2. Parenting stress.................... | Score on Parent Domain of *Parenting Stress Index* |
| 3. Social support: | |
| a) Network size .................... | Sum of 15 possible sources of support on *EICS Parent Support Scale* |
| b) Helpfulness ..................... | Sum of rated helpfulness of supports on *EICS Parent Support Scale* |
| 4. Effects on the family ............... | Score on *Impact-on-Family Scale* |

and Most (1981) and refined by Belsky, Hrncir, and Vondra (1983). Adaptations included a reduction in the total length of observation time, a standardized presentation procedure, and the addition of two categories (visual attention and visually guided reaching/batting) at the lower end of the scale. This 14-step scale (see Table 8) reflects a developmental sequence of play, ranging from simple sensorimotor manipulations (e.g., mouthing, banging, looking) through complex symbolic behavior involving pretense play with double substitution (e.g., treating a shell as a bowl and a stick as a spoon and stirring the shell with the stick). The child is observed for 10 min while interacting with two sets of toys (5 min per set) provided by the investigator. The investigator records the highest level of play and notes the play theme initiated by the child as well as the objects selected. The highest play behavior level shown by the child is recorded using a 15-sec time-sampling procedure. Although the Belsky-Most Scale has not been administered to infants with disabilities, a comparable scale developed by Hill and McCune-Nicolich (1981) was used in previous studies to score the play of young children with Down syndrome. The former scale was chosen for this investigation because its categories are more numerous and defined more elaborately, thus improving its ability to discriminate among children at different levels of development.

*McCarthy Scales of Children's Abilities (McCarthy, 1972).*—Like the Bayley Scales, the McCarthy Scales are composed of a standard series of tasks that

TABLE 8

EICS Observation Scale of Children's Spontaneous Play

| Step | Weight | Categories |
|------|--------|------------|
| 0 ..... | 0 | Unfocused |
| 1 ..... | .2 | Visual attention |
| 2 ..... | .4 | Visually guided reaching/batting |
| 3 ..... | 1.0 | Mouthing |
| 4 ..... | 2.0 | Manipulation |
| 5 ..... | 3.0 | Functional |
| 6 ..... | 4.0 | Juxtapose/relational |
| 7 ..... | 5.0 | Functional relational |
| 8 ..... | 6.0 | Enactive naming |
| 9 ..... | 7.0 | Pretend self |
| 10 .... | 8.0 | Pretend external |
| 11 .... | 9.0 | Substitution |
| 12 .... | 10.0 | Sequence pretend |
| 13 .... | 11.0 | Sequence pretend with substitution |
| 14 .... | 12.0 | Sequence pretend with double substitution |

Source.—Adapted from Belsky and Most (1981).

are presented to the child by an examiner. The McCarthy Scales include 18 tests comprising six subscales: verbal, perceptual-performance, quantitative, general cognitive, memory, and motor. The General Cognitive Index (GCI), used in the present study, was obtained from summing the raw scores for the first three scales. The raw score can be converted into a standard score or a mental age equivalent. The McCarthy Scales were administered at T2 to those children who were over 30 months of age and/or who did not reach a ceiling on the Bayley Scales.

*Vineland Adaptive Behavior Scales: Interview Form (Sparrow, Balla, & Cicchetti, 1984).*—The Vineland is a 577-item questionnaire measuring individual personal and social competence from birth through adulthood. Approximately 100 of these items are appropriate for the age group from birth to age 3. The items comprise four subscales: communication, daily living, socialization, and motor skills. Each subscale generates a raw score, and their sum yields a single Adaptive Behavior Composite. Standard scores and age equivalence scores can be derived from the raw scores.

Administration of the Vineland does not involve direct presentation of tasks, requiring rather an interview with a respondent who is familiar with the child's customary behavior. For this investigation, a semistructured interview was conducted during the home visit with each child's parent (usually the mother) to identify skills the child demonstrates on a regular basis. The Cronbach's alpha reliability coefficient for the Composite variable in the present study was .91.

*Family Measures*

*Child Improvement Locus of Control Scales (DeVillis et al., 1985).*—This 27-item Likert scale was designed to measure parental beliefs concerning who or what influences the improvement of their children. The measure includes five subscales, which reflect the belief that one's child improves because of (*a*) chance, (*b*) divine influence, (*c*) the efforts of professionals, (*d*) the child's own efforts, or (*e*) parents' efforts to help their child. Both mothers and fathers completed this questionnaire independently, following the home visit. The Cronbach's alpha reliability coefficient for each of the subscales was as follows: chance, .67; divine influence, .80; professionals, .74; child's efforts, .72; and parents' efforts, .66.

*EICS Parent Support Scale.*—This scale was adapted from the 18-item Family Support Scale developed by Dunst, Jenkins, and Trivette (1984). This instrument taps a variety of sources of formal and informal support and includes a five-point Likert scale to measure the degree of helpfulness that the respondent attributes to each source. Both mothers and fathers completed this scale independently, following the home visit. The Cronbach's alpha for the helpfulness measure was .69.

*Family Adaptability and Cohesion Evaluation Scales (FACES II; Olson, Bell, & Portner, 1982).*—FACES II is a 30-item self-administered questionnaire measuring two aspects of family functioning: emotional cohesion (16 items) and adaptability (14 items) within the family. Both mothers and fathers completed this questionnaire independently, following the home visit. The Cronbach's alpha reliability coefficient was .86 for the cohesion subscale and .79 for adaptability.

*Home Observation for Measurement of the Environment (HOME; Caldwell & Bradley, 1984).*—The HOME is a measure designed to assess the quality of a young child's caregiving environment. It consists of 45 binary items organized into six subscales that tap the mother's responsivity to the child, use of restriction and punishment, physical qualities of the home, availability of play materials, maternal involvement, and variety in daily stimulation. Administration of the scale requires a semistructured interview with the mother in the home, and items were completed through both observation and maternal report. The Cronbach's alpha reliability coefficient for the total score was .74.

*Impact-on-Family Scale (Stein & Reissman, 1980).*—This 24-item scale was developed originally to measure the effect of a child with a chronic illness on the family system. Slight modifications were made in the wording of scale items for this study to reflect its use with families of children with developmental delays or disabilities. On the basis of a factor analysis of data from the original standardization sample, four factors were identified:

financial burden (called "financial strain," four items), social interaction within and outside the home (called "familial/social strain," nine items), subjective feelings of distress by the parent (called "personal strain," six items), and a positive sense of mastery (called "mastery strain," five items). Both mothers and fathers completed this instrument independently, following the home visit. The Cronbach's alpha reliability coefficient for the total scale was .89.

*Nursing Child Assessment Teaching Scale (NCATS; Barnard, 1978; Barnard et al., 1989; Barnard & Kelly, 1990).*—This observational rating scale was designed to assess a teaching interaction between a mother and her child. A task just beyond the child's ability level is selected for the mother to teach the child. The scale consists of 73 binary items that produce two summary scores: a score for the mother's interaction with her child (based on four subscales: sensitivity to cues, response to distress, social-emotional growth fostering, and cognitive growth fostering) and a score for the child's interaction with his or her mother (based on two subscales: clarity of cues and responsiveness to parent). The mother's summary score was used as a family outcome; its Cronbach's alpha reliability coefficient was .81. The child's summary score was used as a child outcome; its Cronbach's alpha reliability coefficient was .80.

*Parenting Stress Index (PSI; Abidin, 1986).*—This 101-item scale taps several areas of parent attitudes, feelings, and stresses in the parent-child interactive system related to child characteristics, parent characteristics, life events, and demographic variables. The PSI yields two summary scores. The Parent Domain score is derived from seven subscales (depression, attachment, restrictions in role, sense of competence, social isolation, relations with spouse, and parent health) and served as a family outcome measure. Its Cronbach's reliability coefficient was .92. The second summary score is the Child Domain score, derived from six subscales, three of which (adaptability, demandingness, and mood) were used as a measure of child temperament. Its Cronbach's alpha reliability coefficient was .83.

### Service Measures

*Family services information forms* were completed through maternal interview to record the types of services a child and family received prior to enrolling in an early intervention program, as well as the types and frequency of services they received during the 1-year study period, other than from their core early intervention program. Medical, therapeutic, financial, and support services for the child, in addition to financial and support services for other family members, were recorded.

*Monthly services records* were completed by early intervention staff to compile comprehensive data on the quantity, type, and discipline of the provider for all program services delivered to sample children and families. Hours of service provided (in contrast to hours planned) were recorded to within one-quarter of an hour. Data were collected on seven types of service, each corresponding to a category of service included in the standard reporting and billing forms required of the Massachusetts programs for reimbursement by the Department of Public Health and Medicaid. These services included home visits (either child, family, or parent-child focused) and center-based individual child treatments (e.g., physical, occupational, or speech and language therapies), individual parent treatments (e.g., counseling), individual parent-child treatments (e.g., child-oriented therapies provided jointly with parent), child groups (i.e., adult-guided peer experiences), parent-child groups (i.e., educational and social experiences for children and parents together), and parent groups (i.e., professionally guided support groups). Initial intake and periodic assessment services were not included. Each monthly form was checked by the research staff, and any questions or problems were reviewed with the service program. Periodic visits to programs were made by research coordinators to cross-check original service files and corresponding monthly services records for a randomly selected subsample of study children.

The following service variables were created: service intensity (defined as mean hours per month for each specific service and for total services); staffing structure (defined as unidisciplinary when 75% or more of service hours were provided by a single discipline and multidisciplinary when less than 75% of service hours were delivered by a single discipline); service location (defined as 75% or more of service hours delivered in a family's home, in a center, or through a mixed model with a predominance of neither location); and service format (defined as 75% or more of service hours provided as individual service, as group service, or through a mixed model).

## DATA ANALYSIS

### Determination of Sample Sizes

Power analyses (available from the authors) estimated that a total sample of 180 subjects with T1 to T2 data (60 subjects in each type of disability group) would provide a .86 probability of detection of moderate effects. Because attrition between T1 and T2 was lower than we had anticipated, our final sample size ($N$ = 190) exceeded that of our original estimate, although missing data on some outcome measures resulted in variable sample sizes for the study's analyses.

Despite extensive follow-up procedures and payment to parents for completion of the questionnaires, data were missing for some of the family variables that were collected by self-administered questionnaires completed by mothers and fathers following the home visits. Table 9 presents the sample sizes at T1 and T2 and the resulting sample sizes used in the creation of standardized residuals for both the child and the family outcomes (based on maternal and paternal responses). Since fewer fathers than mothers responded to questionnaires, maternal responses were used in all analyses except for those in which mothers' and fathers' responses were compared. As noted earlier, few significant sociodemographic differences were found between families for whom there were complete data and those for whom some data were missing.

## Inspection of the Variables and Data Reduction

After coding, data entry, and preliminary programming, the frequency distributions of all the variables were examined. Any out-of-range values were inspected, and corrections were made for errors due to data coding or entry. Missing values on scales derived from the self-administered questionnaires were double-checked against the raw data for each respondent. Sample members were contacted promptly after the return of their questionnaires to retrieve any missing data. In a small number of cases, scores on single items within the measures' subscales were not obtained. On the basis of procedures described by Anderson, Basilevsky, and Hum (1983), mean score replacement was used if fewer than 10% of the items for a particular subscale were missing. If more than 10% of the items were missing for a subscale, the case was deleted from analyses in which that variable was included.

Next, the subscales of each instrument were checked for internal reliability using Cronbach's alpha and compared to values reported in studies validating the instrument. In general, we found high reliability for the domain scores (i.e., summary scores) on each instrument, as reported earlier in this chapter. Finally, to operationalize several of the key constructs used in this study, we created summary variables for temperament, severity of psychomotor impairment, and early intervention service characteristics, as described in Table 7 above.

## Approach to Statistical Analyses

In general, statistical analyses involved standard nonparametric (i.e., chi square) and parametric procedures (i.e., $t$ tests, analysis of variance, multivariate analysis of variance using the Pillai $V$ test of significance, corre-

TABLE 9

Sample Sizes at T1 and T2 for Child
and Family Outcomes

| Outcome | T1 | T2 | T1 to T2 Residual Scores |
|---|---|---|---|
| Child outcomes: | | | |
| Mental age.............. | 190 | 189 | 189 |
| Spontaneous play......... | 190 | 189 | 189 |
| Adaptive behavior ........ | 190 | 190 | 190 |
| Child-mother interaction... | 190 | 189 | 189[a] |
| Family outcomes (mothers): | | | |
| Mother-child interaction ... | 190 | 189 | 189 |
| Parenting stress .......... | 179 | 155 | 152 |
| Effects on family ......... | 177 | 154 | 150 |
| Social support: | | | |
| Network size ........... | 177 | 155 | 151 |
| Helpfulness............. | 177 | 155 | 151 |
| Family outcomes (fathers): | | | |
| Parenting stress .......... | 140 | 119 | 111 |
| Effects on family ......... | 139 | 117 | 110 |
| Social support: | | | |
| Network size ........... | 140 | 118 | 110 |
| Helpfulness............. | 140 | 118 | 110 |

[a] Standardized T2 score.

lation, partial correlation, and multiple regression). Because many of these tests require that distributional assumptions be met, the distributions of all outcome measures were tested for normality. We found only one outcome measure (child-mother interaction) to deviate significantly from normality. Data transformations (e.g., squaring) were employed for this outcome, and the major statistical analyses were conducted with and without the transformed variable. Because there were no differences in the results of our analyses of the transformed and untransformed data, analyses of the untransformed variables are presented for the sake of consistency and clarity. Furthermore, in order to limit the number of spurious findings and to maintain a reasonable alpha level on significance tests, analyses were conducted primarily on domain or total scale scores rather than on subscales. However, when significant differences were found on domain scores, we also report analyses of subscales to aid in the understanding of those aspects of the domain that contributed to the significant differences.

As anticipated, two critical issues emerged in the analyses of these data. First, we confronted the question of whether to analyze specific outcomes for children using standard scores or age equivalence scores for psychomotor development and adaptive behavior. Despite the acknowledged limitations in interpretation of age equivalence scores, we selected this approach because a substantial portion of our sample (26.3%) had scores so low on the Bayley Scales at T1 that a valid standard score could not be determined. Even after employing extrapolation procedures for the low scores (Naglieri, 1981), 16.9% of our sample could not be assigned a standard score. Furthermore, on conceptual grounds, standard scores (like other norm-referenced scales) are not as useful as age equivalence in measuring change because, with standard scores, absolute levels of change may be masked by changes in the reference group. In this study, we are interested in understanding the predictors and correlates of change in children with disabilities rather than in analyzing their change in relation to that of normally developing children. Moreover, age equivalence scores are known to be more sensitive to changes in growth than are standard scores (Willett, 1988).

A second issue we confronted involved the measurement of change from T1 to T2. Although much has been written about the difficulties of analyzing change in longitudinal research (Appelbaum & McCall, 1983; Cronbach & Furby, 1970), consensus does not emerge around any one approach. The strengths and weaknesses of various statistical options for the measurement of change have been discussed elsewhere (Hauser-Cram & Krauss, 1991). The most straightforward approach to understanding change between two points in time would appear to be an analysis of the simple difference in the scores. Two related problems emerge, however, in using this approach.

First, researchers have demonstrated that, even in cases where the tests used at each time point have reasonably high reliability coefficients, simple difference scores are often unreliable because of the compounding of measurement error from the pretest and posttest (Bereiter, 1963; Cronbach & Furby, 1970; Lord, 1956). Second, many investigators have noted a negative correlation between initial status on a measure and the calculated difference score. Those with low initial scores tend to change a great deal, whereas those with high initial scores tend to change very little. Although debate in the statistical literature indicates that, under certain conditions, the difference score may still be the best unbiased measure of change (Rogosa & Willett, 1983; Zimmerman & Williams, 1982), many researchers have turned to other approaches.

Two specific alternatives for analyzing change have been proposed. Several studies of the effectiveness of early intervention services, for example, have used indices of change based on a calculation of "developmental months" gained per month of participation in an early intervention program (Bagnato & Neisworth, 1980; Dunst, 1986; Wolery, 1983). Although individual indices vary slightly in their method of calculation, they appear to yield similar results (Rosenberg, Robinson, Finkler, & Rose, 1987). These measures are limited, however, by their reliance on age equivalents developed from standardized tests and by their assumption of constant and linear growth. Indexes of change also suffer from some of the same problems as simple difference scores, as they typically are characterized by a negative relation between initial status and change.

The use of residual change scores represents another approach to the analysis of change (Hauser-Cram & Krauss, 1991) and is the one we have selected for this study. Cronbach and Furby (1970) defined the residual change score as "primarily a way of singling out individuals who have changed more (or less) than expected" (p. 70), on the basis of the difference between the actual posttest score that an individual achieves and the score that would be predicted by a regression line derived from his or her pretest score. Given that our primary goal is to understand the correlates and predictors of greater or lesser change in children and families, all of whom are assumed to be demonstrating developmental growth, the use of residual scores provides an efficient and flexible analytic approach.

Using this approach for each outcome, the observed T2 scores were regressed on the observed T1 scores, resulting in the creation of a set of "expected" T2 scores. The difference between the subject's actual (or observed) and expected T2 score was calculated and is termed the "residual." In order to make comparisons of *relative,* not absolute, change across all the study outcomes, the set of residuals for each outcome was then standardized to a mean of zero and a standard deviation of one. On the basis of the T1 to T2 correlations for the full set of outcome measures (see Table 10), residuals were calculated for all outcomes, except child-mother interaction, which had a low and nonsignificant T1 to T2 correlation. (Standardized T2 outcomes were used in analyses of T2 child-mother interaction.) Diagnostic analyses confirmed that the residuals for each outcome conformed to a normal distribution.

Tests for the homogeneity of variance of the residuals across the three diagnostic groups (using Box-M) were nonsignificant for the family outcomes. For the child outcomes, some of the variances demonstrated significant (although slight) differences, with the largest variance occurring in the largest of the three disability groups (e.g., motor impairment). As described by Olson (1976), the Pillai $V$ is the most robust test when variances are not equal. In the multivariate analyses of variance (MANOVA) presented in this *Monograph,* the Pillai $V$ test is used to evaluate the significance of the independent variable. Standard parametric statistical procedures were employed in analyzing residuals to test for significant differences in the residual scores by group membership or for the percentage of variance accounted for in the residuals by the set of independent variables.

The use of standardized residual scores has many benefits and a few drawbacks. The advantages relate to the amount of information that such scores incorporate. For example, the expected scores take into account four critical pieces of information: (1) an individual's T1 score; (2) the distribution of the entire sample at T1; (3) the relation (i.e., the slope of the regres-

TABLE 10

T1 and T2 Correlations
for Child and Family Outcomes

| Outcome | r between T1 and T2 Scores |
|---|---|
| Mental age[a] .................... | .81*** |
| Spontaneous play[a] .............. | .68*** |
| Adaptive behavior[b].............. | .81*** |
| Child-mother interaction[a] ........ | .08 |
| Mother-child interaction[a] ........ | .29*** |
| Parenting stress[c]................ | .75*** |
| Effects on the family[d] ........... | .64*** |
| Social support: | |
| Network size[e].................. | .43*** |
| Helpfulness[e] .................. | .51*** |

[a] $N = 189$.　　[d] $N = 150$.
[b] $N = 190$.　　[e] $N = 151$.
[c] $N = 152$.　　*** $p < .001$.

sion line) between T1 and T2 for the entire sample; and (4) the distribution of the entire sample at T2. The residual takes into account the individual's actual T2 score as well. Individuals who start off with different T1 scores will have different expected T2 scores. Therefore, individuals who demonstrate the same absolute amount of change may have different residual scores because their T1 scores differ and, thus, their expected T2 scores differ. This fact often conforms to our knowledge of how individuals change (i.e., individuals at different ends of the continuum are expected to change differently).

Residual scores do not contain the bias displayed by simple change scores. Residual scores have a zero correlation with initial status and thus permit analyses to focus on questions of efficacy, regardless of initial status.[2] Further, they can be calculated on any interval-level measure and therefore expand the range of child and family outcomes that can be investigated in developmental research.

Because residual scores are measures not of absolute change but rather of relative change, they should be interpreted as scores that are "higher (or lower) than predicted." A full understanding of residual scores requires some knowledge of average group change and an understanding of whether higher or lower scores are associated with beneficial changes. In this study, outcomes that represent benefits to the child or family are not always in the

[2] The computation of the residual scores involves partialing out T1 scores. This results in a zero correlation between initial status and residual scores, but a correlation between residualized gain and T2 scores often occurs. Thus, those individuals who have demonstrated more relative change (regardless of their initial status) often tend to have higher scores at T2.

same direction. Positive signs for the residuals represent benefits for the child outcomes (mental age, spontaneous play, adaptive behavior, and child-mother interaction) and for some family outcomes (mother-child interaction as well as social support network size and perceived helpfulness). A negative residual is associated with family benefits on two outcomes (parenting stress and effects on the family). Because parenting stress and effects on the family have small but positive increases from T1 to T2 for the sample as a whole, those parents who changed less than predicted on those measures (i.e., reported less increase in stress or in adverse family effects) had more beneficial outcomes.

While residual scores have not been widely used as a measure of change, they have been used in prior studies (e.g., Caplan, Vinokur, Price, & van Ryn, 1989; Resnick, 1985) and represent a flexible approach that capitalizes on the full range of information available in pre- and posttest measures.[3] Moreover, residuals provide a direct approach to the task of identifying the correlates of greater or less change within populations who are recipients of deliberate efforts to enhance developmental progress.

[3] Any analysis of two data points requires assumptions derived from a linear model. However, there is a fundamental difference in the linear assumptions underlying raw vs. residualized gain scores. The former are based on an assumption of constant and linear increments for all individuals; the latter are derived from a linear estimate of T2 scores from T1 scores.

# IV. SERVICES RECEIVED DURING THE STUDY PERIOD

## SERVICES RECEIVED WITHIN
## AN EARLY INTERVENTION PROGRAM

Early intervention services data were collected beginning from the T1 visit and extending through the date of the T2 visit. Analyses of service data focused on four key characteristics: *service intensity* (mean hours received per month for each specific service and for all services combined), *staffing structure* (unidisciplinary or multidisciplinary), *service location* (home based, center based, or mixed), and *service format* (individual, group, or mixed). The operational definitions of these four service variables were described in Chapter III.

It should be remembered that our data do not reflect the content or curriculum of the services provided by the early intervention programs. We do not know, for example, the extent to which the content of a home visit may have differed from or mirrored that of a center-based individual session with the parent and child. The basis for our analyses is the quantity of services provided (both overall and for specific types of services) and their organizational or structural characteristics. Although limited, this is nevertheless appropriate given the importance of service intensity and structure from a policy and program perspective and given the multisite conduct of this investigation, which requires comparability in measurement across all sites. With this caveat, this chapter presents a detailed portrait of the service experiences, both within and outside early intervention programs, of the 190 children and their families.

Extensive analyses were conducted to evaluate the presence of systematic between-program differences in the intensity and types of services received by sample members. The median number of study participants per program was five (range = 1–20), and only three of the 29 programs contributed 15 or more families to the sample. Within individual programs, the range of service hours delivered per family was considerable, reaching as high as 17 hours per month. Furthermore, analysis of variation in service formats (e.g., home visits, individual center-based sessions, or center-based group services) revealed substantial differences in both the intensity and the combinations of services received by a given child and family on a month-to-month basis over the course of the 1-year study period (Erickson, 1991).

In order to understand the magnitude of within-program variability further, we conducted separate analyses of the three programs that contributed 15 or more members to the sample. These analyses revealed that families of children with the same type or level of severity of disability received markedly different amounts of service. For example, in one program, families of children with more severe impairment (MDI $<$ 50, $N$ = 5) received a rate of 1.7–17.6 hours of service per month, whereas families of children with relatively mild impairment ($N$ = 14) received between 1.1 and 11.9 hours monthly. In another program, families of children with Down syndrome ($N$ = 3) received between 2.5 and 11.1 hours per month, families of children with motor impairment ($N$ = 12) averaged from less than 1 hour to 9.3 hours per month, and families of children with developmental delay ($N$ = 5) received between 2.8 and 12.3 hours. Thus, because of the small number of sample members provided by most participating programs, and given the large within-program variability in both intensity and patterns of service delivery, all service data were aggregated across programs, and site-specific variability was not considered to be a significant detriment to the understanding of service patterns for the sample as a whole.

### Intensity of Services

The percentage of sample members who received each of the seven types of services provided by early intervention programs and the amount of service hours received are summarized in Table 11 and Figure 1. In preliminary analyses utilizing $t$ tests, we examined whether there was a significant difference in the intensity of services based on the child and family demographic characteristics described in Table 7 above. The results indicated that overall service intensity was not associated with the child's gender, prematurity status, or health characteristics. We did find that older children received more total service hours ($r$ = .25, $p <$ .001), more hours of child groups ($r$ = .35, $p <$ .001), and more hours of center-based individual child services ($r$ = .22, $p <$ .001). Greater maternal participation (in hours) in parent groups was also correlated with the child's age ($r$ = .13, $p <$ .05). Differences based on the child's type of disability and severity of psychomotor impairment were also found; these are discussed below. With respect to family characteristics, utilizing analyses of variance no differences in overall service intensity were found to be related to maternal employment, mater-

TABLE 11

SERVICES RECEIVED WITHIN EARLY INTERVENTION PROGRAM OVER
THE FIRST YEAR ($N = 190$)

| Service | Service Intensity for Full Sample: M Hours/Month (SD) | Range (Hours) | % of Sample Who Received Service | Intensity for Those Who Received Service: M Hours/Month (SD) |
|---|---|---|---|---|
| Home visits . . . . . . . . . . . . | 3.0 (1.9) | 0–9.0 | 96.8 | 3.1 (1.8) |
| Center-based individual: | | | | |
| Child. . . . . . . . . . . . . . . | .1 (.4) | 0–3.5 | 24.7 | .5 (.8) |
| Parent. . . . . . . . . . . . . . | < .1 (.1) | 0–2.0 | 5.3 | .3 (.6) |
| Parent-child . . . . . . . . . . | .5 (.8) | 0–4.4 | 55.8 | .8 (.9) |
| Center-based group: | | | | |
| Child group . . . . . . . . . . | 1.4 (2.3) | 0–11.3 | 54.7 | 2.6 (2.6) |
| Parent-child group. . . . . . | .9 (1.6) | 0–8.1 | 54.2 | 1.7 (1.8) |
| Parent group: | | | | |
| Mothers . . . . . . . . . . . . . | .9 (1.3) | 0–6.0 | 54.7 | 1.6 (1.5) |
| Fathers . . . . . . . . . . . . . | .1 (.2) | 0–1.8 | 14.7 | .5 (.5) |
| Total services. . . . . . . . . . . | 6.9 (4.5) | .1–21.0 | 100 | 6.9 (4.5) |

nal health, marital status, or maternal education. Table 12 presents the
mean hours for each type of service based on the child's type of disability
and severity of impairment. Given the confound between the child's type
of disability and chronological age (as discussed in Chap. III), we also examined whether the pattern of differences in the average hours per month of
services reported in Table 12 persisted when the child's age was used as a
covariate in the two-way analyses of variance. Instances where significant
age-related differences in patterns were established are noted in the discussion that follows.

*Home visits.*—All but six families in the study received home visits during their first year in early intervention programs. The average level of
home visits was 3.1 hours per month, although the range was large (0–9
hours). There were no differences in the frequency of home visits related
to the child's type of disability. Families of children with more severe psychomotor impairment, however, received significantly more hours of home
visits per month, on average, than families of children with relatively mild
impairment (see Table 12).

*Center-based individual services.*—Center-based individual services, pro-

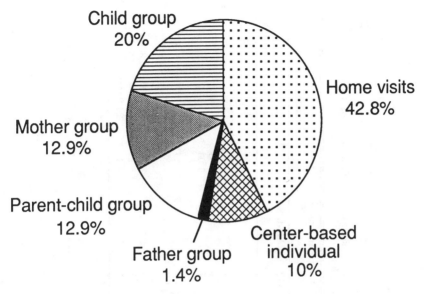

Fig. 1.—Percentage of monthly service hours by type of service over the first year (N = 190).

vided to the child alone, the parent alone, or the parent and child together, were the least commonly received. While slightly over half the families received at least one parent-child individual center-based session, less than one-quarter of the children and only about 5% of parents received individual therapeutic sessions at their early intervention program. The intensity of these services, when provided, was modest (i.e., less than 1 hour per month, on average). No differences were found in the intensity of individual center-based services related to the child's type of disability or severity of psychomotor impairment.

*Center-based group services.*—Over half the sample received either child group services or parent-child group services. Again, the range in average hours per month was large for both these types of services. The average intensity was under 3 hours per month for child group services and under 2 hours per month for parent-child groups. While there were no differences in the intensity of parent-child groups associated with the child's type of disability or severity of psychomotor impairment, a more complicated picture emerged in the analysis of child group services. Specifically, we found an interaction, with and without the child's age as a covariate, $F(2,183) = 4.03$, $p < .05$, and $F(2,184) = 4.5$, $p < .05$, respectively, between type of disability and severity of impairment with respect to the intensity of child groups (see Table 12). For children with Down syndrome and with develop-

TABLE 12

MEAN HOURS OF SERVICES DELIVERED MONTHLY WITHIN EARLY INTERVENTION PROGRAM OVER FIRST YEAR BY TYPE AND SEVERITY OF DISABILITY (N = 190)

| SERVICE | DOWN SYNDROME | | MOTOR IMPAIRMENT | | DEVELOPMENTAL DELAY | | F RATIOS[a] | | |
|---|---|---|---|---|---|---|---|---|---|
| | Mild (N = 51) | Mod./Sev. (N = 3) | Mild (N = 46) | Mod./Sev. (N = 31) | Mild (N = 43) | Mod./Sev. (N = 16) | D | S | D × S |
| Home visits | 2.9 | 3.4 | 2.7 | 4.0 | 2.5 | 4.0 | .40 | 16.77*** | .35 |
| Center-based individual: | | | | | | | | | |
| Child | <.1 | .2 | .1 | .2 | .1 | .4 | .59 | 3.62 | .76 |
| Parent | <.1 | 0 | <.1 | 0 | <.1 | <.1 | .81 | .03 | .10 |
| Parent-child | .5 | <.1 | .5 | .6 | .4 | .1 | 1.04 | .39 | 1.15 |
| Center-based group: | | | | | | | | | |
| Child group | .6 | 3.4 | .9 | 1.2 | 1.9 | 4.3 | 12.81*** | 11.70*** | 4.51* |
| Parent-child group | .8 | .2 | 1.0 | 1.1 | 1.0 | .8 | .30 | .03 | .35 |
| Parent group: | | | | | | | | | |
| Mothers | .7 | 4.1 | .4 | .8 | .9 | 2.3 | 8.79*** | 20.41*** | 8.60*** |
| Fathers | <.1 | <.1 | .1 | .1 | <.1 | .1 | .27 | 1.09 | .93 |
| Total services | 5.6 | 11.4 | 5.7 | 7.9 | 6.9 | 12.0 | 4.44** | 24.24*** | 2.28 |

[a] D = type of disability, $df(2,184)$; S = severity of disability, $df(1,184)$; D × S = interaction term, $df(2,184)$.
* $p < .05$.
** $p < .01$.
*** $p < .001$.

mental delay of uncertain etiology, those with more severe psychomotor impairment received more than twice the average hours per month of child group than those with relatively mild severity. For children with motor impairment, however, the average hours per month of child group was comparable across both levels of severity of impairment.

*Parent groups.*—Slightly over half the mothers in the sample, but less than one in five of the fathers, attended at least one parent group during their first year in an early intervention program. For mothers who attended parent groups, the average hours per month was less than 2, while for fathers who attended any groups, the average was a scant half hour per month. We also found a significant interaction effect between the type of the child's disability and severity of impairment with respect to the hours of mothers' participation in parent groups (see Table 12). Mothers of children with Down syndrome and developmental delays had more intensive participation in parent groups than mothers of children with motor impairment. More intensive participation was also found for mothers of children with more severe, in contrast to relatively mild, psychomotor impairment across all diagnostic groups. The magnitude of difference was less pronounced, however, among mothers of children with motor impairment, whose intensity of participation in parent groups was the lowest within the sample. For fathers, no differences in intensity of parent group participation were found with respect to the child's type of disability or level of severity of impairment.

*Total services.*—The mean number of types of services received by sample families was greater than three. The mean number of total service hours received per month was a modest 6.9 hours. The variability in service experiences was striking, as reflected in the standard deviation of 4.5 hours and a range from a scant few minutes to 21 hours per month. As described above, the child's type of disability and level of severity of impairment contributed to the observed variability in the intensity of specific services received. This pattern also was found in the analysis of total average hours per month of services received. Differences related to the child's type of disability were significant, with families of children with developmental delays receiving the highest intensity of services in comparison to families of children with Down syndrome or motor impairment. When age of the child was controlled, however, this difference was no longer significant.

We also found differences related to the severity of the child's impairment, which remained with and without the child's age as a covariate, $F(1,183) = 22.29$, $p < .001$, and $F(1,184) = 24.2$, $p < .001$, respectively. Specifically, families of children with more severe psychomotor impairment received more hours per month on average of early intervention services than families of children with a relatively mild level of severity.

TABLE 13

SERVICE CHARACTERISTICS
OVER THE FIRST YEAR ($N$ = 190)

| Variable | $N$ | % |
|---|---|---|
| Staffing structure: | | |
| Unidisciplinary .... | 57 | 30.0 |
| Multidisciplinary ... | 133 | 70.0 |
| Locus of service: | | |
| Home based....... | 63 | 33.2 |
| Center based ...... | 30 | 15.7 |
| Mixed ........... | 97 | 51.1 |
| Format of service: | | |
| Individual......... | 89 | 46.8 |
| Group........... | 4 | 2.1 |
| Mixed ........... | 97 | 51.1 |

## Staffing Structure

As shown in Table 13, the majority of families (70%) received services primarily from a multidisciplinary array of service providers. The remainder received most of their services from provider(s) from a single discipline. Families of children with Down syndrome, in contrast to other sample families, more often received their services through a single discipline, $\chi^2(2, N = 190) = 11.7$, $p < .01$. This difference was also related to age, with younger children more likely to receive unidisciplinary services, $F(1,189) = 5.90$, $p < .05$. Again, as a result of our recruitment strategy, sample children with Down syndrome were younger than the other two groups, which may account for their greater participation in services delivered through a single primary discipline. We also found that families of children with more severe psychomotor impairment more often received services through a multidisciplinary model than families of children with relatively mild impairment, $\chi^2(1, N = 190) = 8.3$, $p < .01$.

## Locus of Service Delivery

Only one-third (33.2%) of the families received their services primarily in the home, and less than one in five (15.7%) received their services primarily at the early intervention program site. Indeed, the most common experience for families was the receipt of services both in their homes and at the early intervention program center (i.e., a mixed model). No differences were found (utilizing chi-square tests) in the locus of service with respect to the child's type of disability or severity of impairment.

*Format of Service Delivery*

Very few (*N* = 4) sample members received most of their services in a group setting. Rather, there was a roughly even split between sample members who received primarily individualized services (46.8%) (including home visits and center-based child, parent, or parent-child sessions, as described in Chap. III) and those who received a mixed model of both individualized and group services (51.1%). Utilizing chi-square tests, no differences in the format of services were found with respect to the child's type of disability or severity of impairment.

*Summary of Early Intervention Services Received*

Sample children and their families received a variety of services and a wide range of total service hours during their first year in an early intervention program. Home visits and child groups were the most commonly provided experiences. Overall, services tended to be delivered individually to children and their families, rather than in groups. A notable finding is that the mean level of intensity of service was a modest 7 hours per month.

The type and intensity of service received varied according to certain characteristics of children. Families of children who were older and those of children with more severe psychomotor impairment at the time of study entry received significantly more hours of service, overall, than did other families. Differences in service patterns by family characteristics were not found. In general, early intervention services appeared to have been matched to individual child characteristics rather than reflecting a uniform model of service delivery.

## SERVICES RECEIVED OTHER THAN FROM AN EARLY INTERVENTION PROGRAM

Information was collected from mothers at both T1 and T2 regarding therapeutic and support services received by each family other than from their early intervention program. The considerable degree to which families utilized a variety of such services is summarized in Table 14. Utilization ranged from zero to six services, with a mean of slightly more than one additional service received per family.

The percentage of sample children receiving individual therapeutic services increased almost threefold during the interval from T1 to T2, largely owing to increased use of physical and, to a lesser extent, occupational therapy. Those families who received additional therapeutic services for their child reported a median of 8.5 hours of such services over the 1-year study period. Families who received additional child-oriented support reported a median of 8.0 hours of this service. As expected, families who received child care services reported a relatively high number of hours (median = 627.5 hours).

Family-oriented support services increased almost twofold from 17.9% of the sample at T1 to 31.6% at T2. This substantial increase was explained by an almost ninefold increase in the use of respite care and a doubling of the percentage of families involved in counseling. Families who received family support services reported a median of 30.5 hours of these services over the 12-month study period. Approximately one-third of the sample families received financial support through a variety of publicly funded programs, most commonly in the form of nutritional support through the Women, Infants, and Children Program (WIC) and from participation in Medicaid. There was an overall increase in the percentage of sample families who received both Medicaid and other forms of public assistance between T1 and T2.

Analyses of correlations between the full range of child and family independent variables (see Table 7 above) and the receipt of outside services during the 1-year study period revealed few differences related to child factors but some patterns related to maternal characteristics. No significant differences were found in rates of utilization of additional services by the type or level of severity of the child's disability, except for child therapeutic services, which, as expected, were used more extensively by families of children with motor impairment, $\chi^2(2, N = 190) = 14.25, p < .001$. Not surprisingly, the receipt of financial support was significantly different for mothers by level of education. Over half the mothers with a high school diploma or less (56.7%) received some public financial support during the study year, compared to 23% of those who completed college and 3.8% of mothers with 17 or more years of education, $\chi^2(2, N = 190) = 33.7, p < .001$. Medicaid assistance was provided to 41.1% of those families where the mother had a high school education or less, compared to 13.5% where the mother attended college and none for the families with mothers who completed 17 or more years of education, $\chi^2(2, N = 190) = 26.5, p < .001$.

Chi-square analysis revealed no significant differences in the use of family support services related to maternal characteristics. However, child support services (case management and visiting nurse services) were received more often by families with mothers who completed a high school education or less, $\chi^2(2, N = 190) = 7.5, p < .05$. Slightly over one-quarter of these families (27.8%) received such services, compared to only 12.2% of families with college-educated mothers and 11.5% of families with mothers who had some postbaccalaureate education. Utilization of child care services also varied for mothers with different educational attainment. Over 30% of

TABLE 14

CHILD AND FAMILY SERVICES/SUPPORTS RECEIVED OTHER THAN EARLY
INTERVENTION PROGRAM ($N = 190$)

| Service | Received at Time of Study Entry T1 (%) | Received between T1 and T2 (%) | Change from T1 to T2 $(Z)^a$ |
|---|---|---|---|
| Child therapy.......................... | 5.8 | 15.8 | 3.13*** |
| Physical ............................. | 4.2 | 11.1 | |
| Speech/language ................... | 2.6 | 3.7 | |
| Occupational ...................... | .5 | 4.2 | |
| Child support services ............... | 17.9 | 19.5 | 1.74 |
| Visiting nurse..................... | 16.3 | 16.8 | |
| Case management ................. | 2.1 | 6.3 | |
| Child-care services................... | 7.4 | 10.5 | 1.58 |
| Family day care ................... | 6.3 | 9.5 | |
| Preschool........................ | 1.1 | 2.1 | |
| Family support services .............. | 17.9 | 31.6 | 3.47*** |
| Counseling ....................... | 8.4 | 16.3 | |
| Case management ................. | 5.3 | 4.2 | |
| Visiting nurse..................... | 2.6 | 2.6 | |
| Respite care ...................... | 2.1 | 17.9 | |
| Homemaker...................... | 1.6 | 2.1 | |
| Medicaid........................... | 20.0 | 24.7 | 2.16* |
| Other financial supports.............. | 29.5 | 36.3 | 2.91** |
| WIC............................. | 23.2 | 27.9 | |
| AFDC ........................... | 12.6 | 14.2 | |
| Food stamps...................... | 10.0 | 14.2 | |
| SSI (child)....................... | 3.7 | 11.6 | |
| Services for Handicapped Children ... | 0 | 5.3 | |
| SSDI ............................ | 1.6 | 1.1 | |

$^a$ Two tailed.  ** $p < .01$.
* $p < .05$.  *** $p < .001$.

those with 17 or more years of education used child care services, in comparison to 8.1% of college-educated mothers and 6.7% of those who did not pursue education beyond high school, $\chi^2(2, N = 190) = 13.2, p < .001$.

In summary, it is clear that a formal early intervention program is not necessarily the only service that sample families received during the study period. In fact, over half (52.6%) of the families in the sample received at least one service in addition to those provided through their early intervention program. For many families, the picture of services is indeed complex.

# V. FUNCTIONAL AND BEHAVIORAL CHARACTERISTICS
## OF SAMPLE CHILDREN AND FAMILIES

This chapter describes the functional and behavioral characteristics of the sample children and families at the time of their entry into an early intervention program (T1) and 1 year later (T2). Data are reported first for all the mediating variables assessed at study entry (T1) on the full sample ($N = 190$) and then for the dependent measures for those children ($N = 190$) and families ($N = 152$) for whom both T1 and T2 data were available. In each case, differences among the three sample subgroups based on the child's type of disability (i.e., Down syndrome, motor impairment, or developmental delay of uncertain etiology) are identified. Where possible, the scores we obtained are compared to those obtained from standardization samples or to those reported in the literature by other investigators.

These cross-sectional comparisons are designed to provide a descriptive portrait of our sample. They serve to contextualize our findings by revealing areas in which children with disabilities and their families are similar to or different from each other at the time of entry into an early intervention program as well as by demonstrating comparisons to children and families without significant developmental concerns. Unless otherwise noted, none of the reported standardization samples included children with disabilities or their families. Finally, it should be remembered that the family data reported in this chapter represent maternal responses to either interview questions or self-administered questionnaires. Analyses presented in Chapter VII investigate the differences between mothers and fathers in family outcomes.

## CHILD AND FAMILY MEDIATING VARIABLES

We examined several aspects of the children and their families' functioning that have been shown to mediate patterns of change in child development and/or family adaptation. Specifically, maternal ratings were obtained on the child's temperament, on the family's emotional cohesion and adaptability (as indicators of family functioning), and on maternal locus of control. We also used the HOME assessment to measure the characteristics of the home environment that support children's development. The mean and standard deviation scores for the study sample and normative values for each measure (where available) are summarized in Table 15. Differences by type of disability are presented in Table 16.

The child's *temperament* rating was derived from three subscales (adaptability, demandingness, and mood) of the Child Domain of the Parenting Stress Index (PSI). The scores for the sample as a whole ranged from 25.0 to 99.0 ($M = 53.4$), with higher scores indicating a more difficult temperament. As shown in Table 15, two of the three subscale scores are comparable to those reported for the standardization sample. Children in the present study, however, had significantly higher (more stressful) scores on the demandingness subscale than reported for the standardization sample. In analyses of differences in temperament by type of disability, children with Down syndrome were rated as less difficult than the other two groups (see Table 16).

For each domain and for each subscale of the PSI, a cutoff point in the distribution of scores has been identified by the scale's author (Abidin, 1986) that indicates values suggesting the need for clinical referral. In the EICS sample, slightly more than one-quarter (28.9%) of the mothers' ratings fell above the cutoff point on at least one of the three temperament subscales. The majority of those with high scores were mothers of children with motor impairment (32.5% of this group had clinically significant stress scores) or with developmental delay (37.2% of this group); only eight (14.8%) mothers of children with Down syndrome generated scores above the clinical referral cutoff on any of the three subscales, $\chi^2(2, N = 179) = 8.07, p < .05$.

Examination of the *adaptability and cohesion* subscale scores for sample mothers on the FACES II revealed significantly lower scores for the adaptability subscale in comparison to those reported for the standardization sample (Olson et al., 1982). The cohesion scores, in contrast, were comparable. No significant differences for either adaptability or cohesion were found among the three subgroups defined by the child's type of disability (based on MANOVA analyses). Using the categorization schema proposed for interpretation of this measure, our study sample as a whole scored as "structured" (with respect to adaptability) and "connected" (with respect to cohesion).

The Child Improvement Locus of Control (CILC) Scale was used to assess mothers' *locus of control* with respect to their children's developmental progress. The five subscales focus on control related to the mother's own efforts, the efforts of professionals, the efforts of the child, chance, or divine influence. Examination of the mean subscale scores indicated that, overall,

TABLE 15

Means and Standard Deviations of Mediating Variables at T1

| Variable | Study Sample at T1: $M$ (SD) | Standardization Sample: $M$ (SD) | $t$ |
|---|---|---|---|
| A. Child temperament:[a] | | | |
| PSI Child Domain: | | | |
| Adaptability.................... | 24.7 | 24.5 | .00 |
| | (6.4) | (5.7) | |
| Demandingness ............... | 19.4 | 18.1 | 2.94** |
| | (5.5) | (4.6) | |
| Mood ........................ | 9.2 | 9.6 | 1.49 |
| | (3.3) | (2.9) | |
| Composite index ................ | 53.4 | 52.2 | N.A. |
| | (13.3) | N.A. | |
| B. Family adaptability and cohesion:[b] | | | |
| FACES II subscales: | | | |
| Adaptability.................... | 47.2 | 49.9 | −4.73*** |
| | (6.8) | (6.6) | |
| Cohesion ...................... | 65.5 | 64.9 | .78 |
| | (9.2) | (8.4) | |
| C. Maternal locus of control:[c] | | | |
| CILC subscales: | | | |
| Divine influence ................ | 13.5 | 14.4 | 1.37 |
| | (5.7) | (5.6) | |
| Chance........................ | 10.0 | 9.5 | 1.01 |
| | (4.5) | (4.0) | |
| Child ......................... | 23.9 | 18.1 | 8.46*** |
| | (5.8) | (6.0) | |
| Parent ........................ | 32.1 | 28.8 | 6.65*** |
| | (3.2) | (5.1) | |
| Professional.................... | 25.3 | 28.9 | −5.10*** |
| | (5.7) | (6.2) | |
| D. Home environment:[d] | | | |
| HOME total score ................ | 35.1 | 30.9 | 12.07*** |
| | (4.8) | (7.6) | |
| Responsivity of mother .......... | 8.9 | 8.0 | 4.34*** |
| | (1.7) | (2.2) | |
| Acceptance of the child.......... | 6.6 | 5.3 | .73 |
| | (1.2) | (1.6) | |
| Organization of environment...... | 5.2 | 4.9 | 2.82** |
| | (.8) | (1.2) | |
| Provision of play materials ........ | 6.6 | 6.4 | .89 |
| | (1.8) | (2.4) | |
| Maternal involvement with child ... | 4.8 | 3.3 | 9.49*** |
| | (1.4) | (1.6) | |
| Variety of stimulation ........... | 3.0 | 3.0 | .00 |
| | (1.3) | (1.1) | |

[a] $N$ = 152 for the EICS sample; $N$ = 534 for the standardization sample.
[b] $N$ = 152 for the EICS sample; $N$ = 2,030 for the standardization sample.
[c] $N$ = 152 for the EICS sample; $N$ = 145 for the standardization sample.
[d] $N$ = 190 for the EICS sample; $N$ = 174 for the standardization sample.
** $p < .01$.
*** $p < .001$.

TABLE 16

DIFFERENCES IN MEDIATING VARIABLES BY TYPE OF DISABILITY

| Variable | Down Syndrome (N = 54): M (SD) | Motor Impairment (N = 77): M (SD) | Developmental Delay (N = 59): M (SD) | F[a] |
|---|---|---|---|---|
| Child temperament | 48.1 (11.4) | 55.0 (14.4) | 56.1 (12.2) | 5.90** |
| Family adaptability | 48.0 (6.7) | 46.8 (7.3) | 47.1 (6.3) | .47 |
| Family cohesion | 67.8 (8.0) | 64.1 (9.3) | 65.1 (10.0) | 2.46 |
| Maternal locus of control: | | | | |
|   Divine influence | 13.5 (5.3) | 13.1 (5.7) | 14.1 (6.1) | .49 |
|   Chance | 8.4 (3.3) | 10.5 (4.9) | 10.7 (4.6) | 4.81** |
|   Child | 23.6 (5.3) | 24.3 (5.7) | 23.5 (6.3) | .36 |
|   Parent | 32.6 (3.1) | 32.0 (3.3) | 31.8 (3.2) | .88 |
|   Professional | 25.2 (5.8) | 25.9 (5.5) | 24.4 (5.8) | .96 |
| Home environment | 33.9 (4.4) | 34.5 (5.2) | 37.0 (4.0) | 7.39*** |
|   Responsivity of mother | 8.7 (1.4) | 8.9 (1.9) | 9.0 (1.5) | .51 |
|   Acceptance of the child | 6.9 (.9) | 6.5 (1.4) | 6.4 (1.3) | 2.16 |
|   Organization of environment | 5.0 (.8) | 5.3 (.8) | 5.4 (.7) | 4.50* |
|   Provision of play materials | 5.7 (1.8) | 6.4 (1.6) | 7.6 (1.4) | 19.64*** |
|   Maternal involvement with child | 5.0 (1.2) | 4.5 (1.7) | 5.1 (1.2) | 4.06* |
|   Variety of stimulation | 2.7 (1.2) | 2.9 (1.2) | 3.5 (1.3) | 8.27** |

[a] $df$ range from (2,174) to (2,187).
* $p < .05$.
** $p < .01$.
*** $p < .001$.

sample mothers ascribed more control over their child's future progress to their own efforts than to any other possible source. It is notable, however, that maternal ascription of control to professionals and to the child was also high, suggesting belief in a multiplicity of determinants of child progress rather than a simple internal or external locus of control. MANOVA analyses across all the subscales revealed no significant effect based on type of disability. Univariate analyses, however, revealed greater belief in chance influences by mothers of children with developmental delays. Comparison of these data to findings from studies of parents of children with autism or physical disabilities reveals that our sample mothers attributed significantly more influence to their child's and their own efforts and significantly less influence to professional intervention than was found in the original standardization sample (Devillis et al., 1985).

The total HOME scores for the study sample were higher (indicating a more enriched *child-rearing environment*) than those reported for the original standardization sample of families with children aged 12 months (Caldwell & Bradley, 1984). The three subscales that were significantly higher were maternal responsivity, organization of the environment, and maternal involvement with the child. Although the mean for the total HOME score for the 54 families of infants with Down syndrome was significantly lower than the mean for families of children with developmental delay, it was significantly higher than the average HOME score for families with 6-month-old infants reported for the standardization sample, $M = 28.5$, $SD = 6.6$, $t(355) = 6.92$, $p < .001$. The average HOME score for the 59 families of children with developmental delays was significantly higher than the mean for families in the other two groups. The multivariate analysis of variance across the six subscales was significant, MANOVA $F(12,336) = 5.60$, $p < .001$. Univariate analyses of the subscales revealed that the largest difference was in the "provision of play materials" subscale, with families of children with developmental delays having the highest scores among the three groups. This finding may be explained, in part, by the older mean age of this subgroup and a consequent accumulation of more play materials over time. Families of children with developmental delays also had higher mean scores on the subscales measuring organization of the environment (in comparison to families of children with Down syndrome), maternal involvement (in comparison to families of children with motor impairment), and variety of stimulation (in comparison to both other subgroups).

## CHILD DEPENDENT VARIABLES

The child dependent variables include mental age equivalence, spontaneous play, adaptive behavior age equivalence, and child-mother interaction. The means and standard deviations for each of these dependent measures for the full sample at T1 and T2, and comparisons to standardization samples, are presented in Table 17. Differences by type of disability are summarized in Table 18.

The *mental age* equivalence score was based on performance on the Bayley Scales of Infant Development at T1 and on either the Bayley Scales or the McCarthy Scales of Children's Abilities at T2. At the time of study entry, the sample mean was 6.9 months. Half the sample had an age equivalent of 5.5 months or younger, 21.6% scored at a level of 1 month or less, and the highest age equivalent in the sample at T1 was 22 months. At T2, the mean mental age equivalent for the sample was 14.8 months, demonstrating an average gain of 7.9 months over the 12-month period. As expected, given their differences in chronological age at study entry, there were significant differences in mental age among the three diagnostic groups (see Table 18).

To provide an index of growth (in months) between the T1 and the T2 assessments, a rate-of-development measure was calculated (by developing a ratio of the change in mental age to the change in chronological age). The average developmental rate for the entire sample was 0.66 per month (SD = 0.4). What is important here is that analysis of variance indicated that differences in the rate of change by type of disability were not significant (Table 18). Figure 2 illustrates the parallel rates of change for the three disability groups. Eleven children (seven with motor impairment and four with developmental delay) either displayed no growth or showed regression over the 1-year study period. Thirty-five children (18.5% of the sample) demonstrated a growth in age equivalence of 12 months or more.

*Spontaneous play behavior* (as assessed by a modified version of the Belsky-Most Scales) varied greatly. The average level of child play at T1 involved mouthing or simple manipulation of toys, with only a few children demonstrating at least one episode of pretense play. At T2, the average level of child play involved functional use of objects, and 35 children demonstrated pretense as a modal level in their interaction with toys. Twelve children (6.3% of the sample) had lower average levels of play at T2 than at T1; however, 72.5% had play levels at least one step higher at T2 than at T1.

As anticipated, given their younger age, children with Down syndrome displayed low levels of spontaneous play at the time of study entry, with their average score indicating visual attention to toys. At T2, typical play increased two steps and involved "simple manipulation of objects"; no child with Down syndrome had a modal score of "unfocused," and one typically displayed "pretense."

The average play score of children with motor impairment at T1 indicated mouthing or simple manipulation of objects. By T2, children in this group increased on average almost two steps—that is, to use of toys in a functional manner—and 17.1% demonstrated pretense activities.

Children with developmental delays had spontaneous play scores at T1 that indicated "simple manipulation" of toys as their modal level of interaction. Only two typically were "unfocused" during the play session, and three typically used "pretense" in their play with toys. At T2, the average play of children with developmental delays increased about 1½ steps, reflecting a relational use of objects. However, 34.5% of this subgroup still typically used "simple manipulation," and 31.0% typically showed "pretense." Conse-

## TABLE 17

### MEANS AND STANDARD DEVIATIONS OF DEPENDENT VARIABLES AT T1 AND T2

| VARIABLE | STUDY SAMPLE AT T1: M (SD)[a] | STUDY SAMPLE AT T2: M (SD)[a] | STANDARDIZATION SAMPLE: M (SD) | t — T1 | t — T2 |
|---|---|---|---|---|---|
| *Child dependent variables* | | | | | |
| A. Mental age equivalent (months) | 6.9 (5.6) [1–22] | 14.8 (8.0) [1–37] | ... | ... | ... |
| B. Level of play | 47.0 (41.2) [0–192] | 97.3 (47.4) [0–228] | ... | ... | ... |
| C. Adaptive behavior age equivalent (months) | 7.4 (5.2) [0–21] | 14.1 (5.9) [0–36] | ... | ... | ... |
| D. Child-mother interaction: | | | | | |
| NCATS Child score[b] | 14.1 (4.4) | 17.4 (3.5) | 15.3 (4.0) | −3.50** | 7.37** |
| Clarity of cues | 7.3 (2.1) | 8.7 (1.4) | 8.0 (1.5) | −4.43** | 6.42** |
| Responsiveness to parent | 6.8 (2.8) | 8.7 (2.5) | 7.4 (2.9) | −2.69** | 6.34** |
| *Family dependent variables* | | | | | |
| E. Mother-child interaction: | | | | | |
| NCATS Parent score[c] | 36.3 (6.3) | 37.0 (5.6) | 41.0 (5.8) | −9.49** | −8.93** |
| Sensitivity to cues[c] | 9.2 (1.6) | 9.4 (1.2) | 9.3 (1.4) | −.82 | 1.11 |
| Response to distress[d] | 8.8 (2.3) | 8.1 (2.1) | 10.0 (1.7) | 6.82** | −11.87** |
| Social-emotional growth promoting[c] | 7.9 (1.9) | 7.6 (1.7) | 9.0 (1.5) | −7.59** | −10.77** |
| Cognitive growth promoting[c] | 10.4 (2.9) | 11.8 (2.7) | 12.7 (3.0) | −10.00** | −4.15* |

58

| | | | | |
|---|---|---|---|---|
| **F. Parenting stress:** | | | | |
| PSI Parent Domain[e] | 117.9 | 119.4 | 122.7 | |
| | (24.3) | (25.2) | (24.6) | |
| Depression | 18.6 | 18.8 | 20.4 | |
| | (5.6) | (5.7) | (5.6) | |
| | -2.14* | | | 1.43 |
| Attachment | 11.2 | 11.4 | 12.6 | |
| | (2.9) | (3.0) | (3.1) | |
| | -3.50*** | | | -3.45*** |
| Restrictions in role | 18.7 | 19.1 | 19.0 | |
| | (5.5) | (5.3) | (5.2) | |
| | -5.18*** | | | -4.32*** |
| Sense of competence | 27.4 | 27.9 | 29.2 | |
| | (6.2) | (6.3) | (6.3) | |
| | -.60 | | | .21 |
| Social isolation | 12.4 | 12.6 | 12.8 | |
| | (4.0) | (4.2) | (3.8) | |
| | -3.15** | | | -2.24* |
| Relations with spouse | 17.6 | 17.5 | 16.8 | |
| | (5.6) | (5.6) | (5.1) | |
| | -1.10 | | | -.53 |
| Parent health | 11.9 | 12.1 | 11.9 | |
| | (3.2) | (3.6) | (3.3) | |
| | 1.58 | | | 1.38 |
| | .00 | | | .62 |
| **G. Effects on family:** | | | | |
| IFS summary score[f] | 45.1 | 45.8 | 59.0 | |
| | (10.2) | (9.8) | (9.5) | |
| | -11.04*** | | | -10.66*** |
| Financial strain | 8.0 | 8.2 | 10.4 | |
| | (2.8) | (3.0) | (2.2) | |
| | -7.59*** | | | -6.71*** |
| Familial/social strain | 16.0 | 16.0 | 22.1 | |
| | (4.6) | (4.2) | (4.9) | |
| | -9.91*** | | | -10.22*** |
| Personal strain | 12.4 | 12.7 | 16.6 | |
| | (3.6) | (3.4) | (3.5) | |
| | -9.22*** | | | -8.75*** |
| Mastery strain | 8.7 | 8.9 | 9.9 | |
| | (2.1) | (2.1) | (1.9) | |
| | -4.70*** | | | -3.92*** |
| **H. Social support:** | | | | |
| No. of supports | 9.2 | 10.7 | N.A. | |
| | (2.2) | (2.2) | | |
| | [2-15] | [4-15] | | |
| Helpfulness | 23.1 | 26.2 | N.A. | |
| | (7.8) | (8.6) | | |
| | [2-54] | [6-46] | | |

a Range is given in square brackets.
b N = 179 for EICS sample; N = 918 for standardization sample.
c N = 179 for EICS sample; N = 922 for standardization sample.
d N = 179 for EICS sample; N = 871 for standardization sample.
e N = 152 for EICS sample; N = 534 for standardization sample.
f N = 152 for EICS sample; N = 100 for standardization sample.

* $p < .05$.
** $p < .01$.
*** $p < .001$.

TABLE 18

| Dependent Variable | Down Syndrome (N = 54): M (SD) | Motor Impairment (N = 77): M (SD) | Developmental Delay (N = 59): M (SD) | $F^a$ |
|---|---|---|---|---|
| *Child outcomes* | | | | |
| Mental age equivalent (months): | | | | |
| T1 | 2.0 | 7.0 | 11.2 | 64.52*** |
| | (1.6) | (4.6) | (5.6) | |
| T2 | 9.6 | 14.7 | 19.8 | 30.15*** |
| | (2.4) | (8.1) | (8.1) | |
| Rate of development per month | .62 | .64 | .72 | 1.08 |
| | (.2) | (.5) | (.4) | |
| Level of play score: | | | | |
| T1 | 3.8 | 1.60 | 2.58 | 58.11*** |
| | (.3) | (1.2) | (1.4) | |
| T2 | 2.32 | 3.35 | 4.02 | 19.70*** |
| | (.7) | (1.8) | (1.4) | |
| Adaptive behavior age equivalent (months): | | | | |
| T1 | 2.4 | 7.9 | 11.2 | 70.59*** |
| | (2.1) | (4.1) | (4.9) | |
| T2 | 10.4 | 13.8 | 17.9 | 29.26*** |
| | (2.1) | (5.9) | (6.1) | |
| Rate of development per month | .66 | .48 | .56 | 6.58** |
| | (.2) | (.3) | (.3) | |
| Child-mother interaction: | | | | |
| T1 | 12.1 | 14.9 | 14.8 | 8.32*** |
| | (4.4) | (4.5) | (3.9) | |
| T2 | 17.7 | 17.0 | 17.8 | .98 |
| | (3.4) | (3.8) | (3.2) | |
| *Family outcomes* | | | | |
| Mother-child interaction: | | | | |
| T1 | 37.4 | 36.0 | 35.7 | .30 |
| | (5.8) | (6.4) | (6.4) | |
| T2 | 37.4 | 36.5 | 37.3 | .62 |
| | (4.4) | (5.6) | (6.6) | |
| Parenting stress: | | | | |
| T1 | 112.4 | 124.2 | 115.3 | 3.44* |
| | (28.1) | (20.1) | (24.1) | |
| T2 | 112.5 | 126.4 | 117.5 | 4.24* |
| | (23.2) | (23.8) | (26.8) | |
| Effects on family: | | | | |
| T1 | 44.0 | 46.2 | 44.9 | .63 |
| | (10.1) | (10.9) | (9.5) | |
| T2 | 43.3 | 48.5 | 44.7 | 4.19* |
| | (8.8) | (10.5) | (9.3) | |

TABLE 18 (*Continued*)

| Dependent Variable | Down Syndrome (N = 54): M (SD) | Motor Impairment (N = 77): M (SD) | Developmental Delay (N = 59): M (SD) | $F^a$ |
|---|---|---|---|---|
| Maternal social support network size: | | | | |
| T1 | 9.7 (2.0) | 9.1 (2.0) | 8.9 (2.5) | .21 |
| T2 | 11.0 (2.2) | 10.4 (2.1) | 10.8 (2.4) | .31 |
| Helpfulness of supports: | | | | |
| T1 | 26.6 (7.8) | 21.8 (6.9) | 21.4 (8.0) | 7.02** |
| T2 | 30.3 (7.9) | 23.5 (8.1) | 25.7 (8.6) | 8.71*** |

$^a$ *df* range from (2,147) to (2,187).
\* $p < .05$.
\*\* $p < .01$.
\*\*\* $p < .001$.

quently, levels of play were quite scattered within this subgroup at the T2 assessment. As illustrated in Figure 3, the rates of change in spontaneous play levels were parallel for the three disability subgroups.

The mean *adaptive behavior* age equivalent of sample children (as measured by the Vineland Adaptive Behavior Scales) was 7.4 months at T1 and 14.1 months at T2. The average rate of development of 0.56 per month (SD = 0.3) for the sample as a whole was somewhat lower than that calculated for mental age equivalent. Eight children (4.2% of the sample) demonstrated either no gain or some loss in adaptive behavior over the 12-month

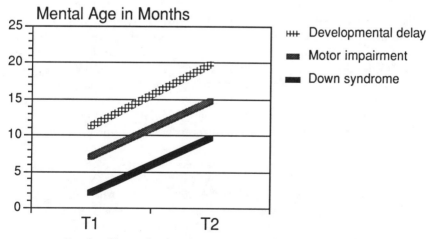

Fig. 2.—Change in mental age over 1 year by type of disability

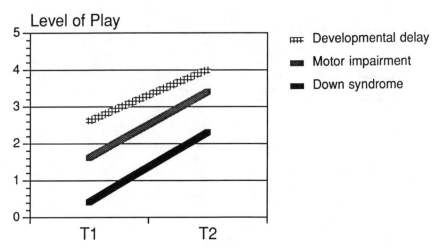

Fig. 3.—Change in spontaneous play over 1 year by type of disability

period; four of those also displayed loss or no gain in their mental age equivalent. Eight children (4.2% of the sample) gained 12 months or more in adaptive behavior skills.

As expected, cross-sectional differences were found among the three subgroups defined by type of disability. Differences in rates of change, however, did not follow a consistent or linear age-related pattern across the three subgroups (see Table 18 above and Fig. 4). For example, the rate of adaptive development for children with developmental delays of uncertain etiology (the oldest subgroup) was 0.56, laying midway between the rates of the other two groups (0.66 for Down syndrome and 0.48 for motor impairment). Furthermore, the rates of adaptive development for children in the developmental delay subgroup on each of the Vineland subscales (Table 19) were similar to those of the other two groups, except in the area of social development, where these children showed a significantly lower rate of change than children with Down syndrome (0.47 vs. 0.80). Children with motor impairment displayed significantly lower rates of development on the daily living and the social subscales, in comparison to children with Down syndrome. No between-group differences were found on the communication and motor subscales. Table 20 presents a descriptive summary of the wide variety of adaptive skills reported by sample mothers for their children.

Child scores on a measure of *child-mother interaction* (the Nursing Child Assessment Teaching Scale) reflected a significantly lower average score at T1 than that reported for the normative population. These scores improved

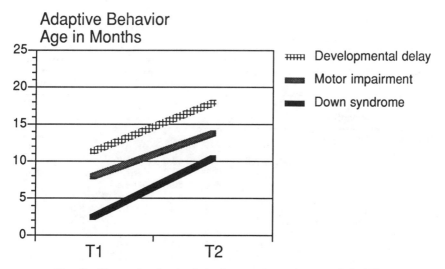

FIG. 4.—Change in adaptive behavior over 1 year by type of disability

at T2, with higher scores reported for sample children in comparison to the standardization sample; the greatest difference occurred on the "responsiveness to parent" subscale.

Interactions with their mothers at T1 were significantly lower for infants with Down syndrome than they were for sample children in the other two groups. Although the average score for a normative sample of infants of comparable age to the Down syndrome subsample (6 months) is lower ($M = 13.9$) than for older children (mean for 7–12 months = 15.3), chil-

TABLE 19

RATE OF ADAPTIVE DEVELOPMENT FOR STUDY CHILDREN BY TYPE OF DISABILITY

| Area of Development | Down Syndrome ($N = 54$): Rate per Month | Motor Impairment ($N = 77$): Rate per Month | Developmental Delay ($N = 59$): Rate per Month | $F^a$ |
|---|---|---|---|---|
| Communication . . . | .56 | .61 | .68 | .99 |
| Daily living . . . . . . . | .57 | .40 | .44 | 5.71** |
| Motor . . . . . . . . . . | .66 | .55 | .67 | 2.41 |
| Social . . . . . . . . . . | .80 | .35 | .47 | 22.31*** |

$^a$ $df(2,187)$.
** $p < .01$.
*** $p < .001$.

TABLE 20

ADAPTIVE SKILLS OF STUDY CHILDREN AT T1 AND T2 ($N = 190$)

| | DOWN SYNDROME ($N = 54$) | | MOTOR IMPAIRMENT ($N = 77$) | | DEVELOPMENTAL DELAY ($N = 59$) | |
|---|---|---|---|---|---|---|
| ADAPTIVE SKILL | T1 (%) | T2 (%) | T1 (%) | T2 (%) | T1 (%) | T2 (%) |
| Communication: | | | | | | |
| Smiles | 94.5 | 98.1 | 96.1 | 100 | 100 | 98.3 |
| Imitates sounds | 5.6 | 83.3 | 42.9 | 77.9 | 50.8 | 88.1 |
| Gestures "yes/no" | 0 | 37.1 | 26.0 | 67.5 | 49.2 | 86.4 |
| Points to body part | 0 | 35.2 | 20.8 | 68.8 | 37.3 | 84.8 |
| Uses phrases of noun-verb or 2 nouns | 0 | 1.9 | 0 | 24.7 | 8.5 | 37.3 |
| Uses 50 words or more | 0 | 0 | 0 | 23.4 | 3.4 | 27.1 |
| Daily living: | | | | | | |
| Eats solids | 11.1 | 74.1 | 55.8 | 84.4 | 76.3 | 98.3 |
| Feeds self with fork | 0 | 0 | 10.4 | 50.7 | 18.7 | 59.3 |
| Urinates in toilet | 0 | 0 | 0 | 10.4 | 5.1 | 20.4 |
| Asks to use toilet | 0 | 0 | 0 | 6.5 | 3.4 | 11.9 |
| Toilet trained at night | 0 | 0 | 0 | 2.6 | 0 | 1.7 |
| Social: | | | | | | |
| Shows interest in others | 18.5 | 83.3 | 72.7 | 87.0 | 74.6 | 94.9 |
| Reaches for person | 9.3 | 94.5 | 52.0 | 87.0 | 78.0 | 98.3 |
| Plays with toy alone | 29.7 | 98.2 | 89.6 | 92.2 | 91.5 | 96.6 |
| Imitates adult moves | 1.9 | 92.6 | 42.9 | 80.5 | 59.3 | 94.9 |
| Plays games with others | 0 | 3.7 | 10.4 | 27.3 | 16.9 | 44.1 |
| Plays make-believe | 0 | 0 | 1.3 | 9.1 | 1.7 | 20.3 |
| Has a preferred friend | 0 | 0 | 0 | 1.3 | 0 | 6.8 |
| Motor: | | | | | | |
| Sits supported 1 min | 38.9 | 98.1 | 81.8 | 94.8 | 91.5 | 98.3 |
| Picks up small objects | 11.1 | 98.1 | 76.6 | 90.9 | 88.1 | 98.3 |
| Crawls | 0 | 42.6 | 22.1 | 66.2 | 61.0 | 94.9 |
| Walks | 0 | 7.5 | 2.6 | 45.5 | 45.8 | 88.1 |
| Climbs on low play equipment | 0 | 13.0 | 9.1 | 42.9 | 32.2 | 76.3 |

dren with Down syndrome had significantly lower scores than the normative average, $t(302) = 2.58$, $p < .01$. Children with motor impairment did not differ significantly from similarly aged children in the normative sample, whereas children with developmental delays demonstrated lower average scores at T1 than those reported for the normative sample of the same chronological age, $t(192) = 3.56$, $p < .01$. At T2, scores increased for all three groups, and the mean between-group differences were not significant. Increases in the scores of sample children with motor impairment and with developmental delays were related largely to the "responsiveness to parent" subscale. For children with Down syndrome, equally large increases occurred in both the "clarity of cues" and the "responsiveness to parent" subscales.

## FAMILY DEPENDENT VARIABLES

The family dependent variables include an observational measure of mother-child interaction, two measures of family adaptation (parenting stress and effects on the family), and a measure of social support (assessing both network size and satisfaction with support). The measures of family adaptation and social support were derived from standardized questionnaires completed by mothers following the home visit. Given the fluctuations in the rate of questionnaire completion (see Table 9 above), the sample sizes for the dependent measures of family adaptation and social support vary between 150 and 152. The means and standard deviations for each of the family dependent measures at T1 and T2 for mothers who provided data at both assessment points are presented in Table 17 above.

Maternal scores on the *mother-child interaction* measure at T1 were significantly lower than those reported for the normative population. These scores increased slightly at T2, with the greatest increase noted for maternal cognitive growth–promoting behavior. The average overall domain score, however, remained significantly below that of the standardization sample, and the study sample was significantly lower than the standardization sample on all subscales except "sensitivity to cues." Although a subgroup of mothers demonstrated large gains, especially on the two growth-promoting subscales, most of the study mothers demonstrated relatively little change in their scores (for a discussion of this subgroup, see Chap. VIII). There were no significant differences in mothers' interactions with their children associated with the type of the child's disability at either T1 or T2 (see Table 18 above).

*Parenting stress* was assessed by mothers' scores on the Parent Domain of the Parenting Stress Index. The mean score on the Parent Domain for mothers in the study sample at T1 was significantly lower than the mean for the standardization sample, although the difference between the means was well within 1 standard deviation of the standardization sample (Abidin, 1986). Only 12 (7.9%) of the study mothers had T1 parenting stress scores above the clinically significant cutoff of 153. Of the seven subscales within the Parent Domain, lower average scores (indicating less stress) were found at both T1 and T2 for the study than for the standardization sample on depression, attachment, and sense of competence as a parent. For the sample as a whole, only modest change was reported in maternal stress scores between T1 and T2 (for both the Parent Domain and the seven subscales). At T2, there was no significant difference in mean scores on the Parent Domain between the study sample and the standardization sample.

Mothers of children with motor impairment had the highest average stress score among the three types of disability groups at both T1 and T2. Four mothers at T1 and seven at T2 scored above the clinical cutoff levels that indicate a need for referral for mental health services. The average stress score for mothers of toddlers with developmental delays was not significantly different from that of other sample members at the time of study entry and increased only slightly 1 year later. Only four mothers at T1 and four at T2 had scores above the cutoff point for clinical referral. Mothers of infants with Down syndrome had the lowest stress scores among the sample at both T1 and T2. Only four mothers at T1 and two mothers at T2 had scores above the clinical cutoff. Their average scores remained constant between T1 and T2.

A second measure of family adaptation, focused on the *effects on the family* of rearing a child with a disability, was assessed through maternal completion of the Impact-on-Family Scale. The mean for the total score and each of the four subscales for sample mothers at T1 and T2 was significantly below the mean scores reported by Stein and Riessman (1980) in their initial administration of the instrument and below the scores of families of children with chronic illnesses served in a large, urban hospital (Stein & Jessop, 1984). On average, there was only a slight increase in the sample mean score from T1 to T2 (indicating more negative family effects over the study period).

No differences among the three disability groups were noted at study entry. However, mothers of children with motor impairment had significantly higher scores on the Impact-on-Family Scale at T2 than mothers of children with Down syndrome and with developmental delays. In contrast, the average scores of the mothers in the other two groups regarding negative family effects decreased (slightly) over the 12-month study period.

Each mother's *social support* network was assessed with respect to its size and the degree of maternal satisfaction with its helpfulness (where each source was rated on a five-point scale from 0 [not at all helpful] to 4 [extremely helpful]). At T1, mothers reported an average of 9.2 (out of 15) sources of support and an average satisfaction rating of 23.1 (out of a possible 60). At T2, there were increases in both the average number of supports (to 10.7) and the rated helpfulness (to 26.2). The social support networks of mothers of infants with Down syndrome were somewhat larger than those of the other two subgroups at both T1 and T2, although the differences were not statistically significant. Compared to the other two groups, these mothers were significantly more satisfied at both T1 and T2 with the assistance and support they received. Comparisons of the study sample to other research are not possible given the adaptation of the scale that was required for this study.

## SUMMARY

The data presented in this chapter describe the study sample as a whole and highlight differences (where they exist) among the three disability subgroups. Multivariate analyses of variance conducted across the full range of child outcomes revealed significant differences based on type of disability, as measured *cross sectionally* at both T1, MANOVA $F(8,370) = 15.20, p < .001$, and T2, MANOVA $F(8,366) = 8.92, p < .001$. In the child outcomes, where the measures of performance are inherently sensitive to age, the observed differences conform to the expected pattern. Significant differences across the full set of family outcomes were also found by type of disability both at T1, MANOVA $F(8,344) = 3.07, p < .01$, and at T2, MANOVA $F(8,298) = 3.02, p < .01$. For the family outcomes, differences related to the child's disability are less consistent and do not appear to be related to the child's chronological age. We recognize, however, that the variability in the data on the children's functional and behavioral status is compounded by the wide age range of the sample at study entry.

All studies of children with disabilities struggle with the potentially confounding influences of diagnostic category and severity of impairment on patterns of development. Naturalistic investigations of infants and toddlers enrolled in early intervention programs, such as the present study, face the additional dilemma of the confound between diagnostic group and age at service initiation. When the recruitment of a study sample is tied to the point of program entry, which is, in turn, dictated by the child's disability or medical diagnosis, age differences among discrete diagnostic subgroups are inevitable. This "problem" is illustrated in the present study by the significant difference in age between the children with Down syndrome and those in the other two subgroups.

The primary goal of this investigation, however, is the analysis of *longitudinal* change and the identification of specific independent and mediating variables associated with different patterns of child performance and family adaptation over time. When data on child outcomes were analyzed longitudinally, subgroup differences based on the child's disability were found to present less of a problem. Specifically, as described earlier in this chapter, the *rates of development* for mental age equivalent scores are comparable across all three diagnostic groups, despite the significant cross-sectional differences in the mean scores at both T1 and T2. Where differences in rate of development do exist across diagnostic groups (i.e., in the adaptive behavior domain), they appear to be related to the characteristics of the disability, not to chronological age.

From a developmental perspective, any differences related to chronological age are of critical importance. From the policymaker's perspective, differences in age at program entry are inevitable and reflect an essential reality of early intervention service delivery. Therefore, an analytic strategy that controlled statistically for age in *all* analyses—as if all children entered programs at the same age—would generate artificial findings. Consequently, as described in the next chapter, our analyses of the predictors of change in children and families were conducted on the full sample, controlling for age *selectively* where significant age-related differences by type of disability were identified.

# VI. PREDICTORS OF CHANGE IN CHILDREN AND FAMILIES

This chapter presents a series of analyses designed to identify the predictors of change in children and families after 1 year of early intervention services. As discussed in Chapter V, there was considerable individual variation within the sample with respect to the amount and direction of the changes we measured. Some children and families demonstrated substantial gains in functioning and adaptation; others illustrated either declines or relatively modest increases in functioning during the 12-month study period. Moreover, for the sample as a whole, there was considerable average change on some measures and less change (or even stable scores) on others. Our analytic approach was to test the predictive power of child and family status characteristics and specified mediating variables in explaining the direction and magnitude of changes (for the full set of independent, mediating, and dependent variables, see Table 1 above). It should be reiterated that analyses of change in families are based solely on data obtained from mothers—we recognize that fathers' perspectives may differ; indeed, Chapter VII reports on the differences we found between the parents.

## Analysis Questions

In an effort to explore possible contributors to child and family change systematically, we begin with analyses of the direct and interactive effects of type of disability and level of severity of psychomotor impairment in explaining changes in outcomes. Our classification by type of disability is consistent with most research on children with developmental disabilities (cf. Chap. II) and represents the most widely used method for characterizing children enrolled in early intervention programs. Relative severity of impairment has been suggested by investigators of childhood chronic illness as a more useful parameter for categorizing and studying children with diverse special needs (Stein & Jessop, 1982). In our analyses, we used a two-group classification for severity, distinguishing children with relatively mild impairment (i.e., Bayley MDI at T1 $\geq$ 50) from those with moderate to severe impairment (i.e., MDI at T1 < 50). The different effects of each classification approach, and their interaction, are examined below.

We then go on to discuss the relations between changes in the study's outcomes and selected child and family independent and mediating variables (see Table 1 above) as measured at T1. Next, we assess the extent to which changes in children and families could be attributed to the types and quantity of services provided by their early intervention programs, applying multivariate analyses to identify whether specific aspects of services explained changes beyond what can be explained by the characteristics of the children and families. Finally, we examine the influence of additional therapeutic and support services on child and family change.

### Correlations among Residuals for Child and Family Outcomes

As described in Chapter III, we assessed change using standardized residual scores, which were generated for all outcomes except child-mother interaction (where standardized T2 scores were used). It should be noted that the meaning of residual scores varies across measures and that they must be interpreted within the context of overall mean change for the full sample. In general, a positive residual reflects a beneficial change, with the exception of parenting stress and adverse effects on the family (where a negative sign on the residual indicates that either decreases or smaller than predicted increases were found).

The full matrix of intercorrelations among residuals is presented in Table 21. These data indicate that changes in child outcomes correlated positively and moderately with each other. The highest correlation was found between mental age and spontaneous play and the lowest between spontaneous play and child-mother interaction.

Correlations among the set of family outcomes were less consistent. Changes in mother-child interaction were not correlated with any other family outcomes. The family outcome most often correlated with changes in other family outcomes was the measure of adverse effects on the family, which correlated positively with parenting stress and with changes in social support network size (but not helpfulness). Thus, families that had greater increases in negative effects also had greater increases in parenting stress as well as greater increases in the size of their social support network. It appears that those families who experienced increasing stress and deleterious effects on family life either sought or were offered more assistance.

The measure of adverse effects on the family was also correlated negatively with three of the four child outcomes. Children who displayed greater increases in adaptive behavior, spontaneous play, and mental age had parents who experienced fewer negative family effects over time. Social support

## TABLE 21

### Intercorrelations among Residual Scores on Child and Family Outcomes

| Outcome | 1 | 2 | 3 | 4 | 5 | 6 | 7 | 8 | 9 |
|---|---|---|---|---|---|---|---|---|---|
| 1. Mental age . . . . . . . . . . . . . . . . | | | | | | | | | |
| 2. Spontaneous play. . . . . . . . . . . | .59** | | | | | | | | |
| 3. Adaptive behavior. . . . . . . . . . | .49*** | .40*** | | | | | | | |
| 4. Child-mother interaction . . . . . | .27*** | .24*** | .31*** | | | | | | |
| 5. Mother-child interaction. . . . . . | .09 | .04 | .09 | .28*** | | | | | |
| 6. Parenting stress . . . . . . . . . . . | -.07 | -.06 | -.04 | -.12 | -.04 | | | | |
| 7. Effects on the family. . . . . . . . | -.18* | -.14* | -.25*** | -.13 | .08 | .44*** | | | |
| 8. Social support: network size. . . . | -.19** | -.07 | -.12 | .08 | .12 | .11 | .23** | | |
| 9. Social support: helpfulness. . . . . | -.12 | -.07 | -.15* | .08 | .07 | -.08 | .08 | .49*** | |

NOTE.—N varies between 150 and 190.

* p < .05.
** p < .01.
*** p < .001.

network size and helpfulness had a modest negative relation to changes in children's mental age and adaptive behavior, respectively. Thus, social support networks appeared to be increasing in size and becoming more helpful for those families whose children were demonstrating less positive change.

In general, the patterns of correlations were in the expected directions, although the magnitude of the coefficients was modest (median absolute value of $r = .25$). Because of this, as well as the finding that the relations among these outcome variables and the independent and mediating variables included in our analyses were often inconsistent (to be discussed below), we did not combine outcomes into composites but instead retained them as separate variables.

## THE EFFECTS OF TYPE OF DISABILITY AND LEVEL OF SEVERITY OF IMPAIRMENT ON STUDY OUTCOMES

Two-way multivariate analyses of variance (MANOVAs) were conducted to test the main effects of type of disability and level of severity of psychomotor impairment, as well as their interaction, on the residual change scores for the child and family outcomes (for means and standard deviations of the residuals by type of disability and severity of impairment, see Tables 22 and 23, respectively).

With respect to the child outcomes, there was a significant main effect for severity of impairment, MANOVA $F(4,179) = 5.15$, $p < .001$, but not for type of disability, MANOVA $F(8,360) = 1.53$, $p = .15$, or their interaction, MANOVA $F(8,360) = 1.26$, $p = .26$. Subsequent univariate tests revealed that differences by level of severity were significant for the residual change scores for mental age equivalence, $F(1,182) = 8.61$, $p < .01$, spontaneous play, $F(1,182) = 17.31$, $p < .001$, and adaptive behavior age equivalence, $F(1,182) = 9.29$, $p < .01$. The only outcome where differences were not significantly associated with severity of impairment was child-mother interaction, $F(1,182) = 1.94$, $p = .17$.

With respect to family outcomes, there was no significant effect for type of disability, MANOVA $F(10,280) = 1.10$, $p = .37$, severity of impairment, MANOVA $F(5,139) = 1.33$, $p = .26$, or their interaction, MANOVA $F(10,280) = .94$, $p = .49$, in the omnibus multivariate test.

These results confirm that type of disability is not useful in explaining differences in developmental patterns of change in either infants or their families. Severity of impairment is a better discriminator among children, but not among families. Children with more severe impairment changed less than children with relatively mild impairment.

TABLE 22

MEANS AND STANDARD DEVIATIONS OF STANDARDIZED RESIDUALS OF STUDY
OUTCOMES BY TYPE OF DISABILITY

| Outcome | Down Syndrome ($N = 54$): $M$ (SD) | Motor Impairment ($N = 77$): $M$ (SD) | Developmental Delay ($N = 59$): $M$ (SD) |
|---|---|---|---|
| Child outcomes: | | | |
| Mental age . . . . . . . . . . . . . . | .09 | −.05 | −.01 |
| | (.41) | (1.27) | (.99) |
| Spontaneous play . . . . . . . . . | .00 | .02 | −.05 |
| | (.57) | (1.18) | (1.06) |
| Adaptive behavior. . . . . . . . . | .25 | −.24 | .08 |
| | (.59) | (1.12) | (1.06) |
| Child-mother interaction . . . | .07 | −.12 | .10 |
| | (.96) | (1.09) | (.91) |
| Family outcomes: | | | |
| Mother-child interaction . . . | .01 | −.08 | .08 |
| | (.76) | (.96) | (1.21) |
| Parenting stress . . . . . . . . . . | −.10 | .05 | .07 |
| | (.89) | (.96) | (1.10) |
| Effects on the family . . . . . . | −.24 | .26 | −.12 |
| | (.90) | (1.03) | (.94) |
| Social support: | | | |
| Network size. . . . . . . . . . . . | .08 | −.13 | .12 |
| | (1.07) | (.91) | (1.05) |
| Helpfulness . . . . . . . . . . . | .29 | −.25 | .08 |
| | (1.09) | (.90) | (.97) |

## THE EFFECTS OF OTHER CHILD AND FAMILY CHARACTERISTICS ON STUDY OUTCOMES

In order to identify other characteristics of the child and family that were associated with change in outcomes, we examined the correlations between a core set of measures collected at T1 (both independent and mediating variables) and the residual scores on the four child and the four family outcomes. These analyses were designed to identify characteristics of children or families that may be "known" or assessed by early intervention professionals at the beginning of the service delivery period and that may be predictive of how the child and family will change regardless of the services they receive.

### Child Outcomes

Table 24 presents the zero-order correlations between the independent and the mediating variable sets (excluding type of disability) and the resid-

TABLE 23

| Outcome | Mild (N = 139): M (SD) | Moderate/Severe (N = 50): M (SD) |
|---|---|---|
| Child outcomes: | | |
| Mental age .............. | .21 (.97) | −.58 (.83) |
| Spontaneous play ......... | .21 (.94) | −.63 (.89) |
| Adaptive behavior......... | .26 (.88) | −.73 (.95) |
| Child-mother interaction ... | .14 (.84) | −.39 (1.28) |
| Family outcomes: | | |
| Mother-child interaction ... | .08 (.96) | −.22 (1.07) |
| Parenting stress........... | .07 (.99) | .05 (1.03) |
| Effects on the family ...... | −.16 (.98) | .41 (.87) |
| Social support: | | |
| Network size............ | −.05 (1.01) | .19 (.96) |
| Helpfulness ............ | −.004 (1.04) | .07 (.89) |

ual change scores for the child and family outcomes. It is notable that changes in the child are rarely associated with family demographic characteristics or aspects of the family environment. Child characteristics—such as age, health factors, and temperament—are more often associated with changes in the child's outcomes, and then only moderately so. For each of the child outcomes, children with less severe psychomotor impairment demonstrated greater than expected changes. Moreover, child gender was not associated with change in any child or family outcome.

Older children and those with seizure disorders demonstrated less change in mental age than predicted. Prematurely born children demonstrated more change than was expected in mental age than children who were full-term babies. Smaller than expected changes in spontaneous play were found for children with seizure disorders and more difficult temperament. Smaller than expected changes in adaptive behavior were associated with older children, the presence of a seizure disorder, the presence of a cardiac problem, or having a more difficult temperament. Finally, changes in child-mother interaction were associated negatively with the presence of cardiac or seizure disorders and positively with greater maternal education and the quality of the home environment. This was the only child outcome for which maternal education and the quality of the home environment were significant correlates.

## Family Outcomes

Changes in family outcomes were much more likely to be associated with family characteristics than with child characteristics (see Table 24). The largest number of significant correlates of change were found for the mother-child interaction scores. Greater than expected changes (i.e., increases in interaction quality) were associated with more maternal education and with higher quality of home environments; smaller than expected changes (i.e., decreases in interaction quality) were associated with single marital status, poorer maternal health, and maternal ascription of influence over the child's development to external sources such as God or fate.

There were few significant correlates of change in parenting stress or in adverse family effects. Smaller than expected increases in parenting stress were found for children who were rated by their mothers as having a more difficult temperament. The only significant correlates of change in effects on the family were the child's severity of psychomotor impairment and the perceived adaptability within the family. Families that reported lower levels of adaptability were found to have larger increases in negative effects on the family than were expected.

Changes in the mothers' social support networks were measured in terms of network size and rated helpfulness. Smaller increases in network size were reported by mothers of children with cardiac problems and by mothers who ascribed influence over their child's development to the child. Increases in network size were significantly associated with more difficult child temperament, with having a higher-quality home environment, and with greater maternal belief in her own power to influence improvements in her child's development. Significantly smaller increases in the helpfulness of the mothers' networks were associated with having a child born prematurely, with having a child with cardiac problems, and with giving greater ascriptions of influence over the child's development to the child. Significant increases in the helpfulness of the mothers' networks were associated with greater belief in the maternal role in the child's development.

## Summary

While a few significant correlates of change in the child and family outcomes were found, the sizes of the correlation coefficients were in the low to moderate range (the range of $r$ extends from .12 to .49), were often

## TABLE 24
### CORRELATIONS BETWEEN CHILD AND FAMILY CHARACTERISTICS AT T1 AND RESIDUALS OF STUDY OUTCOMES

| CHARACTERISTIC | CHILD OUTCOMES | | | |
|---|---|---|---|---|
| | Mental Age | Spontaneous Play | Adaptive Behavior | Child-Mother Interaction |
| Child demographic and health characteristics: | | | | |
| Age at T1 | -.17** | -.09 | -.15* | -.02 |
| Gender | -.04 | -.02 | .05 | .06 |
| Prematurity | .16* | .11 | .09 | .01 |
| Has cardiac problem | -.09 | .03 | -.14* | -.12* |
| Has seizure disorder | -.14* | -.19** | -.21** | -.21** |
| Severity of impairment | .33** | .29** | .49** | .26** |
| Family demographic characteristics: | | | | |
| Maternal education | .08 | .05 | .02 | .18* |
| Marital status | -.04 | .005 | -.10 | .07 |
| Maternal employment status | -.001 | .04 | -.05 | .02 |
| Maternal health status | -.07 | -.06 | -.11 | -.11 |
| Child temperament: | | | | |
| Temperament | .001 | -.18** | -.15* | -.03 |
| Family ecology: | | | | |
| HOME | -.05 | .01 | -.05 | .17* |
| Family adaptability | -.04 | -.01 | -.03 | -.01 |
| Family cohesion | .06 | .09 | .03 | .11 |
| Locus of control: | | | | |
| Divine | .02 | -.03 | .05 | .07 |
| Chance | -.04 | -.06 | -.08 | -.11 |
| Child | .10 | .08 | .13* | .06 |
| Parent | .05 | .07 | .04 | .08 |
| Professional | .06 | .01 | -.10 | .07 |

FAMILY OUTCOMES

|  | Mother-Child Interaction | Parenting Stress | Effects on Family | Social Support | |
|---|---|---|---|---|---|
|  |  |  |  | Network Size | Helpfulness |
| Child demographic and health characteristics: |  |  |  |  |  |
| Age at T1 | .06 | .12 | .13 | .04 | −.002 |
| Gender | −.08 | .09 | −.01 | .03 | .04 |
| Prematurity | −.02 | .005 | −.07 | −.05 | −.14* |
| Has cardiac problem | .05 | .12 | .07 | −.20** | −.26*** |
| Has seizure disorder | −.04 | .13 | .08 | −.04 | −.02 |
| Severity of impairment | .04 | −.06 | −.24** | −.14 | −.04 |
| Family demographic characteristics: |  |  |  |  |  |
| Maternal education | .30** | −.07 | −.06 | .05 | .09 |
| Marital status | −.21** | −.09 | −.03 | −.005 | .09 |
| Maternal employment status | .04 | .03 | −.06 | −.01 | .01 |
| Maternal health status | −.23*** | .05 | .13 | −.10 | −.12 |
| Child temperament: |  |  |  |  |  |
| Temperament | .003 | −.18* | .02 | .14* | .05 |
| Family ecology: |  |  |  |  |  |
| HOME | .23*** | −.10 | −.10 | .15* | .08 |
| Family adaptability | .05 | −.09 | −.14* | .06 | .06 |
| Family cohesion | .11 | −.06 | −.10 | .04 | .07 |
| Locus of control: |  |  |  |  |  |
| Divine | −.14* | −.01 | .05 | .002 | −.02 |
| Chance | −.20** | .09 | .10 | .01 | −.11 |
| Child | −.04 | .11 | −.09 | −.14* | −.15* |
| Parent | .03 | .08 | .04 | .17* | .24*** |
| Professional | .01 | −.01 | −.04 | .07 | .03 |

NOTE.—$N$ varies between 150 and 190.
* $p < .05$.
** $p < .01$.
*** $p < .001$.

77

associated with the child's health status, and were rarely associated with characteristics of the family environment. In general, child characteristics were correlates of change in the child but not in family outcomes; changes in family outcomes were associated typically with parent or family characteristics, particularly with regard to locus of control and qualities of the home environment. The exceptions to this pattern are changes in child-mother and mother-child interactions, where maternal education and the quality of the home environment were significant correlates of both outcomes. Further, other maternal characteristics, such as single parenthood, poorer health status, and having a more external locus of control were correlated with decreases in the quality of the mother-child interaction over time.

## THE EFFECTS OF EARLY INTERVENTION SERVICES ON STUDY OUTCOMES

As described in Chapter IV, we examined various aspects of early intervention services. In this section, analyses of the relation between three specific aspects of service and changes in children and families between T1 and T2 are presented: (1) characteristic approaches to program delivery; (2) participation in parent groups; and (3) service intensity.

### Characteristics of Service Delivery

In delivering services to children and families, early intervention programs make many decisions. Although such decisions may not always be systematic, certain patterns of service delivery become apparent across programs. Programs can provide services through a unidisciplinary or a multidisciplinary model, in an individual or group format, and primarily in homes or at a center. We analyzed the relations between these three aspects of program delivery—program staffing structure, service format, and service location—and changes in child and family outcomes. The results of these analyses are described below. In cases where significant differences were found in the characteristics of those who received a particular service and where those characteristics were related to outcomes (for the sample as a whole), covariates were included in the analyses.

*Program staffing structure.*—Families who received services through a multidisciplinary model ($N = 133$) had an array of service providers from different disciplines; those who received services through a unidisciplinary model ($N = 57$) received at least 75% of their services from a single discipline. This definition of staffing structure is empirical, rather than being based on providers' views of their philosophical approach. Demographic analyses indicated that the multidisciplinary model was used for older children ($M$ = 11.3 and 8.9 months for the multidisciplinary and unidisciplinary models, respectively, $t[188]$ = 2.43, $p < .05$). In contrast, the unidisciplinary model served a significantly lower proportion of children with severe psychomotor impairment, $\chi^2(1, N = 190)$ = 7.27, $p < .01$.

Significant relations between program staffing structure and residual scores were found for one child and two family outcomes (Table 25). For children, more positive changes in mental age were shown by those receiving services from a single discipline. However, this finding did not remain significant statistically when severity of impairment was controlled or when age was controlled (using ANCOVA procedures), although the direction of the finding remained the same.

Among families, those receiving services primarily from a single discipline had significant decreases in parenting stress compared to those who received their services through a multidisciplinary approach. This result persisted when severity was controlled, $F(1,147)$ = 6.04, $p < .05$, when age was controlled, $F(1,147)$ = 5.47, $p < .05$, and when both were controlled simultaneously, $F(1,146)$ = 5.23, $p < .05$.

Although families receiving services predominantly from a single discipline had significant decreases in parenting stress, they also had significantly less change in the size of the mother's social support network. This result was maintained when severity was controlled, $F(1,147)$ = 4.16, $p < .05$, when age was controlled, $F(1,147)$ = 5.12, $p < .05$, and when both severity and age were controlled simultaneously, $F(1,146)$ = 4.12, $p < .05$. No differ-

TABLE 25

MEAN RESIDUAL SCORES FOR CHILD AND FAMILY OUTCOMES BY PROGRAM
STAFFING STRUCTURE

| Outcome | Multidisciplinary ($N$ = 133) | Unidisciplinary ($N$ = 57) | $t$ |
|---|---|---|---|
| Child outcomes: | | | |
| Mental age................ | −.08 | .20 | −2.07* |
| Spontaneous play .......... | .02 | −.07 | .58 |
| Adaptive behavior ......... | −.05 | .12 | .26 |
| Child-mother interaction[a] ... | −.02 | .05 | .67 |
| Family outcomes: | | | |
| Mother-child interaction .... | −.03 | .07 | .53 |
| Parenting stress[b]........... | .21 | −.26 | 2.74** |
| Effects on the family[b]....... | .07 | −.18 | 1.41 |
| Social support:[b] | | | |
| Network size ............. | .15 | −.29 | 2.53* |
| Helpfulness ............. | .08 | −.13 | 1.24 |

[a] Standardized T2 score.   * $p < .05$.
[b] $N$ = 152.   ** $p < .01$.

79

ences were found, however, in changes in maternal reports of the helpfulness of their support networks. Thus, although program staffing structure related to changes in the size of the maternal social support network, it did not affect changes in the perceived helpfulness of that network.

*Service format.*—Services were provided to children and families either in individual sessions (e.g., through a home visit or center-based individual visit) or in group sessions (e.g., in a parent-child group). Very few children and families ($N = 4$) received primarily group services (defined as 75% or more of the services provided through a group format). Approximately half the sample families ($N = 89$) received an individualized service program (defined as 75% or more of the services provided to the parent and/or child individually), and half ($N = 97$) received a mixture of individual and group sessions. Because so few families received a predominance of group services, the analyses described below compared only families receiving primarily individualized services to those receiving a combination of individual and group sessions. Significant age differences existed for these two groups, with families who received individualized services having significantly younger children ($M = 8.9$ and 11.7 months for individual and mixed formats, respectively, $t[184] = -3.03$, $p < .01$). No differences in service format were found related to the severity of the child's psychomotor impairment (based on chi-square analysis).

Children whose families received primarily individualized services displayed significantly greater change in mental age (Table 26), a finding that persisted when age was controlled, $F(1,181) = 4.27$, $p < .05$. The direction of findings for all other child outcomes and for some family effects, although not significant statistically, also favored the individualized services format.

Individualized services, however, were also associated with significantly fewer changes in the size and helpfulness of maternal social support networks, a result maintained when chronological age was controlled in analyses of network size, $F(1,144) = 25.48$, $p < .001$, and of its helpfulness, $F(1,144) = 12.13$, $p < .001$. Thus, the mixed model appeared to be associated with greater benefits for families in relation to maternal social support, whereas the individualized model appeared to be associated with greater gains in psychomotor development for children.

*Service location.*—Services were provided to children and families either at their home or at a center. About half (51.1%) of the sample received a combination of center- and home-based services, whereas some families ($N = 30$) received primarily center-based services and others ($N = 63$) primarily home-based services (i.e., 75% or more of service hours). Analyses were conducted only for the latter two groups. Significant age differences were found between children served at home and those served at a center. Home-based services were delivered to younger children ($M = 8.3$ and 14.1

TABLE 26

Mean Residual Scores for Child and Family Outcomes by
Service Format

| Outcome | Individualized (N = 89) | Mixed (N = 97) | t |
|---|---|---|---|
| Child outcomes: | | | |
| Mental age................ | .19 | -.18 | 2.61** |
| Spontaneous play .......... | .02 | -.02 | .24 |
| Adaptive behavior ......... | .05 | -.07 | .40 |
| Child-mother interaction[a] ... | .02 | -.02 | .79 |
| Family outcomes: | | | |
| Mother-child interaction .... | -.06 | .01 | .63 |
| Parenting stress[b]........... | -.05 | .20 | -1.49 |
| Effects on the family[b]....... | -.16 | .15 | -1.94 |
| Social support:[b] | | | |
| Network size ............ | -.39 | .41 | -5.23*** |
| Helpfulness ............. | -.27 | .29 | -3.51*** |

[a] Standardized T2 scores.  ** $p < .01$.
[b] $N = 149$.  *** $p < .001$.

months for home- and center-based services, respectively, $t[91] = -4.48$, $p < .001$). Chi-square analyses indicated that the distribution of home- or center-based services did not vary on the basis of severity of psychomotor impairment. Analyses of outcome data also failed to reveal any significant differences, either with or without controlling for age (based on ANCOVA tests).

*Summary.*—Although, in general, few differences were found in analyses of characteristics of program delivery, there were some notable exceptions. First, beneficial changes in parenting stress were associated with services delivered primarily through a single discipline. Second, greater gains in children's mental age were associated with individualized services. These results are tempered, however, by the finding that both these service characteristics were associated with significantly less change in maternal social support networks. Not surprisingly, the service models that were associated with beneficial changes in maternal social support were those in which parents had access to multiple service providers (i.e., the multidisciplinary model) or interaction with other parents (i.e., the "mixed" model, which included a substantial amount of group services). These latter models, however, were not associated with other measurable benefits for children or families.

## Parent Groups

As described in Chapter IV, slightly over half the sample mothers (55%) attended at least one professionally guided parent group meeting during the year. The only difference between mothers who did and those who did not participate in such groups with respect to child or maternal characteristics was that those who participated had slightly more education ($M$ = 14.2 years) than those who did not ($M$ = 13.3 years), $t(187)$ = 2.49, $p < .01$.

Our analyses of the effects of parent groups on the children and families addressed two questions. (1) Were there differences in the amount of change on the study's outcomes between mothers who did ($N$ = 104) and those who did not ($N$ = 86) participate in parent groups? (2) For those who participated, what was the effect of the intensity of their participation on the amount of change in children and families?

Significant differences in the magnitude of change were seen only in changes in social support network size, $t(149)$ = 3.59, $p < .001$, and its helpfulness, $t(149)$ = 3.51, $p < .001$. Mothers who attended parent groups had significantly greater changes in both the size and the rated helpfulness of those networks. The increase in network size was attributable largely (and not surprisingly) to more support reportedly received from other parents of children with special needs and from new linkages made to formal support groups, such as those provided in the early intervention programs. The absence of differences on any of the child outcomes or on the other family outcomes, however, suggests that participation alone does not have "spillover" effects to the child or to other domains of parent and family functioning after 1 year of program involvement.

The extent to which the intensity of participation was correlated with change in the child and family was examined next. As described in Chapter IV, the average number of hours per month for those participating in parent groups was 1.6, with a range of from 0.04 to 5.9 hours. Because greater intensity of participation was associated with specific characteristics of the children and the parents, partial correlations were also examined to determine whether the pattern of results was affected by the level of severity of the child's impairment, the child's age, or the mother's education.

Greater participation in parent groups was associated with smaller than expected gains in children's mental age and in level of spontaneous play (Table 27). It was also associated with larger than expected increases in adverse effects on the family, even though, as a group, mothers who participated in parent groups had not reported significantly higher family effects at T1. The increases in negative family effects were evident on two of the four subscales: personal strain ($r$ = .24, $p < .05$) and familial/social strain ($r$ = .27, $p < .01$). Finally, greater participation in parent groups was associated with larger than expected increases in social support network size and in its rated helpfulness. These findings persisted when the child's age or the mother's education was controlled statistically. However, when severity of impairment was controlled, the significant correlation between intensity

TABLE 27

CORRELATIONS BETWEEN RESIDUAL SCORES FOR CHILD AND FAMILY OUTCOMES AND
INTENSITY OF PARTICIPATION IN PARENT GROUP ($N = 104$)

| Outcome | Intensity of Participation in Parent Group | Outcome | Intensity of Participation in Parent Group |
|---|---|---|---|
| Child outcomes: | | Family outcomes: | |
| Mental age............... | −.22* | Mother-child interaction... | −.16 |
| Spontaneous play ......... | −.23** | Parenting stress[b] ......... | .04 |
| Adaptive behavior......... | −.13 | Effects on the family[b] ..... | .26** |
| Child-mother interaction[a]... | −.13 | Social support:[b] | |
| | | Network size .......... | .29** |
| | | Helpfulness .......... | .19* |

[a] Standardized T2 scores.
[b] Sample size = 84.
\* $p < .05.$
\*\* $p < .01.$

of participation and changes in spontaneous play did not persist (partial $r = .17, p = .07$).

In summary, participation in parent groups was associated with maternal reports of larger and more helpful social support networks but also with greater than anticipated increases in strains within the family. Although simply being in a parent group was not associated with any greater or lesser change in parenting stress or in overall adverse family effects, the greater the participation in parent groups, the greater the reported increases in strains in specific domains of family life, such as social/familial relationships and maternal personal strain.

*Service Intensity*

Relations between the intensity of services and changes in children and families were examined. First, we analyzed these relations using average hours per month received across all services; next, we considered separately the intensity of home visits and the intensity of services for child groups. Because more severely impaired children were found to receive significantly more hours of service, partial correlation analyses were also conducted. Both sets of analyses are presented for each of the three service intensity variables.

Although we found a negative relation between intensity of average service hours and changes in two of the child outcomes (i.e., mental age and adaptive behavior), neither of these relations continued to be significant in partial correlations in which severity was controlled (Table 28). For family outcomes, the significant relation between intensity of services and mothers' reports of increases in the size and in the helpfulness of their support

TABLE 28

CORRELATIONS BETWEEN RESIDUAL SCORES FOR CHILD AND FAMILY
OUTCOMES AND AVERAGE TOTAL SERVICE HOURS ($N$ = 190)

| Outcome | $r$ | Control for Severity |
|---|---|---|
| Child outcomes: | | |
|   Mental age............... | −.17* | −.06 |
|   Spontaneous play .......... | −.10 | .00 |
|   Adaptive behavior ......... | −.22** | −.05 |
|   Child-mother interaction[a] ... | −.04 | .06 |
| Family outcomes: | | |
|   Mother-child interaction .... | .04 | .06 |
|   Parenting stress[b]........... | −.03 | −.05 |
|   Effects on the family[b]....... | .12 | .04 |
| Social support:[b] | | |
|   Network size ............ | .32*** | .29*** |
|   Helpfulness ............. | .22** | .21** |

[a] Standardized T2 scores.  
[b] $N$ = 152.  
* $p < .05$.  
** $p < .01$.  
*** $p < .001$.

networks remained significant even when level of severity of impairment was controlled statistically.

The relations between average hours of home visiting and child change were similar to that found for the average number of all service hours. As expected, there was a significant negative relation between the average number of hours of home visits and changes in mental age and in adaptive behavior (Table 29). The first of these did not remain significant when severity of psychomotor impairment was controlled, but it continued to be significant in the latter case. Using partial correlations, subscale analyses revealed that only changes in the motor domain showed a significant negative relation to hours of home visiting ($r = -.24, p < .001$), suggesting that, regardless of the severity of their psychomotor impairment, children with increasingly poor motor development received more hours of home visits.

For families, there was a significant negative relation between average hours of home visiting and changes in parenting stress that persisted in the partial correlation analyses and indicates that parenting stress decreased with more hours of home visiting. Subscale analyses (using partial correlations) revealed significant relations between hours of home visiting and decreased stress associated with parental competence ($r = -.23, p < .01$), restriction of role ($r = -.21, p < .01$), and relations with spouse ($r = -.24, p < .001$).

In analyses of the relations between average hours of child group attendance and changes in children and families, no significant findings emerged for child outcomes. For families, a positive relation was found for changes in size ($r = .31, p < .01$) and helpfulness ($r = .17, p < .05$) of the maternal

TABLE 29

CORRELATIONS BETWEEN RESIDUAL SCORES FOR CHILD AND FAMILY
OUTCOMES AND AVERAGE HOURS OF HOME VISITING ($N = 190$)

| Outcome | $r$ | Control for Severity |
|---|---|---|
| Child outcomes: | | |
| Mental age............... | −.17* | −.06 |
| Spontaneous play ......... | −.09 | .02 |
| Adaptive behavior ........ | −.30** | −.15* |
| Child-mother interaction[a] ... | −.07 | .02 |
| Family outcomes: | | |
| Mother-child interaction .... | −.05 | −.04 |
| Parenting stress[b]........... | −.19* | −.22** |
| Effects on the family[b]....... | .01 | −.08 |
| Social support:[b] | | |
| Network size ............ | .06 | .01 |
| Helpfulness ............. | .01 | .00 |

[a] Standardized T2 scores.  *$p < .05.$
[b] $N = 152.$   **$p < .01.$

support network, and the relation continued to be significant in partial
correlation analyses. Although mothers did not actually participate in the
child groups, many programs offered parent groups that met at the same
time, which may account for the increased support noted by mothers whose
children attended child groups. In fact, we found a moderately high correlation between the average number of hours of child and parent group attendance ($r = .65$, $p < .001$). Other possible explanations are that mothers
developed friendships during the child groups that encouraged parents to
become acquainted with each other or that parents met with each other
informally during arrival for or dismissal from the child group sessions.

In summary, there was wide variation in the number of service hours
provided for sample children and families, and intensity was predicted significantly by the level of severity of the child's psychomotor impairment.
However, we did not find intensity of services to be related significantly to
most outcomes for children when these relations were adjusted for severity
of impairment. For families, total service hours and hours of child group
attendance were related significantly to increases in the size and helpfulness
of maternal support networks. While not related to increases in social support, more hours of home visiting were related significantly to decreases in
parenting stress.

## Multivariate Analyses of the Effects of Early Intervention Services on Child and Family Change

We conducted a series of hierarchical multiple regression analyses on
the residual scores of the study's child and family outcomes. Our goal was

to determine whether characteristics of early intervention services added significantly to the amount of explained variance in the dependent measures, above and beyond that explained by child and/or family characteristics. As described above, however, the magnitude of the correlations between child and family characteristics and changes in child and family outcomes was low. The regression analyses reported below build on the correlation results reported in Table 24 above. Specifically, child and/or family characteristics that were significantly associated with study outcomes were entered first into the regression equation. Next, various aspects of early intervention services were entered, to determine the unique contribution that services make to changes in child or family outcomes, controlling for other known significant correlates. With two exceptions, no aspect of early intervention services (either service approach or intensity) contributed more than 3% of additional explained variance to a study outcome. The exceptions were changes in parenting stress and in social support (in terms of both network size and perceived helpfulness). The multiple regression analyses for changes in these two types of study outcomes are presented below.

*Predictors of change in parenting stress.*—The only significant child or family characteristic that correlated with changes in parenting stress, as reported in Table 24 above, was child temperament. In the regression analysis, it was found that 3% of the variance in changes in parenting stress was explained by the child's temperament (Table 30). The only early intervention service characteristic that explained a significant amount of unique variance in parenting stress was staffing structure. Specifically, an additional 4.7% of the variance was explained by the receipt of services through a unidisciplinary model.

*Predictors of change in social support network size.*—It was found that 16.7% of the variance in change in social support network size was explained by child and family characteristics (i.e., having a cardiac problem, being premature, and maternal locus of control beliefs; Table 31). Entering intervention

TABLE 30

HIERARCHICAL REGRESSION OF RESIDUAL OF
PARENTING STRESS ON INDEPENDENT VARIABLE SETS

| Independent Variable | $R^2$ | $R^2$ Change |
|---|---|---|
| Child behavior: | | |
| Temperament . . . . . . . . . . . | .03 | .03* |
| Early intervention services: | | |
| Staffing structure . . . . . . . . | .08 | .047** |

* $p < .05$.
** $p < .01$.

TABLE 31

HIERARCHICAL REGRESSION OF RESIDUAL OF SOCIAL SUPPORT NETWORK
SIZE ON INDEPENDENT VARIABLE SETS

| Independent Variable | $R^2$ | $R^2$ Change |
|---|---|---|
| Child characteristics: | | |
| Has a cardiac problem ⎫ ................... | .072 | .072** |
| Severity of impairment ⎭ | | |
| Child behavior: | | |
| Temperament........................... | .084 | .012 |
| Family ecology: | | |
| HOME ⎫ ................ | .167 | .083** |
| Maternal locus of control ⎭ | | |
| Early intervention services:[a] | | |
| 1. Service format ........................ | .285 | .118*** |
| 2. Staffing structure...................... | .203 | .036* |
| 3. Participation in parent group ............ | .224 | .057** |
| 4. Average service hours per month......... | .226 | .059** |
| 5. Average parent group hours per month ... | .231 | .064*** |
| 6. Average child group hours per month .... | .226 | .059** |

[a] Each characteristic of early intervention services was tested separately, resulting in six unique regression equations. The $R^2$ and $R^2$ change represent the amount of additional variance contributed by each characteristic above and beyond the other variables in the equation.

* $p < .05$.
** $p < .01$.
*** $p < .001$.

service format (i.e., individualized vs. mixed) into the equation explained an additional 11.8% ($p < .001$) of the variance. Thus, controlling for child and family characteristics, almost 12% of the variance in change in the size of maternal support networks from T1 to T2 was explained by a family receiving services in a combination of individual and group formats.

As noted earlier, some other aspects of early intervention services correlated significantly with changes in maternal support network size. Each was tested separately for the significance of the additional amount of explained variance that it contributed to this outcome, controlling for the set of child and family characteristics described in Table 31. We found statistically significant increases in explained variance attributable to receiving services in a multidisciplinary staffing structure ($R^2$ increase = 3.6%, $p < .05$), to participation in parent groups ($R^2$ increase = 5.7%, $p < .01$), to more total service hours per month ($R^2$ increase = 5.9%, $p < .01$), to more service hours in parent groups ($R^2$ increase = 6.4%, $p < .001$), and to more service hours of child group ($R^2$ increase = 5.9%, $p < .001$). Thus, changes in social support network size were sensitive to both the service model and the intensity of early intervention programs.

*Predictors of change in rated helpfulness of social support.*—Child and family characteristics (i.e., having a cardiac problem, being premature, and maternal locus of control beliefs) explained 19.1% of the variance in change in

TABLE 32

HIERARCHICAL REGRESSION OF RESIDUAL OF SOCIAL SUPPORT
HELPFULNESS ON INDEPENDENT VARIABLE SETS

| Independent Variable | $R^2$ | $R^2$ Change |
|---|---|---|
| Child characteristics: | | |
| Has a cardiac problem ⎱ ................... | .092 | .092*** |
| Prematurity ⎰ | | |
| Family ecology: | | |
| Maternal locus of control................... | .191 | .100*** |
| Early intervention services:[a] | | |
| 1. Service format ........................ | .259 | .068*** |
| 2. Participation in parent group ............ | .258 | .067*** |
| 3. Average service hours per month......... | .227 | .036* |
| 4. Average parent group hours per month ... | .238 | .047** |

[a] Each characteristic of early intervention services was tested separately, resulting in four unique regression equations. The $R^2$ and $R^2$ change represent the amount of additional variance contributed by each characteristic above and beyond the other variables in the equation.

* $p < .05$.
** $p < .01$.
*** $p < .001$.

mothers' ratings of the helpfulness of their social support networks (Table 32). The largest additional amount of unique variance was contributed by service format (i.e., receiving a combination of individualized and group services; $R^2$ increase $= 6.8\%$, $p < .001$). However, participation in parent groups explained nearly as much unique variance when it was tested separately ($R^2$ increase $= 6.7\%$, $p < .001$). Two of the three service intensity variables also contributed statistically significant increases in explained variance, after child and family characteristics were controlled: receiving more total service hours per month ($R^2$ increase $= 3.6\%$, $p < .01$) and receiving more service hours per month of parent group ($R^2$ increase $= 4.7\%$, $p < .01$). Thus, changes in both support network size and helpfulness were attributable, in part, to the type and intensity of early intervention services provided.

## THE EFFECTS OF SERVICES RECEIVED OTHER THAN FROM AN EARLY INTERVENTION PROGRAM ON STUDY OUTCOMES

Services delivered through a single early intervention program are often not the only professional assistance that families receive when they have a young child with a developmental delay or disability. As described in Chapter IV, we found that slightly more than half the families in our sample (52.6%) received additional services of some type during the 12-month study period. About one-fifth (19.5%) of the families received child-oriented support services, 15.8% received additional child-oriented therapeutic services, and about one-third (31.6%) received additional family support services from other agencies.

In this section, we present analyses of the relation between these three types of additional services—child-oriented support, child-oriented therapy, and family-oriented support—and changes in children and families (Table 33). (Child-care services were not included in the analyses because they were received by only a few families and differed substantially in kind and intensity from early intervention services.) We also examined whether, in comparison to other families, those who received additional services had more or fewer average hours of service from their early intervention program. While our data do not indicate *why* families received additional services, one plausible possibility is that, having decided they were not receiving enough service from their early intervention program, families procured additional services independently. Alternatively, early intervention programs may have linked families to additional services in order to supplement their own capacity for service intensity. One final caveat: since the data on services received other than from an early intervention program are based solely on maternal report, our findings should be interpreted with caution.

### Child-oriented Support Services

A total of 37 families reported receiving child-related visiting nurse services and child-related case management in addition to their early intervention services. Compared to the others, these families received significantly fewer hours of service from their early intervention programs ($M$ = 5.6 and 7.2 hours, respectively, $t[188]$ = 2.60, $p < .05$). They also demonstrated significantly less positive change in mother-child interaction, $t(187)$ = 3.34, $p < .001$; however, this latter result was not sustained when mother's education was controlled. In addition, these families reported significantly less change in negative effects on their family, $t(148)$ = 2.52, $p < .05$, which indicates that they had fewer adverse effects over time. Subscale analyses showed a significant relation between receipt of child-oriented support services and decreased adverse effects on the familial/social aspects of family life ($M$ = .36 and .06 for those with and without additional services, respectively, $t[148]$ = 2.17, $p < .05$), even with controls for maternal education.

### Child-oriented Therapy Services

A total of 30 children received therapeutic services in addition to those received in early intervention; these included physical therapy, occupational therapy, and speech and language therapy. The majority of these children had motor impairment (70%), but neither they nor their families differed

## TABLE 33

MEAN RESIDUAL SCORES FOR CHILD AND FAMILY OUTCOMES BY TYPES OF SERVICES RECEIVED OTHER THAN EARLY INTERVENTION PROGRAM

| OUTCOMES | CHILD SUPPORT | | CHILD THERAPY | | FAMILY SUPPORT | |
|---|---|---|---|---|---|---|
| | Yes (N = 37) | No (N = 153) | Yes (N = 30) | No (N = 160) | Yes (N = 60) | No (N = 130) |
| Child outcomes: | | | | | | |
| Mental age | .09 | −.02 | −.23 | .05 | .06 | −.02 |
| Spontaneous play | −.05 | .01 | −.20 | .03 | −.04 | .01 |
| Adaptive behavior | .06 | −.02 | −.26 | .05 | −.19 | .09 |
| Child-mother interaction[a] | −.19 | .05 | −.29 | .05 | −.05 | .02 |
| Family outcomes: | | | | | | |
| Mother-child interaction | −.48 | .11** | −.03 | .01 | .01 | −.01 |
| Parenting stress[b] | .04 | .07 | .11 | .05 | .41 | −.11** |
| Effects on the family[b] | −.39 | .09** | .41 | −.08* | .20 | −.12 |
| Social support:[b] | | | | | | |
| Network size | −.16 | .06 | −.03 | .02 | .26 | −.12* |
| Helpfulness | .11 | −.01 | .11 | −.01 | .13 | −.05 |

NOTE.—Values marked with asterisks indicate significant differences based on $t$ test analysis.

[a] Standardized T2 scores.

[b] $N = 152$.

* $p < .05$.

** $p < .01$.

significantly from the rest of the sample in any other way, based on chi-square and $t$ test analyses. The families of children receiving additional therapeutic services received approximately the same average number of total hours of early intervention services as did other families (based on $t$ test analysis). In terms of outcomes, this subgroup of mothers reported significantly greater increase in adverse family effects in comparison to other sample families, $t(148) = 2.21, p < .05$. Two subscales account for the significant differences in the composite: financial strain ($M = .49, M = -.06, t[148] = 2.45, p < .05$) and familial/social strain ($M = .42, M = -.11; t[148] = 2.37, p < .05$). No difference was obtained on any of the child outcomes.

### Family-oriented Support Services

A total of 60 families received additional family support services such as counseling, family-related case management, family-related visiting nurse services, respite care, and homemaker services. Surprisingly, chi-square and $t$ test analyses indicated that there were no demographic differences between those who did and those who did not receive such services (considered in aggregate), and $t$ test analysis indicated that there were also no significant differences in the average number of total service hours received from the early intervention programs.

Significant differences were established for two outcome measures. In comparison to others, mothers in families who received additional support services had greater change in the size (but not helpfulness) of their support networks, $t(149) = 2.22, p < .05$, and greater increases in parenting stress, $t(150) = 3.12, p < .01$. Subscale analyses of the latter indicated significant differences for attachment ($M = .34, M = -.13, t[150] = 2.82, p < .01$), depression ($M = .31, M = -.11, t[150] = 2.45, p < .05$), restriction of role ($M = .35, M = -.15, t[150] = 2.99, p < .01$), and relations with spouse ($M = .32, M = -.13, t[150] = 2.68, p < .01$).

### Summary

In the case of two of the three types of additional services we investigated (child-oriented therapy and family-oriented support), those who received additional services showed significantly greater adverse changes on a family outcome measure. A causal relation cannot be inferred, however, as we cannot determine from these data whether those who sought additional services did so because they felt the family to be under increasing stress or whether the services themselves contributed to the increases in stress or disadvantageous family effects.

In contrast, families who received child-oriented support services showed significant decreases in the adverse effects of raising a child with disabilities. Moreover, these families also received fewer hours of early intervention services. Taken together, these data suggest that receipt of additional child-oriented services, which are very similar to the services offered by early intervention programs, may have served an important function for some families in this sample, especially in circumstances where the intensity of early intervention services was diminished.

## SUMMARY OF PREDICTORS OF CHANGE

In this chapter, we presented analyses designed to identify characteristics that are predictive of changes in child and family outcomes after 1 year in an early intervention program. In general, the severity of the child's psychomotor impairment proved a better predictor of change in most child and family outcomes than type of disability. We also found that child health characteristics were the most consistent correlates of child change and that changes in child outcomes were rarely associated with characteristics of the family. In contrast, family demographic and ecological characteristics were the most consistent correlates of change in family outcomes.

As regards the effect of specific characteristics of early intervention services, the four most powerful correlates of change proved to be program staffing structure (multidisciplinary vs. unidisciplinary models), service format (individualized vs. a combination of individual and group services), intensity of participation in parent groups, and intensity of home visit services. Children and families who received services primarily through a single discipline had better family outcomes after 1 year, especially in relation to decreased maternal parenting stress. Individualized services tended to provide greater benefits for the child (i.e., significantly greater increases in mental age), while a "mixed" model of both individual and group services tended to provide greater social support benefits for the family (i.e., larger and more helpful support networks). More hours of participation in parent groups were associated with greater increases in maternal social support (both in size and in perceived helpfulness), despite generally less beneficial outcomes for children and greater family strains. Finally, there was a significant positive relation between average number of hours of home visiting and decreases in maternal parenting stress.

Although receipt of additional services from agencies other than the early intervention program was associated with increasingly poor child or family outcomes, services that offered child-oriented support to families (e.g., visiting nurse and case management services) were associated with less adverse effects on the social aspects of family life. This finding suggests that the effects of early intervention services need to be considered within a broader context of diverse service delivery efforts.

# VII. DIFFERENCES BETWEEN MOTHERS AND FATHERS IN PARENTING A CHILD WITH DISABILITIES

Data on parenting stress, effects on the family, and social support were collected through self-administered questionnaires completed independently by both mothers and fathers following the T1 and T2 home visits (cf. Chap. III). The purpose of the analyses reported in this chapter is to determine the extent of *within*-family differences on the three family outcomes for which we have data from both parents (parent-child interaction was observed only for mothers) so as to provide a more refined picture of whether and how parental experiences differed for fathers and mothers.

Differences in family outcomes based on maternal scores were found by type of disability (cf. Chap. VI), and severity of psychomotor impairment was found to be correlated with maternal perception of change in adverse family effects (cf. Chap. VI). Analyses presented in this chapter examine the extent to which the variation in fathers' and mothers' scores on the family outcomes (as measured at T1 and T2 and in change scores) is attributable to parent gender, to the child's type of disability, or to the severity of the child's psychomotor impairment. In the first set of analyses, we tested the main effects of parent gender and type of disability (and their interaction); in the second, we examined the main effects of parent gender and severity of impairment (and their interaction).

To examine specific ways that mothers and fathers may differ in their experience of parenting a child with a disability, we focused on the dimensions of parenting stress, effects on the family, and social support. Analyses within each of these domains were conducted using repeated-measures multivariate analysis of variance (MANOVA). When the omnibus test yielded significant main effects or interaction terms, follow-up univariate tests for each subscale were undertaken.

TABLE 34

CHILD AND FAMILY DEMOGRAPHIC CHARACTERISTICS ($N = 97$)

| Characteristic | | Characteristic | |
|---|---|---|---|
| Type of disability ($N$): | | Child's gender ($N$): | |
| Down syndrome ....... | 34 | Male ................ | 54 |
| | (35.1) | | (55.7) |
| Motor impairment ..... | 33 | Female .............. | 43 |
| | (34.0) | | (44.3) |
| Developmental delay ... | 30 | Prematurity ($N$): | |
| | (30.9) | No................... | 77 |
| Severity of impairment | | | (79.4) |
| ($N$): | | Yes ................. | 20 |
| Mild................. | 72 | | (20.6) |
| | (74.2) | Mother's age (years) ...... | 30.3 |
| Moderate/severe ....... | 25 | | (4.5) |
| | (25.8) | Father's age (years)....... | (32.4) |
| Child's age (months): | | | (5.3) |
| $M$.................... | 9.5 | Mother's education (years) | 14.6 |
| SD .................. | 6.4 | | (2.5) |
| | | Father's education (years) | 14.6 |
| | | | (3.0) |

NOTE.—Percentages are given in parentheses.

## CHARACTERISTICS OF THE SAMPLE

The sample consisted of married couples for whom complete data were available ($N = 97$); its demographic characteristics are summarized in Table 34. Roughly one-third of these couples' children fell into each type of disability group, and almost two-thirds had mild psychomotor impairment. There was a significant relation between type of disability and severity of impairment; 40% of the children with motor impairment and one-third of those with developmental delay were classified as having more severe psychomotor impairment, whereas virtually all the children with Down syndrome were classified as relatively mildly impaired, $\chi^2(2, N = 97) = 14.94$, $p < .001$.

There were few significant differences that distinguished this subsample from the rest of the study sample. Children of parents in this analysis were younger at T1 ($M = 9.6$ months) than children of the remaining 93 families ($M = 11.7$ months), $t(118) = 2.25$, $p < .05$, and both the mothers and the fathers were older ($M = 30.3$ vs. 27.9, $M = 32.4$ vs. 30.5, respectively, $t[187] = -3.33$, $p < .001$, $t[184] = -2.35$, $p < .05$, respectively) and had more years of education ($M = 14.6$ vs. 13.0, $M = 14.6$ vs. 13.0, respectively, $t[188] = 4.67$, $p < .001$, $t[182] = 3.87$, $p < .001$, respectively) than the other parents.

## THE EFFECTS OF TYPE OF DISABILITY ON DIFFERENCES BETWEEN MOTHERS AND FATHERS IN FAMILY OUTCOMES

*Differences at T1 and T2.*—Tables 35 and 36 present mean subscale scores for the family outcomes for mothers and fathers by type of child's disability at T1 and T2, respectively. (Summary and standard deviation scores for the measures are available from the authors.) Multivariate analyses of variance (MANOVA) tests conducted on parenting stress subscale scores as measured on entry into the study revealed a significant main effect for parent gender, MANOVA $F(14,178) = 6.45, p < .001$. Fathers typically had a lower score than mothers in their level of parenting stress (Table 35); subsequent univariate tests indicated significant between-parent differences on four of the seven subscales. While fathers reported more stress with respect to feelings of attachment to their child, mothers reported more stress with respect to personal and interpersonal strains associated with parenting (i.e., parental health, restrictions in role, and relations with spouse). There was also a significant main effect of the child's diagnostic group, MANOVA $F(14,178) = 2.35, p < .01$, on two of the parenting stress subscales—social isolation and relations with spouse—where univariate tests showed parents of children with motor impairment to have the highest scores.

With respect to adverse effects on the family, MANOVA $F(8,184) = 3.75, p < .01$, mothers perceived the personal strain of parenting a child with special needs more strongly than did fathers. While the interaction term was not significant in the omnibus test, univariate analyses did indicate a significant interaction term for the mastery strain subscale. In contrast to other fathers, fathers of children with developmental delays reported less strain associated with mastery than did their wives. With respect to social support at study entry, MANOVA procedures yielded a significant main effect for type of disability, MANOVA $F(4,188) = 3.80, p < .01$. Both parents of children with Down syndrome reported significantly greater helpfulness from their support networks than did parents of children with motor impairment or developmental delay.

At T2, the results of the analyses of the subscales of parenting stress mirrored those found at T1 (Table 36). There was a significant main effect for both parent gender, MANOVA $F(14,178) = 5.11, p < .001$, and type of disability, MANOVA $F(14,178) = 2.52, p < .01$. Fathers reported greater stress with respect to feelings of attachment or emotional closeness to their children, while mothers reported greater stress with respect to their own health, restrictions in their role, and relations with their spouse. Both parents of children with motor impairment reported greater stress than did other parents with respect to parental health (a difference not found at T1) and relations with spouse. Whereas the interaction was not significant in

95

# TABLE 35

## MEAN SCORES ON FAMILY OUTCOMES AT T1 BY TYPE OF DISABILITY AND PARENT GENDER ($N = 97$)

| OUTCOME | DOWN SYNDROME ($N = 34$) | | MOTOR IMPAIRMENT ($N = 33$) | | DEVELOPMENTAL DELAY ($N = 30$) | | F RATIOS[a] | | |
|---|---|---|---|---|---|---|---|---|---|
| | Mothers | Fathers | Mothers | Fathers | Mothers | Fathers | D | G | D × G |
| Parenting stress: | | | | | | | | | |
| Attachment | 11.7 | 13.7 | 11.6 | 12.2 | 10.9 | 12.9 | 1.40 | 12.99*** | 1.35 |
| Sense of competence | 25.7 | 27.4 | 28.5 | 26.6 | 26.6 | 25.6 | .64 | .34 | 2.29 |
| Depression | 19.3 | 19.1 | 19.2 | 16.9 | 17.5 | 17.1 | 1.60 | 2.52 | 1.25 |
| Parent health | 11.2 | 11.1 | 12.7 | 11.0 | 11.9 | 11.0 | .79 | 5.51* | 1.28 |
| Social isolation | 10.7 | 12.1 | 14.0 | 13.5 | 11.6 | 12.5 | 5.90** | 1.90 | 1.55 |
| Restrictions in role | 17.2 | 16.4 | 20.1 | 16.0 | 18.4 | 16.2 | .78 | 16.23*** | 2.72 |
| Relations with spouse | 16.0 | 15.2 | 18.9 | 16.9 | 16.3 | 15.5 | 3.40* | 6.17* | .73 |
| Effects on the family: | | | | | | | | | |
| Mastery strain | 7.9 | 8.4 | 8.6 | 9.3 | 9.0 | 8.3 | 2.08 | .78 | 3.90* |
| Financial strain | 8.1 | 8.4 | 9.0 | 8.8 | 7.9 | 7.4 | 2.13 | .13 | .75 |
| Personal strain | 12.3 | 11.9 | 13.5 | 12.4 | 12.7 | 11.3 | 1.06 | 10.14** | .80 |
| Familial/social strain | 15.8 | 17.2 | 17.9 | 17.1 | 16.1 | 15.0 | 2.19 | .16 | 2.77 |
| Social support: | | | | | | | | | |
| Network size | 9.9 | 10.3 | 9.1 | 9.1 | 9.1 | 9.3 | 2.66 | .80 | .37 |
| Helpfulness | 26.4 | 28.6 | 21.4 | 20.8 | 22.7 | 22.5 | 8.17*** | .39 | 1.79 |

[a] D = disability group, $df(2.94)$. G = parent gender, $df(1.94)$. D × G = interaction term, $df(2.94)$.

* $p < .05$.
** $p < .01$.
*** $p < .001$.

TABLE 36

Mean Scores on Family Outcomes at T2 by Type of Disability and Parent Gender ($N = 97$)

| | Down Syndrome ($N = 34$) | | Motor Impairment ($N = 33$) | | Developmental Delay ($N = 30$) | | $F$ Ratios[a] | | |
|---|---|---|---|---|---|---|---|---|---|
| Outcome | Mothers | Fathers | Mothers | Fathers | Mothers | Fathers | D | G | D × G |
| Parenting stress: | | | | | | | | | |
| Attachment | 11.2 | 14.0 | 12.0 | 12.8 | 12.4 | 12.6 | .05 | 9.98** | 4.19* |
| Sense of competence | 25.8 | 27.5 | 29.4 | 28.0 | 26.7 | 25.7 | 1.91 | .10 | 1.67 |
| Depression | 18.6 | 19.2 | 19.1 | 17.7 | 18.4 | 16.6 | .92 | 2.40 | 1.81 |
| Parent health | 10.6 | 11.2 | 13.6 | 11.8 | 12.1 | 10.6 | 5.78** | 5.70* | 4.23* |
| Social isolation | 11.7 | 12.9 | 13.3 | 13.9 | 12.5 | 12.3 | 1.59 | 1.12 | .72 |
| Restrictions in role | 17.3 | 17.1 | 20.2 | 17.8 | 19.0 | 16.3 | 2.05 | 12.94*** | 2.57 |
| Relations with spouse | 15.7 | 15.8 | 19.5 | 17.5 | 18.8 | 16.7 | 4.29* | 6.91** | 2.02 |
| Effects on the family: | | | | | | | | | |
| Mastery strain | 8.1 | 8.6 | 9.2 | 9.7 | 8.9 | 8.8 | 4.19* | 1.62 | .59 |
| Financial strain | 8.1 | 9.1 | 9.1 | 8.7 | 7.7 | 7.8 | 1.79 | .52 | 2.36 |
| Personal strain | 11.6 | 12.0 | 13.7 | 12.8 | 13.2 | 11.7 | 2.36 | 3.45 | 2.69 |
| Familial/social strain | 15.1 | 16.9 | 18.2 | 17.6 | 15.8 | 15.3 | 3.92* | .37 | 3.53* |
| Social support: | | | | | | | | | |
| Network size | 11.1 | 10.3 | 10.3 | 9.3 | 10.4 | 10.4 | 2.25 | 8.74** | .09 |
| Helpfulness | 29.3 | 28.7 | 23.3 | 22.6 | 26.7 | 24.1 | 7.01*** | 2.03 | .46 |

[a] D = disability group, $df(2,94)$. G = parent gender, $df(1,94)$. D × G = interaction term, $df(2,94)$.
* $p < .05$.
** $p < .01$.
*** $p < .001$.

97

the MANOVA analysis, there were two significant interaction terms in the follow-up univariate analyses. These results (which should be interpreted cautiously) indicate that fathers of infants with Down syndrome experienced considerably higher stress than their wives with respect to their feelings of attachment. They also reported greater stress than their wives with respect to parental health, a pattern not found among parents of children with motor impairment or developmental delay.

Differences on the subscales of the effects on family measure at T2 were not consistent with those found at T1. Specifically, at T2, there was a main effect of diagnostic group, MANOVA $F(8,184) = 2.38, p < .05$, with both parents of children with motor impairment reporting higher levels of strain associated with feelings of mastery as a parent and in their familial/ social relationships. While there was a significant effect for parent gender, MANOVA $F(8,184) = 2.85, p < .05$, with mothers reporting generally more strain, no specific subscale of the measure accounted for this difference. In the follow-up univariate tests, the one significant interaction (not detected in the omnibus MANOVA test) showed that, in contrast to fathers of children with motor impairment or developmental delays, fathers of children with Down syndrome reported higher levels of stress in their social/familial relationships than did their wives. With respect to social support, there was a significant effect for parent gender, MANOVA $F(4,186) = 8.74, p < .01$, and for type of disability, MANOVA $F(4,186) = 3.99, p < .01$. Mothers reported larger support networks than fathers, and both parents of children with motor impairment rated network helpfulness lower than the other two groups (a finding consistent with T1).

*Differences in residual change scores.*—Analysis of differences in the residual change scores on the subscales for parenting stress yielded a significant main effect for diagnostic group, MANOVA $F(14,178) = 1.94, p < .05$, largely accounted for by differences in the subscale measuring parental health (Table 37). Parents of children with motor impairment had larger than expected increases in stress related to their own health than did other parents (a finding that complements the results of the cross-sectional analyses reported above). We also found a significant interaction term in the follow-up univariate analyses (but not in the omnibus test) for the attachment subscale. Fathers of infants with Down syndrome had significant increases in the stress associated with their feelings of attachment, whereas other fathers had either reduced stress (i.e., fathers of children with developmental delays) or virtually no change in their stress level (i.e., fathers of children with motor impairment). MANOVA analyses revealed no significant differences in the residual change scores for the subscales of the effects on family measure. Similarly, no significant differences were detected (based on MANOVA analyses) in the residual change scores for the size or helpfulness of parents' social support networks.

TABLE 37

MEAN SCORES ON RESIDUALS OF FAMILY OUTCOMES BY TYPE OF DISABILITY AND PARENT GENDER (N = 97)

| OUTCOME | DOWN SYNDROME (N = 34) | | MOTOR IMPAIRMENT (N = 33) | | DEVELOPMENTAL DELAY (N = 30) | | F RATIOS[a] | | |
|---|---|---|---|---|---|---|---|---|---|
| | Mothers | Fathers | Mothers | Fathers | Mothers | Fathers | D | G | D × G |
| Parenting stress: | | | | | | | | | |
| Attachment.......... | -.17 | .11 | .19 | .002 | .50 | -.25 | .43 | 2.99 | 5.43** |
| Sense of competence... | -.13 | -.12 | .23 | .12 | -.10 | -.20 | 1.66 | .26 | .09 |
| Depression .......... | .11 | .06 | .03 | .02 | .11 | -.26 | .14 | .35 | 1.76 |
| Parent health ....... | -.33 | -.03 | .39 | .27 | .03 | -.28 | 4.49* | .13 | 1.96 |
| Social isolation ..... | .09 | .02 | -.05 | .03 | .14 | -.22 | .15 | .97 | 1.12 |
| Restrictions in role ... | -.20 | -.08 | .09 | .20 | .05 | -.27 | 1.23 | .07 | 1.50 |
| Relations with spouse .. | -.17 | -.15 | .28 | .09 | .49 | .06 | 2.73 | 4.06* | 1.58 |
| Effects on the family: | | | | | | | | | |
| Mastery strain ........ | -.16 | -.16 | .23 | .27 | -.08 | -.02 | 2.52 | .07 | .03 |
| Financial strain....... | -.05 | .17 | .15 | -.05 | -.15 | -.17 | .69 | .00 | 1.65 |
| Personal strain....... | -.34 | -.08 | .15 | .11 | .12 | -.09 | 1.47 | .00 | 1.62 |
| Familial/social strain ... | -.26 | -.08 | .31 | .13 | -.09 | -.22 | 2.33 | .18 | 1.14 |
| Social support: | | | | | | | | | |
| Network size.......... | .06 | .06 | -.17 | -.19 | .24 | .22 | 1.88 | .01 | .01 |
| Helpfulness........... | .19 | .25 | -.25 | -.15 | .11 | -.04 | 2.31 | .00 | .43 |

[a] D = disability group, $df(2,94)$. G = parent gender, $df(1,94)$. D × G = interaction term, $df(2,94)$.

* $p < .05$.
** $p < .01$.

## THE EFFECTS OF LEVEL OF SEVERITY OF CHILD PSYCHOMOTOR
## IMPAIRMENT ON DIFFERENCES BETWEEN MOTHERS
## AND FATHERS IN FAMILY OUTCOMES

*Differences at T1 and T2.*—Tables 38 (T1) and 39 (T2) present mean subscale scores of the family outcomes for mothers and fathers for the two levels of severity of psychomotor impairment. Multivariate analysis of the parenting stress measure's seven subscales revealed a significant effect for parent gender, MANOVA $F(7,89) = 4.63$, $p < .001$, which mirrored the findings reported earlier in the analysis based on parent gender and type of disability (Tables 35 and 36 above). Specifically, mothers reported greater stress related to parental health, restrictions in role, and relations with spouse; fathers reported greater stress associated with their feelings of attachment to their child.

There were no T1 differences (based on MANOVA procedures) in the parents' social support network size or helpfulness or on the subscales of the effects on family measure related to the child's severity of impairment or parent gender; however, in follow-up univariate analyses, we found that mothers reported more personal strain than did fathers.

At T2, there was a main effect of both parent gender, MANOVA $F(7,89) = 3.53$, $p < .01$, and of severity of the child's psychomotor impairment, MANOVA $F(7,89) = 2.88$, $p < .05$, on the parenting stress subscales (Table 39). The differences between mothers and fathers obtained at T1 with respect to attachment, parental health, restrictions in role, and relations with spouse persisted at T2. In addition, both parents of children with more severe psychomotor impairment reported greater stress associated with restrictions in their roles than did parents of children with milder impairments. Severity of the child's impairment was also related to the subscales of the effects on family measure, MANOVA $F(4,92) = 5.68$, $p < .001$. Both fathers and mothers of more severely impaired children had higher scores (more negative effects) on all four dimensions. Although no differences based on the severity of the child's impairment were found for either network size or rated helpfulness, mothers reported larger social support networks than did fathers, MANOVA $F(2,94) = 4.55$, $p < .05$.

*Differences in residual change scores.*—Analyses of the residual change scores for parenting stress (Table 40) revealed a main effect for severity of the child's impairment, MANOVA $F(7,89) = 3.81$, $p < .001$, with both parents of more severely impaired children indicating greater increases in stress associated with their feelings of attachment to their child and with restrictions in their role. A similar effect prevailed for the subscales of the effect on family measure, MANOVA $F(4,92) = 4.58$, $p < .01$; both mothers and fathers of more severely impaired children reported larger increases in financial strain, strain in their social/familial relationships, and personal

## TABLE 38

### MEAN SCORES ON FAMILY OUTCOMES AT T1 BY SEVERITY OF PSYCHOMOTOR IMPAIRMENT AND PARENT GENDER ($N = 97$)

| OUTCOME | MILD ($N = 72$) | | MODERATE/SEVERE ($N = 25$) | | $F$ RATIOS[a] | | |
|---|---|---|---|---|---|---|---|
| | Mothers | Fathers | Mothers | Fathers | S | G | S × G |
| Parenting stress: | | | | | | | |
| Attachment | 11.4 | 13.2 | 11.4 | 12.3 | .65 | 7.29** | .77 |
| Sense of competence | 26.6 | 26.5 | 27.9 | 26.8 | .39 | .52 | .31 |
| Depression | 18.7 | 17.6 | 18.7 | 18.1 | .06 | 1.46 | .14 |
| Parent health | 11.9 | 11.1 | 12.1 | 10.9 | .01 | 4.93* | .16 |
| Social isolation | 11.8 | 12.3 | 12.8 | 14.0 | 3.90 | 2.37 | .49 |
| Restrictions in role | 18.3 | 15.9 | 19.3 | 17.0 | 1.29 | 11.37*** | .02 |
| Relations with spouse | 16.9 | 15.7 | 17.4 | 16.5 | .53 | 4.14* | .09 |
| Effects on the family: | | | | | | | |
| Mastery strain | 8.3 | 8.6 | 8.9 | 8.8 | 1.13 | .29 | .47 |
| Financial strain | 8.3 | 8.1 | 8.6 | 8.7 | .65 | .00 | .28 |
| Personal strain | 12.6 | 11.5 | 13.4 | 13.1 | 3.30 | 4.67* | 1.49 |
| Familial/social strain | 16.1 | 16.2 | 18.1 | 17.4 | 3.44 | .41 | .60 |
| Social support: | | | | | | | |
| Network size | 9.5 | 9.9 | 9.0 | 8.7 | 3.24 | .01 | 2.22 |
| Helpfulness | 23.5 | 24.6 | 23.8 | 22.4 | .29 | .04 | 2.71 |

[a] S = severity group, $df(1,95)$. G = parent gender, $df(1,95)$. S × G = interaction term, $df(1,95)$.

* $p < .05$.

** $p < .01$.

*** $p < .001$.

TABLE 39

Mean Scores on Family Outcomes at T2 by Severity of Psychomotor Impairment and Parent Gender ($N = 97$)

| | Mild ($N = 72$) | | Moderate/Severe ($N = 25$) | | F Ratios[a] | | |
|---|---|---|---|---|---|---|---|
| Outcome | Mothers | Fathers | Mothers | Fathers | S | G | S × G |
| Parenting stress: | | | | | | | |
| Attachment | 11.5 | 13.0 | 12.8 | 13.4 | 2.83 | 5.29* | 1.01 |
| Sense of competence | 26.9 | 26.5 | 28.5 | 28.8 | 2.38 | .00 | .16 |
| Depression | 18.9 | 18.0 | 18.2 | 17.6 | .35 | 1.30 | .08 |
| Parent health | 11.7 | 11.1 | 13.0 | 11.5 | 2.14 | 5.74* | .87 |
| Social isolation | 12.4 | 12.6 | 12.9 | 14.3 | 2.13 | 2.31 | 1.22 |
| Restrictions in role | 18.5 | 16.4 | 19.8 | 19.2 | 5.64* | 5.79* | 1.68 |
| Relations with spouse | 17.7 | 16.3 | 18.7 | 17.6 | 1.33 | 4.37* | .05 |
| Effects on the family: | | | | | | | |
| Mastery strain | 8.6 | 8.8 | 9.1 | 9.8 | 4.59* | 2.87 | 1.18 |
| Financial strain | 7.9 | 8.3 | 9.6 | 9.3 | 5.93* | .01 | 1.46 |
| Personal strain | 12.2 | 11.6 | 14.6 | 14.0 | 17.10*** | 2.20 | .00 |
| Familial/social strain | 15.3 | 15.9 | 19.4 | 16.4 | 18.77*** | .00 | 1.72 |
| Social support: | | | | | | | |
| Network size | 10.7 | 10.0 | 11.1 | 9.9 | .08 | 9.15** | .70 |
| Helpfulness | 26.4 | 25.9 | 26.8 | 23.2 | .47 | 3.68 | 2.09 |

[a] S = severity group, $df(1,95)$. G = parent gender, $df(1,95)$. S × G = interaction term, $df(1,95)$.
* $p < .05$.
** $p < .01$.
*** $p < .001$.

TABLE 40

MEAN SCORES ON RESIDUALS OF FAMILY OUTCOMES BY SEVERITY OF PSYCHOMOTOR IMPAIRMENT AND PARENT GENDER ($N = 97$)

| OUTCOME | MILD ($N = 72$) Mothers | Fathers | MODERATE/SEVERE ($N = 25$) Mothers | Fathers | $F$ RATIOS[a] S | G | S × G |
|---|---|---|---|---|---|---|---|
| Parenting stress: | | | | | | | |
| Attachment | .02 | −.13 | .56 | .22 | 7.51** | 2.56 | .37 |
| Sense of competence | −.04 | −.17 | .13 | .25 | 2.69 | .00 | .73 |
| Depression | .05 | −.01 | −.13 | −.19 | 1.08 | .18 | .00 |
| Parent health | −.06 | −.06 | .29 | .14 | 2.36 | .24 | .28 |
| Social isolation | .07 | −.09 | .04 | .06 | .12 | .26 | .36 |
| Restrictions in role | −.07 | −.21 | .12 | .43 | 4.96* | .45 | 2.86 |
| Relations with spouse | .15 | −.06 | .30 | .15 | .94 | 2.34 | .08 |
| Effects on the family: | | | | | | | |
| Mastery strain | −.03 | −.11 | .09 | .43 | 3.22 | 1.09 | 2.80 |
| Financial strain | −.17 | −.09 | .44 | .21 | 5.76* | .48 | 2.13 |
| Personal strain | −.21 | −.16 | .48 | .40 | 11.80*** | .02 | .21 |
| Familial/social strain | −.24 | −.21 | .62 | .38 | 15.87*** | .76 | 1.23 |
| Social support: | | | | | | | |
| Network size | −.04 | .01 | .27 | .09 | .97 | .26 | .78 |
| Helpfulness | .01 | .09 | .03 | −.15 | .31 | .16 | .95 |

[a] S = severity group, $df(1,95)$. G = parent gender, $df(1,95)$. S × G = interaction term, $df(1,95)$.
* $p < .05$.
** $p < .01$.
*** $p < .001$.

strain. Neither parent's gender nor the severity of the child's impairment showed any significant effects (based on MANOVA procedures) on social support network size or helpfulness.

## SUMMARY OF MOTHER-FATHER DIFFERENCES

Our cross-sectional and longitudinal analyses yielded a consistent distinction between married mothers and fathers related to their patterns of parenting stress. Fathers reported greater stress associated with their feelings of attachment to their child at both T1 and T2, whereas mothers reported more stress associated with the personal and familial aspects of parenting. In all our other analyses of potential between-parent differences, however, the findings for fathers were consistent with those established for mothers (see Chap. VI).

# VIII. VULNERABILITY AND ADAPTATION: SELECTED SUBGROUP ANALYSES

Analyses presented in Chapter VI demonstrated the extent of child and family change over the 1-year period for the full study sample as well as their correlates. For children, the association between severity of psychomotor impairment and magnitude of developmental gains is pervasive. Beyond the effect of severity of disability, however, some subgroups exhibited greater gains, while others showed less developmental growth. As concerns families, although the sample as a whole did not manifest significant sociodemographic risk or maladaptation either on entry into the study or 1 year later, almost half the mothers had no education beyond high school, and a subgroup of both mothers and fathers reported clinically significant levels of stress. Furthermore, mothers and fathers differed in systematic ways with respect to both level and sources of parenting difficulties with their child.

In this chapter, we extend our analyses by undertaking a closer examination of four selected subgroups. Two of these (children with seizure disorders and parents exhibiting relatively high levels of stress) were selected because they represent particularly vulnerable populations served by early intervention programs. The third group (defined by fewer years of maternal education) was chosen because it represents a population that has been viewed traditionally as at risk for deleterious outcomes. Finally, the fourth group (families in which mothers demonstrated large gains in the quality of their interaction with their children) was selected because it highlights the capacity for significant growth among some families who have a child with a disability. Despite the distinctions among these four subgroups, there were no significant differences in either intensity (based on $t$ tests) or types of early intervention services (based on chi-square analyses) that each of them received in comparison to the rest of the sample. Consequently, we structured our analyses of T1 and T2 change data to investigate which child or family demographic characteristics, or aspects of functioning, might distinguish each of the subgroups from the remainder of the sample. Interpretation of our findings is discussed in the concluding chapter.

## CHILDREN WITH SEIZURE DISORDERS

Thirty-five children (three with Down syndrome, 20 with motor impairment, and 12 with developmental delay) had a seizure disorder confirmed by medical record review. A significantly higher proportion of children in this group than in the sample as a whole was categorized as having a severe psychomotor impairment (48.6% vs. 26.5%, respectively), $\chi^2(1, N = 189) = 10.80, p < .01$, at study entry. Within this group of children, 45.7% were firstborn, 57.1% were male, 14.3% had a cardiac anomaly, and 25.7% were born prematurely. Statistical analyses revealed that the group did not differ significantly from other sample children in their gestational age, birth weight, Apgar scores, or time spent in a neonatal intensive care unit or special care nursery. In terms of demographic differences, the mothers of these children did not differ from other mothers in marital status (based on chi-square analyses) or years of education (based on $t$ test analyses), but they were more likely to be employed full or part time outside the home (54.3%), $\chi^2(1, N = 186) = 5.46, p < .05$.

Children with seizure disorders were remarkably similar to other sample members on the full set of child outcomes at T1. However, they showed significantly less developmental growth over the 1-year period, MANOVA $F(4,183) = 3.70, p < .01$. Univariate tests indicated a slower pattern of growth on three of the child outcomes: adaptive behavior, $F(1,186) = 8.78, p < .01$; spontaneous play, $F(1,186) = 6.74, p < .01$; and child-mother interaction, $F(1,186) = 7.80, p < .01$ (Figs. 5–7). The fourth child outcome, mental age, displayed the same trend, $F(1,180) = 3.80, p < .06$. Thus, as a group, these children demonstrated a different overall trajectory of development.

At study entry, measures of the child-rearing environment and levels of family functioning were no different for children with seizure disorders than for the other sample members. Multivariate analyses of the set of parent outcomes, however, revealed an overall significant difference, MANOVA $F(5,170) = 3.38, p < .01$. Univariate analyses indicated that mothers of children with seizure disorders reported significantly more adverse family effects, $F(1,174) = 9.30, p < .01$, particularly related to increased financial, $F(1,174) = 10.80, p < .001$, personal, $F(1,174) = 5.97, p < .05$, and familial/social strain, $F(1,174) = 8.72, p < .01$. This overall pattern was sustained at T2, as multivariate analyses indicated a significant difference, MANOVA $F(5,147) = 2.54, p < .05$, across the family outcomes, and univariate tests revealed a significant difference in maternal report of negative effects on the family, $F(1,151) = 9.30, p < .01$. The differences again reflected increased financial, $F(1,151) = 4.58, p < .05$, personal, $F(1,151) = 6.35, p < .05$, and familial/social strain, $F(1,151) = 12.99, p < .01$. Multivariate analysis of the residual change scores on family outcomes,

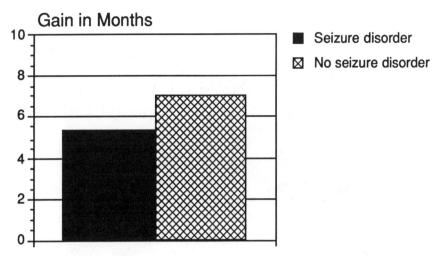

Fɪɢ. 5.—A comparison of the gains made by children with and without seizure disorders: adaptive behavior.

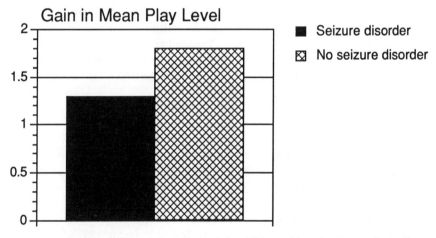

Fɪɢ. 6.—A comparison of the gains made by children with and without seizure disorders: spontaneous play.

however, was not significant. This suggests that mothers of children with seizure disorders did not have a different pattern of change in family outcomes; rather, they maintained their relatively higher levels of strain associated with adverse family effects across the study period.

In summary, children with seizure disorders did not differ from other children with disabilities at entry to early intervention in measures of their

## Gain in Child Subscale Score

■ Seizure disorder

⊠ No seizure disorder

Fɪɢ. 7.—A comparison of the gains made by children with and without seizure disorders: child-mother interaction.

developmental status. Their families, however, reported greater adverse effects of the child's disability on many aspects of family life. Over the course of the year, the progress of these children was not as great as that of other sample children in almost all assessed aspects of development, and their mothers continued to report greater adverse family effects.

### FAMILIES REPORTING ATYPICALLY HIGH STRESS

Most sample mothers had parenting stress levels that fell well within the normative range reported by mothers of young children without disabilities (cf. Chap. V), and most fathers reported lower overall levels of parenting stress than their wives (cf. Chap. VII). Although the absence of unusually high stress levels generally persisted over time, there was a subgroup of families in which both mother and father reported a level of stress indicative of a need for clinical intervention. Specifically, in 19.6% of the 97 married couples for whom complete study data were collected, both parents reported at study entry clinically significant scores on at least one of the seven dimensions of parenting stress. Our analyses compare characteristics of these (relatively) "high-stress" families ($N = 19$) with the remaining married couples ($N = 78$) who were characterized by normative levels of parenting stress on all seven subscales (see Fig. 8).

Statistical comparisons of the two groups of families revealed an unexpected absence of differences either in demographic or functional characteristics of children at T1 or T2 or in the patterns of children's development

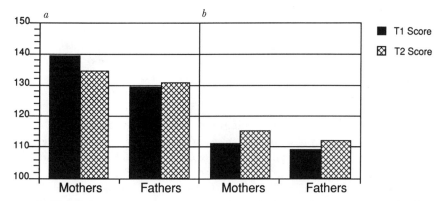

FIG. 8.—Mean scores on parenting stress for high-stress and normative-stress families at T1 and T2. a, High-stress families (N = 19). b, Normative-stress families (N = 78).

over the study period. Specifically, no differences between the high- and normative-stress groups were found with respect to the child's type of disability, health status, gender, prematurity status (based on chi-square analyses), or age (based on $t$ test analysis). Multivariate analyses (MANOVA) indicated no significant differences in the children's mean level of psychomotor performance, adaptive behavior skills, spontaneous play, or interaction with their mothers either at study entry or 1 year later. Indeed, the only difference in this domain between the two groups of families was that both mothers and fathers in the high-stress group rated their children as more difficult temperamentally on study entry ($M$ = 61.0 vs. 51.2 for mothers, $t[95]$ = 3.09, $p < .01$; $M$ = 61.6 vs. 54.4 for fathers, $t[95]$ = 2.67, $p < .01$).

In terms of family characteristics, chi-square analyses indicated that the two groups were comparable in family income, maternal and paternal education levels, and maternal and paternal employment status. Thus, the traditional correlates of parenting stress—child functional and family sociodemographic characteristics—were not helpful in distinguishing between married couples experiencing higher or lower levels of stress at the time of entry into early intervention services.

The high-stress group did differ from the remaining couples in other ways. On entry into the study, both mothers and fathers in this stress group perceived their family as less adaptable and less cohesive, MANOVA $F(2,94)$ = 3.82, $p < .05$, and MANOVA $F(2,94)$ = 3.79, $p < .05$, respectively. Further, as expected, both mothers and fathers in this subgroup had more adverse ratings on the full set of parent outcomes, MANOVA $F(5,91)$ = 6.43, $p < .001$, and MANOVA $F(4,92)$ = 3.96, $p < .01$, respectively. Univariate tests indicated that mothers not only reported higher levels of parenting stress at study entry, $F(1,95) = 26.39$, $p < .001$, but also perceived more negative effects on their families, $F(1,95) = 15.99$, $p < .001$, and reported their social support network as less helpful, $F(1,95) = 8.00$, $p < .01$. Moreover, they had lower scores on the measure of mother-child interaction, $F(1,95) = 6.23$, $p < .05$, especially in ratings of their responsiveness to the child's distress, $F(1,95) = 6.15$, $p < .05$, and their provision of social-emotional growth–promoting behaviors, $F(1,95) = 4.08$, $p < .05$. These latter findings are particularly striking since the children in this group were not rated as interacting with their mothers in any significantly different ways from other sample children (based on MANOVA tests). Although fathers in the high-stress group had more adverse family outcomes than other fathers at T1, univariate tests indicated that no outcome other than parenting stress, $F(1,95) = 15.23$, $p < .001$, was significantly different from that reported by other married fathers.

One year later, neither the mother nor the father in nine of the 19 high-stress families had scores above the clinical cutoff on any of the measured dimensions of parenting stress. All 19 couples, however, continued to have significantly higher parenting stress scores than the comparison group of normatively stressed couples. Multivariate analyses of the set of parent outcomes at T2 indicated persistent differences for the mothers who had been in the high-stress group, MANOVA $F(5,91) = 3.43$, $p < .01$. In addition to their persistently high scores for parenting stress, univariate tests showed them to have lower scores for helpfulness (but not size) of their support networks, $F(1,95) = 6.83$, $p < .01$. These mothers also reported significantly more adverse family effects, $F(1,95) = 8.29$, $p < .01$, especially with respect to personal strain, $F(1,95) = 5.15$, $p < .05$, and familial/social relationships, $F(1,95) = 6.86$, $p < .01$. Nevertheless, despite reports of such pervasive negative effects, these mothers' interaction with their children improved by T2 and no longer differed significantly from mothers in the comparison group.

Multivariate analyses of fathers' reports at T2 indicated that those who had been in the high-stress group continued to differ significantly from other married fathers on the full set of parent outcomes, MANOVA $F(4,92) = 4.07$, $p < .01$. Univariate tests indicated some similarities with the T2 pattern of the mothers. In addition to sustained higher levels of parenting stress, $F(1,95) = 10.21$, $p < .01$, these fathers reported significantly greater adverse effects on their family, $F(4,92) = 4.01$, $p < .05$, especially in terms of their feelings of mastery as a parent, $F(1,95) = 5.43$, $p < .05$, and of personal strain, $F(1,95) = 4.45$, $p < .05$, and a less extensive social support network, $F(1,95) = 4.73$, $p < .05$. However, patterns of change in family outcomes (as measured by multivariate tests) were not significantly different between parents in the high-stress group and those in the comparison group.

In summary, the differences between married couples reporting some dimensions of high stress and those reporting normative stress cannot be attributed to characteristics of the child, such as type of disability or extent of psychomotor impairment, or even to aspects of the child's functioning, such as level of adaptive behavior. High-stress mothers as well as fathers reported their child to be temperamentally difficult; the extent to which this may reflect an intrinsic characteristic of the child and not an attribute of parental perception is impossible to assess. However, higher levels of parenting stress were clearly associated with other indicators of troubled family and personal functioning. While the precise causes of the heightened difficulties found in the more stressed families cannot be ascertained at both time points, these parents were less likely to perceive themselves as supported by their social networks, less likely to view their families as cohesive and adaptable in response to situational demands, and more likely to view their child as a source of financial and social strain. The extent to which this subgroup of parents continues to report greater difficulties, and whether their children's development remains unaffected by these problems, will be answered by continued longitudinal study.

## MOTHERS WITH A HIGH SCHOOL EDUCATION OR LESS

In our sample of mothers from whom both T1 and T2 data were collected, 43% had attended 12 years of school. Low maternal education is usually defined as failure to complete high school; however, since only 8.9% of the sample mothers failed to do so, we compared mothers with 12 years of schooling or less ($N = 65$) to those with more than a high school education ($N = 85$) in our analyses.

As expected, mothers with less education had significantly lower income, $\chi^2(3, N = 148) = 45.49, p < .001$, and were more likely to be unmarried, $\chi^2(1, N = 152) = 17.81, p < .001$. Significant differences were also found between these two groups with respect to the child-rearing qualities of the home environment, $t(150) = 4.89, p < .001$, and the reported levels of cohesion and adaptability within the family, MANOVA $F(2,178) = 4.44$, $p < .05$. Mothers with less education were disadvantaged in each case; their homes were rated as less oriented to their child's development and social needs, and their families were characterized by less cohesion and adaptability.

In multivariate analyses of the T1 set of parent outcome measures, mothers with lower levels of education differed significantly from more educated mothers, MANOVA $F(5,144) = 5.10, p < .001$. Univariate significance tests indicated that their interactions with their children were significantly less positive, $F(1,148) = 20.46, p < .001$. Specifically, these mothers displayed less sensitivity to their child's distress, $F(1,148) = 9.73$, $p <$ .01, and were less promoting of both social-emotional, $F(1,148) = 10.69$, $p < .001$, and cognitive growth, $F(1,148) = 11.83$, $p < .001$. Multivariate analyses of T2 data indicated that the differences between the two groups persisted, MANOVA $F(5,143) = 6.01$, $p < .001$. Univariate tests revealed the same pattern of differences in mother-child interaction as had been found at T1, $F(1,147) = 20.14$, $p < .001$, as well as significantly higher levels of parenting stress, $F(1,147) = 6.24$, $p < .05$, and significantly less helpful social support networks, $F(1,147) = 4.49$, $p < .05$, reported by mothers with less education. However, although the differences between these two groups became more pronounced over time, the patterns of change across the family outcomes were not significantly different.

Despite the scope and magnitude of the differences in family environments and reported stress related to parenting, there were no statistically significant differences between mothers with different levels of education with respect to the characteristics and developmental status of their children. Multivariate analyses of data collected at T1 and T2 and of the residual change scores indicated no overall difference between the two groups in child outcomes. One difference did emerge in univariate tests, although, in view of the lack of multivariate results, it should be interpreted with caution. At T2, children of mothers with less education were less positive in their interaction with their mothers, $F(1,146) = 6.71$, $p < .05$. In light of the significantly less nurturing maternal interactive behavior observed for this subgroup, the less responsive scores on the part of children are not surprising. Nevertheless, the robustness, durability, and subsequent effect of these differences in the quality of child-mother interaction await further confirmation and study.

## FAMILIES IN WHICH MOTHERS DEMONSTRATED LARGE GAINS IN THEIR INTERACTIVE SKILLS

Mothers' interactions with their children are critical influences on the developmental process, especially during the first few years of life. Although distinctive patterns of mother-child interaction have been reported for infants with special needs, the extent of change in maternal interactive behavior with such children has rarely been addressed, despite the fact that quality of interaction is generally considered to be amenable to intervention effects. In our sample, mother-child interaction scores at T1 were significantly lower than those of the standardization sample (cf. Chap. V). Although average scores remained low at T2, a subgroup of mothers ($N = 23$) demonstrated remarkable growth in their cognitive and social growth–promoting behaviors with their children; their scores at T2 were more than 1 standard deviation higher than their T1 scores on both these subscales.

Surprisingly, these 23 mothers did not differ significantly from other sample mothers on any of the demographic variables we tested. No single or combined set of these variables—namely, maternal education, marital status, employment status, and family income—differentiated between the two groups. Similarly, statistical tests indicated that the children of these mothers did not differ significantly from the other sample children in gender, severity of psychomotor impairment, health status, prematurity status, age, or type of disability (the group comprised six children with Down syndrome, nine with motor impairment, and eight with developmental delay).

Other aspects of the family environment, such as maternal reports of the level of family cohesion and adaptability and observer ratings of the home environment, also did not differ for the two groups (based on MANOVA tests). Multivariate analyses of the set of parent outcomes indicated no differences at T1 or T2 or in the residual change scores. Thus, the changes in quality of mother-child interaction were not part of some overall pattern of changes in this group of mothers.

The children of these mothers did not differ significantly from other children on the set of child outcome measures at T1, but they did show significant differences at T2, MANOVA $F(4,183) = 4.89$, $p < .001$, and significantly different patterns of change from T1 to T2, MANOVA $F(4,183) = 3.82$, $p < .01$. Univariate tests indicated that their gains occurred in adaptive behavior, $F(1,186) = 4.52$, $p < .05$, spontaneous play, $F(1,186) = 5.73$, $p < .05$, and interactions with their mothers, $F(1,186) = 10.38$, $p < .01$ (Figs. 9–11).

Unfortunately, our data do not elucidate the mechanisms that underlie such large maternal gains. Although this group of mothers received the same intensity (based on ANOVA tests) and types of early intervention services (based on chi-square analyses) as other sample members, the specific nature of the interchanges among the early intervention service providers and the mothers—which could be key to understanding why this subgroup demonstrated such improvement—was not assessed in this study. We also do not know whether the mother or the child served as the primary catalyst for the co-occurring change. It is possible that, if children demonstrate improving developmental profiles, their mothers become more responsive in their interactions. It is also possible that some mothers are capable of significant growth in their ability to provide an optimal caregiving environment, which results in a range of developmental advantages for the child. Although we cannot specify the underlying cause of the observed change, our analyses point to an association between substantial improvement in

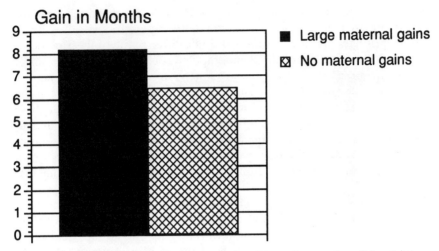

FIG. 9.—A comparison of the gains made by children whose mothers did and did not show large increases in growth-promoting behaviors: adaptive behavior.

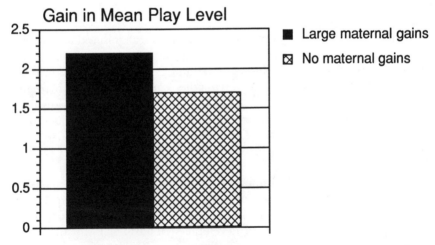

FIG. 10.—A comparison of the gains made by children whose mothers did and did not show large increases in growth-promoting behaviors: spontaneous play.

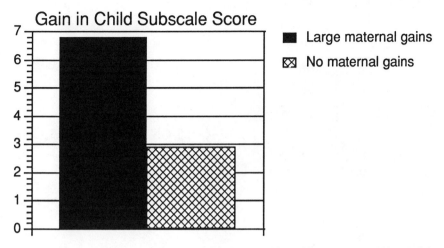

FIG. 11.—A comparison of the gains made by children whose mothers did and did not show large increases in growth-promoting behaviors: child-mother interaction.

mother-child interactive behavior and increasing developmental gains for children. Furthermore, our findings indicate that the resilient mothers were not limited to certain socioeconomic groups or to having children with any particular type of disability or severity of psychomotor impairment. The wide-ranging circumstances of these mothers support an optimistic view of the possibility of positive change and adaptation to nurturing a child with disabilities in all types of families.

# IX. DISCUSSION AND IMPLICATIONS

This first phase of the Early Intervention Collaborative Study was aimed at three interrelated objectives: (1) to enhance our understanding of variations in the development of young children with disabilities and in the adaptation of their families during their first year of participation in an early intervention program; (2) to study the mediating influences of family ecology and formal services on selected child and family outcomes; and (3) to generate conceptual models of child and family development to guide future research on children with special needs.

Two tensions are inherent in a complex investigation of this nature. First, there is the danger of stereotyping both the children and their families while attempting to extract useful generalizations for theory building and program planning. This problem is particularly salient given the current political movement toward an intervention system capable of implementing individualized family service plans within prescribed program models that adhere to measurable standards of practice. The second source of tension is related to the competing perspectives of short- versus long-term developmental research. This presents a special concern in the area of social policy, where the lessons learned from an intensive analysis of infant and family change after only 12 months of intervention must be balanced by a more extended view of child development and family adaptation over time.

In preparing this *Monograph*, we have been guided by a determination to respond to each of these challenges; thus, our conclusions focus on both commonalities and subgroup variation. The implications of our findings are presented in a spirit of respect for the limitations of what one may infer from studying a single year in the lives of young children and their families, in conjunction with an investment in the value of using such knowledge to generate hypotheses about their future.

## STUDY FINDINGS

### Changes in Children

Growth in four aspects of child development—psychomotor skills, spontaneous play, adaptive behavior, and the child's interaction with his or her mother—was documented for the study sample. On average, sample children demonstrated a gain of 8 months age equivalence in their psychomotor skills and 7 months age equivalence in adaptive behavior. The mean level of spontaneous play advanced from mouthing and simple manipulation at study entry to functional use of toys 1 year later. Children's interactions with their mothers at the time of entry into an early intervention program were, on average, below normative expectations for their chronological age. Twelve months later, their interactive behaviors were comparable to age-matched norms, with the greatest amount of change noted in their responsiveness.

Although description of average change provides a useful perspective on aggregate growth, investigation of variability among the study children is far more instructive. For example, over the 1-year study period, slightly more than one out of six children demonstrated psychomotor gains in age equivalence of 12 months or more, while only one in 25 showed comparable growth in adaptive behaviors. At the other end of the spectrum, approximately one out of 20 sample children displayed either no psychomotor gains or an apparent regression in performance, and four of those youngsters showed the same pattern in their adaptive behavior scores as well.

Analyses of a wide range of child and family variables as potential predictors of differences in the magnitude of child change revealed several consistent patterns. Not unexpectedly, children who were born prematurely showed greater gains in their psychomotor performance than children who were born at term. This finding supports the concept of "catch-up" development in children whose delivery was premature. In contrast, youngsters with chronic medical conditions generally had less favorable outcomes than those without special health care needs. Specifically, children with cardiac problems demonstrated less growth than expected in their adaptive behavior and interactive skills, whereas children with seizure disorders showed less improvement than expected in all four domains of child outcome (mental age, adaptive behavior, spontaneous play, and interaction with mother).

Although cross-sectional analyses revealed differences in child functioning that were related to type of disability both at the time of entry into early intervention services and 1 year later, severity of psychomotor impairment was the single most significant predictor of change across all the child measures (including most of the subscales) used in the study. Children with relatively mild psychomotor impairment (as categorized by the Bayley MDI at study entry) showed greater gains than predicted, whereas those with more severe delays showed relatively less growth than expected; it is important to note, however, that the extent of developmental variation was considerable. In contrast, the family characteristics we measured failed to predict differential change in any of the child outcomes; the only exceptions here were the modest influence of maternal education and of the home environment on children's interactions with their mothers and the identification of a small subgroup whose substantial gains in mother-child interactive behaviors were associated with greater developmental gains by their children.

### Changes in Families

Four aspects of family life were assessed at both the beginning and the end of the 12-month period—the mother's interaction with her child, parenting stress, effects on the family of rearing a child with a disability, and social support. At the time of study entry, the sample mothers' interactions with their children were, on average, of poorer quality than those reported for the normative population. Twelve months later, maternal interactive behaviors had improved slightly, on average, but many of the mothers demonstrated little change, and the sample mean was still below that of the original standardization group. Although mean maternal ratings of parenting stress at the time of study entry were comparable to those of a normative sample, 8% of the mothers ($N = 15$) had summary scores that exceeded the threshold recommended for clinical referral. One year later, the sample mean was essentially unchanged. Mothers' ratings of adverse effects on their family at study entry revealed fewer, or a lower rate, of negative effects than had been established in the original standardization sample of urban mothers of children with chronic illnesses. After 1 year, average levels of adverse family effects had not changed. Maternal social support networks showed a modest increase in size between T1 and T2 (with an average gain of 1.5 additional sources of support), and their ratings of perceived network helpfulness demonstrated a corresponding rise.

Perhaps the most striking aspect of these data is the relatively stable level of adaptation demonstrated by most sample families. In focusing on potential sources of variability, our analyses revealed a different and less concise set of findings than those found for the children. Whereas severity of the child's psychomotor impairment was the single most consistent predictor of change across all child outcome measures, it predicted change on only one of the family variables; the greater the psychomotor impairment, the more negative the effects on the family reported over the 1-year study period. Given that children with more severe impairment also made less developmental progress, this subgroup must be considered as especially vulnerable.

When family outcomes were examined for differences related to the type of the child's disability, results from several analyses converged in indicating that families of children with motor impairment represent another vulnerable segment of the study sample. At both entry into early intervention programs and 12 months later, mothers of such children reported the highest levels of parenting stress and of adverse family effects; additionally, they rated their social support networks at T2 as less helpful than other mothers did. Analyses of data from both mothers and fathers showed that parents of children with motor impairment had larger increases in multiple dimensions of parenting stress than other parents. In general, whenever family adaptation was found to be associated with type of disability, families of children with motor impairment appeared to report the most deleterious outcomes.

The only family outcome for which change was not predicted either by severity of psychomotor impairment or by type of disability was mother-child interaction. Under the challenging conditions of a developmental delay or disability, early deficiencies in the child's responsiveness and/or clarity of cues (as detected at T1) were not unexpected. However, the initially low maternal scores, and their relative lag at T2, could not be predicted given other indices of the caregiving environment. For example, the HOME scores of the sample were high (indicating a relatively enriched child-rearing environment), particularly as reflected on the subscales assessing organization of the environment, maternal responsivity, and maternal involvement with the child. In addition, on a measure of locus of control, sample mothers ascribed more influence over their child's future developmental progress to their own efforts than to all other alternative sources. Thus, our findings suggest that maternal difficulties in interactions with their children could not be attributed to a diminished sense of personal effectiveness or to a home environment that was unresponsive to child needs. Rather, our data indicate persistent maternal difficulties specific to dyadic teaching activities.

Paternal difficulties were found in the parent-child relationship as well. At the time of study entry, parenting stress reported by fathers was focused largely on issues related to attachment to the child, whereas maternal stress tended to focus more on the personal effects of parenting, such as physical health, restrictions in role, and marital relations. These findings suggest that the sample fathers were experiencing a less secure sense of emotional closeness to their children and indicate the possibility of a real or perceived difficulty in understanding the child's feelings and/or needs. After 1 year of intervention services, the fathers continued to report higher levels of stress in their attachment to their children, particularly fathers of children with Down syndrome. In comparisons across the three disability groups, mothers (at T1 and T2) and fathers (at T2) of children with motor impairment reported the highest levels of overall parenting stress and of negative family effects. Moreover, both parents of children with motor impairment reported larger increases than other parents in several dimensions of parenting stress over the study period. Thus, the precipitants and the dimensions of parenting stress were found to differ in a consistent pattern for mothers and for fathers, both cross sectionally and longitudinally.

### Early Intervention Services

In the conceptual framework that has guided the design of this study, early intervention programs are viewed as one of several factors that may mediate child and family outcomes. Two aspects of the services received by our sample are particularly worthy of examination: (1) the marked variability in service experiences and (2) the differential associations between specific program features and both child and family outcomes.

*Service experiences.*—Although each of the sample families was involved in an early intervention program for a full year, the amount of actual service received varied considerably, averaging from as little as a few minutes to as much as 21 hours per month, with a mean intensity of a modest 7 hours each month. Virtually all the sample members experienced home visits, and slightly more than half were involved in center-based individual or group services. Fifty-five percent of the mothers attended at least one parent group session, and their participation consisted of slightly more than 1½ hours per month, on average.

We defined alternative models of service empirically: 30% of the sample received more than three-quarters of their services from one discipline, whereas the rest were served through a multidisciplinary model. Approximately one-third had predominantly home-based services, and about one-sixth had more than 75% of their services at a center. Slightly less than half the sample received most of their services in an individualized format, whereas half were recipients of a mixed individual-group model.

Analyses of associations between child characteristics and service intensity indicated that severity of psychomotor impairment was the most significant correlate of the amount of service received; there were no differences in service experiences related to maternal marital status, employment, health, or educational level. Involvement with services beyond those provided by the early intervention program was not uncommon, with approximately one out of six children receiving supplementary child therapeutic services (most commonly physical therapy), one out of five families receiving additional child support services (such as from a visiting nurse association), and about one-third receiving additional family support services (such as counseling, case management, and respite care). These data illustrate the heterogeneity of early intervention services and highlight the complexity inherent in questions about the effects of involvement in a formal early intervention program.

*Service correlates of child and family change.*—Although the nonexperimental nature of our study precludes definitive conclusions, the correlations between selected aspects of early intervention services and changes in children and families over the study period reveal several important findings.

First, as noted above, intensity of service provision (i.e., average number of hours received each month) correlated significantly with the severity of the child's psychomotor impairment. After controlling for severity level, service intensity was related to several important family outcomes. Mothers whose families received more total hours (on average) of service reported larger and more helpful social support networks than did other sample mothers. Furthermore, mothers whose families averaged more hours per month of home visits reported significant decreases in several aspects of parenting stress.

Second, analyses of service patterns suggest that alternative service delivery models are associated with different effects. Program models that generally encouraged or required parents to interact with other parents (e.g., through parent groups and a mixture of group and individual services) or with a range of service providers (i.e., the multidisciplinary model) were associated with greater increases in the size of maternal social support networks. Increased network size, however, is not necessarily beneficial unless it is associated with increases in mothers' perceptions of the helpfulness of their supports. In this context, it is noteworthy that the service model that involved the parent in interactions with a greater variety of professional disciplines was associated with increases in support network size but not in perceived helpfulness, whereas models of service provision that facilitated parental access to other parents were associated with increases in both the network size and its reported helpfulness.

Sample families whose social support networks showed the greatest increase in size (and were perceived as increasingly helpful) were those whose children were making substantially less developmental progress. However, although social support is generally believed to serve as a buffer against adversity, we did not find that changes in either network size or support helpfulness were associated with concomitant changes in other aspects of family functioning, such as parenting stress or effects that rearing a child with a disability have on the family. Although this finding may appear to contradict the extensive literature on the benefits of support, two explanations must be considered. First, it is important to keep in mind that both reported stress and adverse family effects were not elevated beyond clinically significant levels at the time of study entry and that they remained within the normal range over the 12-month study period. Second, the limited time frame of this investigation may be insufficient to demonstrate the buffering function of helpful social supports. Further longitudinal study of samples that include families with greater variation in their levels of initial maladaptation will enhance our understanding of this issue.

Two additional relations between service delivery models and child and family outcomes are noteworthy. First, families who received most of their services through a single professional discipline (and therefore most likely from a single provider) showed significant decreases in parenting stress. Second, services that were provided through one-on-one contact between the service provider and the child and/or parent (i.e., the individual model) were associated with greater increments in the child's psychomotor growth. When viewed together, these findings point to the potential benefits of individualization and of limiting the number of service providers interacting with a family, at least when children are very young.

The correlates of maternal participation in a parent group (led by a service provider) suggest the need for a more reflective approach to this particular program component. Only slightly more than half the study mothers participated in a formal parent group. Not unexpectedly, mothers' involvement in such groups was associated with increases in both the size and the perceived helpfulness of their social support networks. In fact, participation in a parent group contributed the largest additional amount of unique variance (above and beyond that explained by child and family characteristics) from among all service characteristics in predicting changes in maternal ratings of support helpfulness. However, as reported elsewhere, parent groups were ranked less positively by both mothers and fathers than most other aspects of their early intervention experience (Krauss, Upshur, Shonkoff, & Hauser-Cram, in press; Upshur, 1992). Furthermore, the frequent coordination of such groups with concurrently scheduled child group activities suggests that involvement in a parent group may not always have been completely voluntary. Although maternal participation was not associated with changes in parenting stress or overall effects on the family, mothers who attended more hours of parent groups reported greater increases in personal strain and strain related to social/familial relationships. Whether that increased strain resulted from more frequent parent group participation or whether mothers who were experiencing greater strain chose to attend more hours of a parent group cannot be determined from the available data. The fact that children of mothers who attended more hours of a parent group demonstrated fewer developmental gains than other sample children lends weight to the latter hypothesis. Future investigations of this issue should consider both possibilities.

Finally, the relatively common use of various child and family services in addition to those provided by the early intervention program illustrates the difficulty of trying to develop an accurate definition of the intervention experience. The involvement of multiple service agencies may either enhance or complicate service delivery, depending on the relationships among providers and on whether additional services are viewed as supplementing or supplanting the primary early intervention program. Although the data presented in this *Monograph* do not address these distinctions, they highlight the complex and multidimensional nature of the early intervention "system" for many families.

## IMPLICATIONS OF STUDY FINDINGS FOR RESEARCH

Longitudinal research on the development of infants with disabilities and on the adaptation of their families has been limited and largely descriptive. Previous studies generally have documented benefits for those enrolled in early intervention programs, yet no prior research has generated comparable data on the range of child, family, and service variables that have been assessed in this investigation (Casto & Mastropieri, 1986; Dunst & Rheingrover, 1981; Farran, 1990; Guralnick, 1989; Shonkoff & Hauser-Cram, 1987; Simeonsson et al., 1982). Multidimensional developmental data on infants and toddlers with motor impairment or developmental delays of uncertain etiology are particularly scarce. In view of the paucity of knowledge about the determinants of developmental change in children with special needs and in their families, the creation of an extensive data base for 190 infants and toddlers with Down syndrome, motor impairment, or delays of uncertain etiology presents an important opportunity to study a range of potential influences on early adaptation.

### Assessment of Family Adaptation

The developmental tasks facing all families during the early childhood period typically involve the establishment of positive, nurturing relationships between parents and their children and the reformulation of roles among family members (Belsky, 1981; Bretherton, Biringen, & Ridgeway, 1991; Kreppner, 1989). In order to assess the processes of family adaptation to normative and nonnormative stress, contemporary conceptual models focus on the extent to which personal, family, and community resources are activated to meet changing life situations (McCubbin & Patterson, 1983). Within this context, adaptive families generally are characterized by an ability to support the needs of all their members and to be responsive to acute and chronic adversities as they arise. Families of children with disabilities traditionally have been seen as "at risk" for maladaptation. This risk has been attributed primarily to the atypical and persistent caregiving demands presented by the children and to the presumed difficulty faced by parents in developing a personal sense of competence as a parent (Farber & Rowitz, 1986; Krauss, 1986).

More recently, several investigations have provided empirical documentation of the general adaptiveness of most families who have a child with a developmental disability or a chronic health impairment. For example, normative levels of parenting stress have been reported in studies of mothers of children with developmental delays (McKinney & Peterson, 1987) and of parents of children with cystic fibrosis or congenital heart disease (Cowen et al., 1986; Goldberg, Morris, Simmons, Fowler, & Levinson, 1990). Our data on families of young children with three types of disabilities provide further support for the position that special needs in a child do not necessarily precipitate maladaptive or atypical family functioning. Indeed, we found that sample mothers felt no greater stress as parents than mothers of normally developing young children, that the family environments were of similar (and on some dimensions higher) quality to those found in other families, that mothers felt personally effective as facilitators of their children's development, and that they were able to acquire increasingly helpful support over time. We also found that, for most families, there was a high degree of stability over the 12-month study period with respect to levels of parenting stress and perceived effect of having a child with disabilities on the family. The broad picture that emerges is an affirmation that, although families of children with disabilities may face special or distinct challenges, their responses to these challenges are typically normative and stable, and they are coupled with a readiness to provide a positive, nurturing environment for their children.

Within this generally adaptive sample of families, two relatively vulnerable subgroups were identified on the basis of maternal adjustment. The first, consisting of families of children with relatively severe impairment, was more likely to perceive more adverse effects on the family over time. However, this subgroup reported larger increases in maternal support networks during the study period than did families of children with milder disabilities. These findings may reflect more intense mobilization of resources on behalf of mothers experiencing significant strain. Alternatively, they might indicate a basic resilience within these families that is manifested in their ability to seek more assistance in coping with difficult parenting demands and to appraise the greater challenges of their situation realistically.

Families of children with motor impairment made up the second distinctive subgroup. As noted earlier, these parents had the highest parenting stress levels both on entry into early intervention and 1 year later, and they reported decreasing social support over time. The persistence of their heightened parenting difficulties, coupled with their diminishing informal support network, signals troubling vulnerability during the early childhood period. Tracking the durability of this higher risk and exploring the difficulties these families experience in sustaining helpful support systems represent an important agenda for continued longitudinal study.

Beyond documenting family differences related to the child's disability, differences in adaptation between mothers and fathers were also found. This is particularly noteworthy in view of the frequent exclusion of fathers from studies of families of children with special needs. The importance of an independent assessment of paternal adaptation is underscored by a growing body of literature that documents differences in parental roles assumed by mothers and fathers (Lamb, 1986; McBride, 1990), differences in family interactions when father-mother-child triads are studied in comparison to mother-child dyads (Clarke-Stewart, 1978; Stoneman & Brody, 1981), and differences between the development of emotional attachments between fathers and their children and the evolution of mother-child bonds (Beckman, 1991).

Our data indicate that fathers typically reported greater stress associated with their feelings of emotional closeness to their children than did mothers. Furthermore, fathers of infants with Down syndrome (the youngest child subgroup) reported higher levels of parenting stress and more negative effects on their family than did their wives; they also were the only group of fathers in our sample who scored higher on these outcomes than their spouses. While the magnitude of the differences was not large, this finding was unanticipated, given the reports of other studies that fathers, in general, experienced either lower stress (Bristol et al., 1988; Goldberg et al., 1986; Goldberg et al., 1990) or stress levels similar to those of mothers (Noh et al., 1989).

Finally, we identified a small subgroup of married couples who demonstrated unusually high maternal and paternal parenting stress at the time of study entry. The absence of significant differences between this subgroup and the remainder of the sample either in family demographics or in the functional or developmental characteristics of their children indicates that clinically significant maladaptation among parents of children with special needs may not be determined primarily by the family's socioeconomic status or by the child's disability. In fact, the vulnerability of this subgroup may well have predated the birth of the study child. A greater understanding of the specific personal and family variables (e.g., less helpful social supports, diminished family adaptability and cohesion, etc.) that contribute to substantial elevations in parenting stress will require further investigation.

The extent to which these preliminary findings on family adaptation remain stable over time remains a critical and unanswered question. Although there is a growing interest in the developmental consequences of nonnormative events, longitudinal studies of family adaptation are scarce

(Seltzer & Ryff, in press). Wikler, Wasow, and Hatfield (1981) described specific developmental periods and family life stages that are comparatively more problematic for families who have a member with a disability. In this regard, families of children with special needs have been characterized as less likely to feel "different" from families of children without disabilities during the early childhood period because the similarity in the tasks associated with parenting *any* young child, and with reorganizing the family to incorporate a new member, is universal (Birenbaum, 1971). From this perspective, differences in parenting stress and family functioning would be expected to be minimal in the infant-toddler period and to emerge over time, as the child's caregiving requirements and developmental progress become increasingly distinctive from that of his or her peers.

### Perspectives on the Influences of Social Support

The role of social support as a buffer of family dysfunction and a protective factor for child development has been a focus of extensive research (Cochran & Brassard, 1979; Crnic et al., 1986; Dunst & Trivette, 1990), particularly in studies of high-risk populations. In fact, most models of family adaptation attribute considerable importance to the effects of formal and informal supports on a family's capacity to function optimally in the face of adversity (McCubbin & Patterson, 1983). Viewed broadly, the families in our study had access to a diverse range of support networks. The finding that their informal support increased over time (with respect to both its amount and its perceived helpfulness) suggests that the sample families lived within a responsive and reinforcing environment. They were also recipients of a variety of formal services, from both within and beyond their early intervention programs. Furthermore, they were relatively advantaged socioeconomically. Thus, the study participants benefited from access to educational and financial resources and a from a demonstrated ability to marshal support from friends, families, and professionals. Finally, their involvement in a family-oriented service system meant that these families were not, in general, coping with their situations in isolation.

Of the multiple family dimensions examined in the study, social networks were the most dynamic. Social support was also sensitive to program effects, as parents who received services that involved interactions with other families reported greater increases in both network size and helpfulness than families who received more individualized services. In view of the documented malleability of social support, the absence of a significant relation between changes in support and in other family outcomes, or between changes in social support and in indices of child development, was unexpected. These findings suggest that the extent to which social support (at least with respect to network size and perceived helpfulness) modifies the effects of normative and nonnormative stresses may not be as clear or as immediate as is generally assumed. Alternatively, this buffering function may depend on the magnitude of the stressor or on the magnitude of change in the support. In this regard, it is important to note that much of the data that confirm the beneficial effects of increased support networks have been collected from populations considered to be at risk socially. Furthermore, research has demonstrated that the effects of enhanced support are greater when the need for support is higher (Affleck, Tennen, Rowe, Roscher, & Walker, 1989), suggesting that increasing support within an already well-functioning environment may have a negligible effect, at least in the short term. Thus, future investigations of the effects of changes in social support on families of children with disabilities must account for the variability among families in their baseline support networks.

## Influences on Child Development and the Concept of Canalization

Generally speaking, the developmental trajectories of young children with special needs are poorly understood. Multidimensional longitudinal data are particularly sparse, and the opportunity to study different effects on child development over time has been limited. For the 190 infants and toddlers in our sample, two characteristics stand out as influences on developmental change over the 1-year study period—the severity of the child's psychomotor impairment at the time of study entry and the diagnosis of a seizure disorder. Together, these findings underscore the potent effect of neurobiology on the early developmental process.

Infants with seizure disorders appear to be particularly vulnerable to slower rates of development. The source of that vulnerability is, however, unclear. By its very nature, this condition is characterized by an episodic loss of consciousness that is variable in frequency, highly unpredictable (by both the child and the caregivers), and potentially disruptive of sustained learning opportunities. Furthermore, it reflects a basic dysfunction in the excitatory and inhibitory mechanisms that control higher cortical activity. Consequently, the slower rates of development for children with seizures may be an intrinsic feature of the disorder. An alternative possibility is that some of the documented developmental impairment may be secondary to medication. Most of the drugs prescribed for the treatment of children with seizure disorders have well-documented side effects that influence behavior, activity levels, and attention/alertness. Moreover, some anticonvulsant medications have been hypothesized to have specific adverse effects on cognitive development, including effects on memory and performance on neuropsychological tests (Camfield et al., 1979; Farwell et al., 1990). Further research on the different developmental effects of specific types of seizures, varying degrees of seizure control, and alternative therapeutic regimens is clearly needed.

The pervasive influence of the level of severity of the children's psychomotor impairment on the magnitude of their gains in the range of developmental areas assessed was not surprising. The failure to detect significant correlations between aspects of family adaptation and child change in psychomotor performance over the 12-month study period, however, was initially puzzling. Indeed, the influence of the caregiving environment on the child has been a central tenet of developmental theory for the past 3 decades (e.g., Bloom, 1964; Bronfenbrenner, 1979; Hunt, 1961). The empirical validation of this association has been well documented and has focused largely on broad socioeconomic indicators (such as maternal education level and family income) as markers of the family milieu (e.g., Golden & Birns, 1976; Sameroff & Chandler, 1975). Extensive data on the effects of early intervention programs on the later abilities of children with low birth weight or those living in dysfunctional or impoverished environments have provided further support for the effects of social context on child development (e.g., Infant Health and Development Program, 1990; Lazar, Darlington, Murray, Royce, & Snipper, 1982). A closer examination of the data on the relation between environmental influences and developmental outcomes in children, however, highlights the limited effects of family variables and the relatively powerful role of biological factors on the emergence of psychomotor skills during the first 2 years of life. This phenomenon has been confirmed in a variety of populations (McCall, 1979; Rutter, 1987) and has been considered to be a manifestation of "canalization" of early human development.

The concept of canalization was introduced by Waddington (1957) and adapted by Gottlieb (1991), McCall (1979, 1981, 1987), and Scarr-Salapatek (1976) to describe a postulated species-specific pathway (called a "creode") that governs the normative developmental process. Given a reasonably typical environment (i.e., one that is free of severe neglect), the creode serves to set the boundaries within which developmental patterns unfold. When development is highly canalized, biological determinants are strong, and environmental influences are diminished. In contrast, when development is less canalized, functional variation is increased, and the effects of environmental heterogeneity are greater.

Extensive empirical data have been generated over several decades of research with young children to support the assertion that psychomotor development (as measured by standardized instruments such as the Bayley Scales of Infant Development) is highly canalized during the first 2 years of life (Golden & Birns, 1976; McCall, 1979, 1981; Rutter, 1987). That is to say, despite considerable variation in both genetic endowment and early life experiences, normally developing children generally master basic psychomotor skills according to a fairly predictable timetable. In contrast, with the growth of symbolic functioning toward the end of the second year, human development becomes less canalized, and variations, such as those related to socioeconomic status, become more evident. Although a wealth of data is available documenting this emerging association between home environment and early childhood development (as measured by standardized assessments *after* the sensorimotor period) for children of diverse ethnic backgrounds and socioeconomic circumstances (Bradley et al., 1989; Gottfried, 1984; Sameroff, Seifer, Barocas, Zax, & Greenspan, 1987), there has been little systematic investigation of this relation for children with established disabilities.

The degree to which the emerging skills of young children with disabilities parallel normative developmental patterns is a matter of both theoretical and empirical interest (Zigler & Balla, 1982). Weisz, Yeates, and Zigler (1982) reviewed 28 studies of children and young adults with a variety of disabling conditions to test the hypothesis that individuals with mental retardation differ from those with normal intellectual abilities only in their rate of cognitive development and in the ultimate ceiling they attain, not in the developmental pathways or stages they traverse. With few exceptions, consistent support for this "similar sequence hypothesis" was found. Since the children in our study sample had a mean chronological age of 23 months at T2 (and a mean developmental age of 14 months), their developmental level was within the sensorimotor stage. In this context, the paucity of family influences on their psychomotor skills is to be expected. However, if the principle of canalization governs the progress of children with disabilities in a comparable fashion to that observed in the normally developing population, then the influence of environmental variables, such as the quality of caregiving in the home, will be reflected in their standardized test scores (especially in aspects related to symbolic functioning) to a greater degree as they progress beyond the sensorimotor period.

Children with Down syndrome have been the focus of a number of longitudinal studies whose data provide support for the applicability of the concept of early developmental canalization to infants and toddlers with disabilities. Carr (1975) followed two groups of children beginning in early infancy. The first group lived at home with their families but did not receive formal intervention services, while the second was "boarded out" to a variety of nonhome settings. Sequential administrations of the Bayley Scales of Infant Development between 1.5 and 48 months of age revealed negligible differences in mental age between the two groups during the early months of life, with modest discrepancies in performance (favoring the home-reared group) beginning to appear at 15 months of age and increasing differences found as the children aged. Dunst (1990), Schnell (1984), and Sharav and Shlomo (1986) administered the Bayley Scales at regular intervals (from 6 to 36 months of age) to young children with Down syndrome who were enrolled in formal early intervention programs, and all reported test scores that reflected a similar pattern. Up to 24 months of age, the three intervention groups achieved an average mental age equivalent comparable to that reported for the nonintervention, home-reared sample, followed by Carr (1975). However, after 24 months of age, the average scores of the intervention groups increasingly began to exceed those of the home-reared but untreated children. Thus, these data sets support the hypothesis that emergent differences in development related to environmental influences on children with Down syndrome may not be manifested on standardized tests until after the first 2 years of life.

The results of randomized, controlled trials designed to test the effects of early intervention services on other high-risk groups of infants have provided further support for this pattern of a latent developmental effect on standardized test performance. In a 4-year follow-up of a relatively modest intervention designed to facilitate maternal adjustment to the care of a premature newborn, Rauh, Achenbach, Nurcombe, Howell, and Teti (1988) documented early treatment effects on the mothers but delayed effects on the sample children. Specifically, despite measurable changes in the mothers during the first year of their child's life, no significant differences in mean Bayley scores were found between the experimental and the control groups at 6, 12, or 24 months of age. However, at 36 months, the experimental group achieved significantly higher scores on the McCarthy Scales, and both the magnitude and the significance of the difference favoring the experimental group increased at age 48 months. Similarly, in a follow-up study of children considered to be at risk for developmental retardation because of their impoverished socioeconomic status, Ramey, Yeates, and Short (1984) found nonsignificant differences in Bayley scores between their experimental and control groups at 6 and 12 months of age, the emergence of significant differences at 18 months, and increasing differences on the Stanford-Binet Intelligence Scale favoring children in the experimental group at 24, 36, and 48 months of age.

In summary, our findings are consistent with other longitudinal investigations that demonstrate low correlations between measures of family functioning and calculated developmental quotients or mental ages *during infancy*. Indeed, except in cases of severe deprivation (e.g., Provence & Lipton, 1962; Spitz, 1945), the effects of the caregiving environment on age-standardized developmental test scores have seldom been demonstrated before children have emerged from the sensorimotor period.

*A Proposed Framework for Further Investigation*

A fundamental challenge facing developmental scholars is the need to construct testable conceptual models that account for the influences of both biology and the caregiving environment on the development of children with disabilities over time, beginning in early infancy and extending throughout the childhood years. Contemporary developmental theory, previous empirical research, and the data presented in this *Monograph* highlight the complexity of this task.

Building on those three sources, we suggest that future research on young children with special needs be built around the following two propositions. First, it is proposed that the effects of the early caregiving environment on the age-standardized developmental test scores of children with disabilities (as for children with normal development) are generally latent and typically are not detected until after the sensorimotor period. Second, we propose that significant enhancement of the caregiving environment during infancy may have beneficial effects on other aspects of child development (e.g., symbolic and communicative skills) that are not necessarily reflected in developmental quotients yet serve as later mediators of enduring differences in cognitive and social competence.

Both these propositions are consistent with the basic concept of canalization, which focuses on the emergence of fundamental, species-specific, psychomotor functions (e.g., reaching, grasping, and orienting, as cited by Bornstein & Sigman, 1986) as distinct from functions related more closely to the processing of information. In fact, in contrast to findings based on standardized developmental tests that assess psychomotor functioning during the sensorimotor period, there is a growing body of empirical research that demonstrates significant correlations between maternal interactive behaviors and discrete domains of infant-toddler function that rely on symbolic and communicative development. For example, associations have been documented between maternal encouragement of attention at 5 months and toddler language comprehension and representational competence at 13 months (Tamis-LeMonda & Bornstein, 1989); between maternal teaching and infant object-focused communication at 13 months (Olson et al., 1984); between maternal depression and child persistence as well as competence at challenging problem-posing tasks at 1 and 2 years of age (Redding, Harmon, & Morgan, 1990); and between maternal contingency and responsiveness and infant measures of information processing, such as habituation, during the first year (Bornstein & Sigman, 1986). The extent to which early developmental functions that are influenced by caregiver-infant interaction in the normative population show comparable malleability in young children with developmental disabilities requires considerable further investigation.

The caregiving environment for a young child is characterized by both proximal and distal dimensions. Distal characteristics are manifested in the overall functioning of the family as a system and are reflected positively through such features as cohesion, adaptability, the availability of helpful social supports, and manageable stress. The central determinant of the proximal caregiving environment is the nature of the relationship between the infant and his or her primary caregivers. Optimal relationships are characterized by contingent responsiveness, affective attunement, and emotional investment. Biological vulnerability in an infant often presents significant challenges to the caregiver; parental anxieties, fears, or misinterpretations of atypical child behaviors may result in impaired early relationships. Diminished adult expectations, learned helplessness, and significant family stresses may generate potent adverse influences on both the proximal and the distal aspects of the caregiving environment.

Our data demonstrate that, for most sample families, the distal caregiving milieu was generally adaptive. In contrast, mothers' proximal interactions with their delayed or disabled infants were often difficult, even in the face of otherwise positive family functioning. The data also indicate that feelings related to their attachment to the child were a source of particular stress for fathers, suggesting that interactional difficulties may be salient for both parents of young children with developmental concerns. On the other hand, correlations obtained between substantial gains in maternal growth-promoting behaviors and greater gains in multiple domains of child development suggest that proximal caregiving experiences can serve as a source of resilience for young children with disabilities. These findings underscore the potential protective characteristics of proximal caregiving behaviors for infants with disabilities as well as their vulnerability. Conversely, clinically elevated parenting stress (when documented in both parents) was correlated with other evidence of family dysfunction but was not associated with significant differences in the quality of the mother's interaction with her infant or with significant effects on child performance during the 12-month study period. This latter finding suggests that early child development may be relatively buffered from more distal ecological influences.

The hypothesis that characteristics of the proximal caregiving environment can modify biological influences and produce measurable effects on child development during the sensorimotor period is a complex proposition that demands serious examination. Studies of young children subjected to severe deprivation have demonstrated that extreme adversity can have early and devastating developmental effects (e.g., Provence & Lipton, 1962; Spitz, 1945). Within a broad range of normative, expectable environmental variation, however, performance on age-standardized psychometric instruments is generally unrelated to caregiving experiences in the first 2 years, whereas symbolic and communicative skills in the normative population have been shown to be influenced by maternal interactive behaviors in early infancy. During our 12-month study period, average developmental change in mental age, adaptive behavior, and play was not correlated with family characteristics and was predicted best by the severity of the child's psychomotor impairment at the time of study entry. These findings would appear to support a concept of broad-based canalization of developmental functions during the sensorimotor period for children with disabilities. On the other hand, a small group of mothers demonstrated substantial progress in the growth-promoting aspects of their interactions with their child, and their children showed significant gains in aspects of development that required communicative and symbolic skills (such as interaction with their mothers and spontaneous play). These findings underscore the limitations of age-standardized developmental tests (e.g., Bayley Scales) for detecting environmental effects on young children with disabilities and highlight the need to investigate a broad range of developmental functions, including those related to communication and symbolic competence.

## IMPLICATIONS OF STUDY FINDINGS FOR POLICY AND SERVICE DELIVERY

### Understanding the Complexity of the Early Intervention Experience

The results of this investigation address a number of important challenges currently facing the field of early childhood intervention. Perhaps the most basic among our findings relevant to policy and service delivery is the documentation of the multidimensional nature of the early intervention experience and of the different effects that the organization and distribution of service components within programs (e.g., individual vs. group, home vs. center based) appear to have on a range of child and family outcomes. This underscores the importance of creating flexible service models that are capable of addressing a variety of specific objectives for children (e.g., improved motor development, enhanced social competence) and for their families (e.g., decreased parenting stress, an expanded and more helpful social support network). The need for randomized studies of the effectiveness of individualized versus group services and of multidisciplinary versus unidisciplinary models is clearly highlighted by the results of our nonexperimental investigation; however, the feasibility of such studies is questionable under current legislative mandates.

The considerable variability that characterized the early intervention experience of the 190 children and families in our sample raises a number of fundamental questions about how decisions are made (by both providers and recipients) regarding the allocation of service resources. In our natural laboratory composed of 29 independent programs extending over two state-wide early intervention systems, the distribution of service hours appears to have been driven largely by the severity of the child's psychomotor impairment. Although our data indicate particular vulnerability for families with fewer years of maternal education and for mothers of children with motor impairment or seizure disorders, overall levels of service were not significantly higher for these subgroups. These findings clearly suggest the need for systematic development of criteria to determine the best use of program resources. Furthermore, the relatively greater stress experienced by fathers regarding their feelings of attachment to their infant underscores the importance of considering the needs of the entire family and taking a view of family adaptation that goes beyond the mother-child dyad.

Our findings on the relation between participation in professionally run parent groups and both child and family outcomes also raise questions, particularly in light of previous research reports. Contrary to an earlier study by Minde et al. (1980), we found no significant association between maternal participation in parent groups and quality of mother-child interaction. While other studies have noted positive effects on mothers' behavior and attitudes toward their children that can be attributed to parent group participation (Slaughter, 1983), mothers who had higher levels of participation in parent groups in the present study also reported higher levels of adverse effects on their families. Although the direction of this association between group attendance and increased strain cannot be discerned, these findings point to the need for a careful examination of the parent group experience. Issues related to the explicit goals of parent groups, the professional training of the staff facilitators, and the criteria for individual parent participation clearly require further study. It should be emphasized that our findings apply to professionally organized groups and must not be generalized to support groups that are initiated and run by parents themselves. Nevertheless, given the mandate for family-oriented services and the interest in parent-to-parent support activities, the need to identify "best practices" for formal parent groups is essential.

The increasing involvement of outside therapeutic and support services during the first year of a family's participation in an early intervention program highlights additional policy concerns. Most fundamentally, this finding points to the frequent need for coordination across service agencies and systems and for examination of the extent to which the current models and staffing structures of early intervention programs are able to respond to the breadth of needs identified in individualized family service plans. Respite care, for example, is a support service that is generally not provided as part of an early intervention program, yet we do not know the extent to which early intervention programs serve as effective linkages to such services. Physical therapy, on the other hand, is provided more appropriately as an integrated component in a core intervention program, yet we found that almost one-quarter of the children with motor impairment in our sample received additional therapy services from another source. Both these examples point to the need for the "whole" service system to be defined precisely before it can be studied effectively and modified rationally.

## Clarifying the Goals of Early Childhood Intervention

The theoretical issues that we have discussed in this chapter suggest a critical question for policy formulation, service provision, and program evaluation. If parents of young children with special needs demonstrate generally positive adaptation, and if psychomotor development is relatively canalized during the sensorimotor period, how should decisions regarding the goals and age of initiation of early intervention services be made for infants and toddlers with disabilities and their families?

The answer to this question demands thoughtful consideration of the relative importance of attempting to enhance adaptive, growth-promoting interactions between young children with disabilities and their primary caregivers in the early years, in contrast to focusing primarily on the direct promotion of sensorimotor skills. Our data indicate that, at the time of program entry, young children with atypical development demonstrated delayed interactive behaviors. Furthermore, in comparison to parents of age-matched youngsters without disabilities, their fathers experienced more stress in feelings of attachment to their children, and their mothers had greater difficulty in reading the children's signals and in facilitating their learning. It is also important to note that differences in interactive skills favored the more highly educated mothers throughout the study period and appeared to be linked to emerging differences in their children's responsiveness after 1 year of service. In fact, interactive behavior was the single domain we measured in which family characteristics were associated with child performance.

The finding that the average mother's interactions with her child remained problematic after 12 months of intervention was unanticipated, particularly in view of the fact that the mean HOME scores for the study participants were high and that there was abundant evidence of otherwise positive adaptation among these mothers with respect to parenting stress and their perceptions of their family's cohesion and adaptability. The contrasting normalization of the children's interactive behaviors during that same 12-month period is comparable to that described in a study of premature infants who were found to demonstrate increasing responsiveness during the latter part of the first year while their mothers' interaction skills remained relatively stable or declined slightly (Barnard, Bee, & Hammond, 1984). The degree to which a relative lag in maternal performance is a predictable consequence of early interaction difficulties and the extent to which increased responsiveness by the child is a prerequisite for growth in the mother's interactive skills remain important empirical questions. The finding that substantial gains in mother-child interactive behaviors for a small subgroup of mothers were associated with relatively accelerated growth in their infants' skills further highlights the need for greater understanding of the direction of effects and of the reciprocal relation between maternal and child interactive behaviors over time.

All these data underscore the need for early intervention services to focus intensively on the caregiver-child relationship. This focus is essential, not simply because mothers' interactions with their children are developmentally critical, but because qualities of relationships do not improve automatically with either maturation or experience. Moreover, attention to the early caregiving environment of young children with disabilities is important for its potential effect on subsequent child development, as manifested in the latent effects on standardized intelligence tests that have been demonstrated by previous investigations of other vulnerable populations (e.g., Ramey et al., 1984; Rauh et al., 1988). The model of early canalization indicates that a search for short-term change on age-standardized developmental measures (such as the Bayley Scales) would be misguided. Early intervention services and the evaluation of their short-term effects ought rather to focus on the proximal caregiving environment, with greater attention to the assessment of developmental variables (such as symbolic and communicative behaviors) that are likely to mediate later child competencies (Barocas et al., 1991; Freund, 1990).

Finally, the findings of this investigation indicate the need for a clear demarcation between the sensorimotor period and subsequent stages of development when studying the effect of environmental variables on child skills. Research reviews of early intervention effectiveness that aggregate standardized scores on cognitive measures from early infancy through the preschool years may be particularly misleading. The failure to make distinctions related to chronological age and developmental level in the analysis of program effects on child performance is most problematic in studies of heterogeneous samples of children with disabilities whose ages and functional skills often overlap multiple developmental periods. Future research must recognize that the relative malleability of human development may vary, depending not only on the nature of an established disability but also on the developmental function of interest (e.g., psychomotor skills vs. communication, social interaction, and symbolic functioning) and the child's developmental stage (e.g., sensorimotor vs. preoperational).

## STUDY LIMITATIONS

Three potential limitations must be considered. The first relates to the generalizability of the data to a more diverse early intervention population. The fact that the study sample is predominantly white and that more than half the families identified themselves as Catholic requires caution in extending our findings to groups of greater cultural, religious, or ethnic diversity. Indeed, the need for cross-cultural data on children with disabilities and their families is considerable and should be a priority for empirical research. On the other hand, the racial homogeneity of the sample provides an opportunity to study differences related to socioeconomic status that are not confounded by ethnic diversity.

A second limitation relates to the nonexperimental nature of the research design. This suggests the need for a conservative approach to the interpretation of the different effects of alternative service models that were not assigned randomly to sample families. Thus, even though statistical controls were applied to compensate for group differences, findings that relate specific service characteristics to child and family outcomes must be viewed as correlational rather than causal.

Finally, it is important to acknowledge the limitations of the data set regarding services. Although the quantitative aspects of these data are reliable, important qualitative information is unavailable. Our counts of hours of home visits are highly accurate, but we have no information regarding the content of those visits. Indeed, for any of the service variables that we derived (e.g., center-based child groups, individual parent-child sessions, etc.), the variation in the child's and family's experiences may be substantial. Therefore, although the structural dimensions that differentiate our service variables are clear, the potential confounding effect of qualitative differences within each service component (e.g., issues related to the relationship between the family and the service provider) must be acknowledged. Ultimately, the validity of our analyses is based on an assumption of random variability on these qualitative aspects across sample members, programs, and service models/formats.

## CONCLUSIONS

A prospective study of 190 infants with developmental disabilities or delays and their families during their first year of participation in an early intervention service system generated four principal findings. *First,* the variability in multiple aspects of child competence, measured both cross sectionally and longitudinally, was substantial. It is clear that a full understanding of the development of young children with disabilities requires an appreciation for within-group differences. *Second,* most participating parents demonstrated relatively stable levels of personal and familial adaptation over the 1-year study period. Significant maladaptation, when detected, was related to difficulties along several dimensions of family functioning and was not associated with characteristics of the child. *Third,* early intervention was found to be a complex and multidimensional experience (including a wide range of intensity and types of services) that defies simple description. Some aspects of services were correlated with enhanced child and family development, others were associated with less desirable outcomes or with trade-offs among child and family benefits, and some had fewer measurable (or measured) effects over the 1-year study period. *Fourth,* the correlates of change in sample children and families differed depending on the domain of interest. No single variable predicted change in both child and family outcomes.

The theoretical and applied importance of these findings is considerable. They suggest the need to question several prevailing assumptions about children with disabilities and their families and to reframe the fundamental research and policy questions to be addressed in the field of early childhood intervention. Rather than asking, What is the prognosis for an infant with Down syndrome or for a toddler with cerebral palsy? we must ask, How do both constitutional variations in the child and differences in the caregiving environment influence change in children's adaptive skills over time? Rather than assuming that maladaptation is common in families with young children with diagnosed disabilities, we must ask, Which difficulties experienced by families can be attributed to the child, and which are precipitated by factors that are independent of the child's special needs? Rather than asserting that early intervention programs assure optimal child progress and family adaptation, we must ask, What types of services are most likely to facilitate specific outcomes for children and families with specific characteristics? Rather than determining service eligibility primarily on the basis of the child's developmental diagnosis, we must ask, What are the unmet child and family needs for each potential service recipient, and how can limited resources be mobilized most effectively to best respond to those needs? Understanding the short- and long-term determinants of variations in infants with disabilities and in their families constitutes a central task for both empirical research and the formulation of public policy.

Current policy initiatives for early intervention services and the findings presented in this *Monograph* highlight the emergence of a new appreciation of the complexity of early childhood disability and of family adaptation to the challenges of rearing a young child with special needs. Further refinement of our knowledge of the development of children with disabilities and their families, and the design of more effective intervention programs, will require considerable creativity. Multiple research strategies will be needed.

The data reported in this *Monograph* identify a number of key variables that correlate with differential vulnerability or resilience for a range of child and family outcomes.

The next step for researchers and service providers is to generate integrated conceptual models, anchored to theories of normative development, in order to test hypotheses designed to explain the underlying mechanisms of developmental adaptation for special populations. Our finding that the predictors of change in children and families over 1 year differed from the correlates of child and family function measured cross sectionally underscores the importance of both short- and long-term longitudinal investigation. Identifying factors that are associated with immediate benefits for children and families is vitally important for the human service community. Tracking the durability of such effects over time is critical to long-range policy planning. Finally, elucidating the underlying processes that mediate the successful adaptation of young children with disabilities and their families is essential to furthering our basic understanding of the commonalities, the variability, and the essential mystery of human development.

# REFERENCES

Abidin, R. (1986). *Parenting stress index: Manual* (2d ed.). Charlottesville, VA: Pediatric Psychology.

Ackerman, N. (1958). *The psychodynamics of family life.* New York: Basic.

Affleck, G., Tennen, H., Rowe, J., Roscher, B., & Walker, L. (1989). Effects of formal support on mothers' adaptation to the hospital-to-home transition of high-risk infants: The benefits and costs of helping. *Child Development, 60,* 488–501.

Ainsworth, M., & Bell, S. (1974). Mother-infant interaction and the development of competence. In K. J. Connolly & J. S. Bruner (Eds.), *The growth of competence.* New York: Academic.

American Psychiatric Association. (1987). *Diagnostic and statistical manual of mental disorders* (3d ed., rev.). Washington, DC: American Psychiatric Association.

Anderson, A., Basilevsky, A., & Hum, D. P. (1983). Missing data. In P. H. Rossi, J. D. Wright, & A. B. Anderson (Eds.), *Handbook of survey research.* San Diego, CA: Academic.

Anderson, S., & Messick, S. (1974). Social competency in young children. *Developmental Psychology, 10,* 282–293.

Appelbaum, M., & McCall, R. (1983). Design and analysis in developmental psychology. In W. Kessen (Ed.), P. H. Mussen (Series Ed.), *Handbook of child psychology: Vol. 1. History, theory, and methods.* New York: Wiley.

Bagnato, S., & Neisworth, J. (1980). The intervention efficiency index: An approach to preschool program accountability. *Exceptional Children, 46,* 264–269.

Bailey, E., & Bricker, D. (1984). The efficacy of early intervention for severely handicapped infants and young children. *Topics in Early Childhood Special Education, 4,* 30–51.

Barnard, K. (1978). *Nursing child assessment teaching scales.* Seattle: University of Washington School of Nursing.

Barnard, K., Bee, H., & Hammond, M. (1984). Developmental changes in maternal interactions with term and preterm infants. *Infant Behavior and Development, 7,* 101–113.

Barnard, K., Hammond, M., Booth, C., Bee, H., Mitchell, S., & Spieker, S. (1989). Measurement and meaning of parent-child interaction. In F. Morrison, C. Lord, & D. Keating (Eds.), *Applied developmental psychology* (Vol. 3). New York: Academic.

Barnard, K., & Kelly, J. (1990). Assessment of parent-child interaction. In S. Meisels & J. Shonkoff (Eds.), *Handbook of early childhood intervention.* New York: Cambridge University Press.

Barocas, R., Seifer, R., Sameroff, A., Andrews, T., Croft, R., & Ostrow, E. (1991). Social and interpersonal determinants of developmental risk. *Developmental Psychology, 27,* 479–488.

Barrera, M. (1981). Social support in the adjustment of pregnant adolescents. In B. Gottlieb (Ed.), *Social networks and social support.* Beverly Hills, CA: Sage.

Bayley, N. (1969). *The scales of infant development.* New York: Psychological Corp.

Beckman, P. (1983). The influence of selected child characteristics on stress in families of handicapped infants. *American Journal of Mental Deficiency,* **88,** 150–156.

Beckman, P. (1991). Comparison of mothers' and fathers' perceptions of the effect of young children with and without disabilities. *American Journal on Mental Retardation,* **95,** 585–595.

Beckman, P., & Kohl, F. (1987). Interactions of preschoolers with and without handicaps in integrated and segregated settings: A longitudinal study. *Mental Retardation,* **25,** 5–11.

Beckwith, L. (1990). Adaptive and maladaptive parenting—implications for intervention. In S. Meisels & J. Shonkoff (Eds.), *Handbook of early childhood intervention.* New York: Cambridge University Press.

Bee, H., Barnard, K., Eyres, S., Gray, C., Hammond, M., Spietz, A., Snyder, C., & Clark, B. (1982). Prediction of IQ and language skill from perinatal status, child performance, family characteristics and mother-infant interaction. *Child Development,* **53,** 1134–1156.

Beeghly, M., & Cicchetti, D. (1987). An organizational approach to symbolic development in children with Down syndrome. *New Directions for Child Development,* **36,** 5–29.

Belsky, J. (1981). Early human experience: A family perspective. *Developmental Psychology,* **17,** 3–23.

Belsky, J., Goode, M., & Most, R. (1980). Maternal stimulation and infant exploratory competence: Cross-sectional, correlational, and experimental analyses. *Child Development,* **51,** 1163–1178.

Belsky, J., Hrncir, E., & Vondra, J. (1983). *Manual for the assessment of performance, competence, and executive capacity in infant play.* Unpublished manuscript.

Belsky, J., & Most, R. (1981). From exploration to play: A cross-sectional study of infant free play behavior. *Developmental Psychology,* **17,** 630–639.

Bereiter, C. (1963). Some persisting dilemmas in the measurement of change. In C. W. Harris (Ed.), *Problems in measuring change.* Madison: University of Wisconsin Press.

Berry, P., Gunn, V., & Andrews, R. (1984). Development of Down's syndrome children from birth to five years. In J. M. Berg (Ed.), *Perspectives and progress in mental retardation: Vol. 1. Social, psychological, and educational aspects.* Austin, TX: PRO-ED.

Birenbaum, A. (1971). The mentally retarded child in the home and the family life cycle. *Journal of Health and Social Behavior,* **12,** 55–65.

Bloom, B. (1964). *Stability and change in human characteristics.* New York: Wiley.

Bornstein, M. H., & Sigman, M. D. (1986). Continuity in mental development from infancy. *Child Development,* **57,** 251–274.

Bradley, R., Caldwell, B., Rock, S., Barnard, K., Gray, C., Siegel, L., Ramey, C., Gottfried, A., & Johnson, D. (1989). Home environment and cognitive development in the first 3 years of life: A collaborative study involving six sites and three ethnic groups in North America. *Developmental Psychology,* **25,** 217–235.

Bretherton, I., Biringen, Z., & Ridgeway, D. (1991). The parental side of attachment. In K. Pillemer & K. McCartney (Eds.), *Parent-child relations throughout life.* Hillsdale, NJ: Erlbaum.

Bristol, M. (1987). Mothers of children with autism or communication disorders: Successful adaptation and the double ABCX model. *Journal of Autism and Developmental Disabilities,* **17,** 469–486.

Bristol, M., Gallagher, J., & Schopler, E. (1988). Mothers and fathers of young developmentally disabled and nondisabled boys: Adaptation and spousal support. *Developmental Psychology*, **24**, 441–451.

Bronfenbrenner, U. (1979). *The ecology of human development—experiments by nature and design*. Cambridge, MA: Harvard University Press.

Bronfenbrenner, U., Moen, P., & Garbarino, J. (1984). Child, family, and community. In R. D. Parke (Ed.), *Review of child development research: The family* (Vol. 7). Chicago: University of Chicago Press.

Brooks-Gunn, J., & Lewis, M. (1982). Development of play behavior in handicapped and normal infants. *Topics in Early Childhood Special Education*, **2**, 28–38.

Buckhalt, J., Rutherford, R., & Goldberg, K. (1978). Verbal and nonverbal interaction of mothers with their Down's syndrome and nonretarded infants. *American Journal of Mental Deficiency*, **82**, 337–343.

Buium, N., Rynders, J., & Turnure, J. (1974). Early maternal linguistic environment of normal and Down's syndrome language-learning children. *American Journal of Mental Deficiency*, **79**, 52–58.

Byrne, E., & Cunningham, C. (1985). The effects of mentally handicapped children on families—a conceptual review. *Journal of Child Psychology and Psychiatry*, **26**, 847–864.

Caldwell, B., & Bradley, R. (1984). *Home observation for measurement of the environment*. Unpublished manuscript, University of Arkansas at Little Rock.

Camfield, C., Chaplin, S., Doyle, A., Shapiro, S., Cummings, C., & Camfield, P. (1979). Side effects of phenobarbital in toddlers: Behavioral and cognitive aspects. *Journal of Pediatrics*, **95**, 361–365.

Caplan, R., Vinokur, A., Price, R., & van Ryn, M. (1989). Job seeking, reemployment, and mental health: A randomized field experiment in coping with job loss. *Journal of Applied Psychology*, **74**, 759–769.

Carr, J. (1975). *Young children with Down's syndrome: Their development, upbringing, and effect on their families*. London: Butterworth.

Carter, E., & McGoldrick, M. (1980). *The family life cycle: A framework for family therapy*. New York: Gardner.

Casto, G., & Mastropieri, M. (1986). The efficacy of early intervention programs: A meta-analysis. *Exceptional Children*, **52**, 417–424.

Cicchetti, D., & Sroufe, L. (1976). The relationship between affect and cognitive development in Down's syndrome infants. *Child Development*, **47**, 920–929.

Cicchetti, D., & Wagner, S. (1990). Alternative assessment strategies for the evaluation of infants and toddlers: An organizational perspective. In S. Meisels & J. Shonkoff (Eds.), *Handbook of early childhood intervention*. New York: Cambridge University Press.

Clarke-Stewart, K. (1973). Interaction among mothers and their young children: Characteristics and consequences. *Monographs of the Society for Research in Child Development*, **38**(6–7, Serial No. 153).

Clarke-Stewart, K. (1978). And daddy makes three: The father's impact on mother and young child. *Child Development*, **49**, 466–478.

Clunies-Ross, G. (1979). Accelerating the development of Down's syndrome in infants and young children. *Journal of Special Education*, **13**, 169–177.

Cochran, M., & Brassard, J. (1979). Child development and personal social networks. *Child Development*, **50**, 601–616.

Cohen, S., & Syme, S. L. (Eds.). (1985). *Social support and health*. Orlando, FL: Academic.

Comfort, M. (1988). Assessing parent-child interaction. In D. B. Bailey & R. Simeonsson (Eds.), *Family assessment in early intervention*. New York: Merrill.

Cowen, L., Mok, J., Corey, M., MacMillan, H., Simmons, R., & Levison, H. (1986). Psychologic adjustment of the family with a member who has cystic fibrosis. *Pediatrics*, **77**, 745–753.

Crnic, K., Friedrich, W., & Greenberg, M. (1983). Adaptation of families with mentally retarded children: A model of stress, coping and family ecology. *American Journal of Mental Deficiency,* **88,** 125–138.

Crnic, K., Greenberg, M., Robinson, N., & Ragozin, A. (1984). Maternal stress and social support: Effects on the mother-infant relationship from birth to eighteen months. *American Journal of Orthopsychiatry,* **54,** 224–235.

Crnic, K., Greenberg, M., & Slough, N. (1986). Early stress and social support influences on mothers' and high-risk infants' functioning in late infancy. *Infant Mental Health Journal,* **7,** 19–33.

Cronbach, L., & Furby, L. (1970). How should we measure "change"—or should we? *Psychological Bulletin,* **74,** 68–80.

Cummings, S. (1976). The impact of the child's deficiency on the father: A study of fathers of mentally retarded and of chronically ill children. *American Journal of Orthopsychiatry,* **46,** 246–255.

Cummings, S., Bayley, H., & Rie, H. (1966). Effects of the child's deficiency on the mother: A study of mothers of mentally retarded, chronically ill and neurotic children. *American Journal of Orthopsychiatry,* **36,** 595–608.

Cunningham, C., Glenn, S., Wilkinson, P., & Sloper, P. (1985). Mental ability, symbolic play and receptive and expressive language of young children with Down's syndrome. *Journal of Child Psychology and Psychiatry,* **26,** 255–265.

Cunningham, C., Rueler, E., Blackwell, J., & Deck, J. (1981). Behavioral and linguistic developments in the interactions of normal and retarded children with their mothers. *Child Development,* **52,** 62–70.

Davis, M., & MacKay, D. (1973, October 27). Mentally subnormal children and their families. *Lancet,* 5.

Dean, A., & Lin, N. (1977). Stress-buffering role of social support. *Journal of Nervous and Mental Disease,* **165,** 403–417.

Devillis, R., Devillis, B., Revicki, D., Lurie, S., Runyan, O., & Bristol, M. (1985). Development and validation of the Child Improvement Locus of Control (CILC) Scales. *Journal of Social and Clinical Psychology,* **3,** 307–324.

Dodge, K. A., Pettit, G. S., McClaskey, C. L., & Brown, M. M. (1986). Social competence in children. *Monographs of the Society for Research in Child Development,* **51**(2, Serial No. 213).

Dunst, C. (1986). Overview of the efficacy of early intervention programs. In L. Bickman & D. L. Weatherford (Eds.), *Evaluating early intervention programs for severely handicapped children and their families.* Austin, TX: PRO-ED.

Dunst, C. (1990). Sensorimotor development of infants with Down syndrome. In D. Cicchetti & M. Beeghly (Eds.), *Children with Down syndrome—a developmental perspective.* New York: Cambridge University Press.

Dunst, C., Jenkins, V., & Trivette, C. (1984). The Family Support Scale: Reliability and validity. *Journal of Individual, Family, and Community Wellness,* **1,** 45–52.

Dunst, C., & Rheingrover, R. (1981). An analysis of the efficacy of infant intervention programs with organically handicapped children. *Evaluation and Program Planning,* **4,** 287–323.

Dunst, C., & Snyder, S. (1986). A critique of the Utah State University early intervention meta-analysis research. *Exceptional Children,* **53,** 269–276.

Dunst, C., & Trivette, C. (1990). Assessment of social support in early intervention programs. In S. Meisels & J. Shonkoff (Eds.), *Handbook of early childhood intervention.* New York: Cambridge University Press.

Dunst, C., Trivette, C., & Cross, A. (1986). Mediating influences of social support: Personal, family, and child outcomes. *American Journal of Mental Deficiency,* **90,** 403–417.

Dunst, C., Trivette, C., & Deal, A. (1988). *Enabling and empowering families: Principles and guidelines for practice*. Cambridge, MA: Brookline.

Duvall, E. (1962). *Family development*. Philadelphia: Lippincott.

Eheart, B. (1982). Mother-child interactions with nonretarded and mentally retarded preschoolers. *American Journal of Mental Deficiency*, **87**, 20–25.

Epstein, N., Bishop, D., & Baldwin, L. (1982). McMaster model of family functioning: A view of the normal family. In F. Walsh (Ed.), *Normal family processes*. New York: Guilford.

Erickson, M. (1991). *Evaluating early intervention services: A cost effectiveness analysis*. Unpublished doctoral dissertation, Brandeis University.

Farber, B. (1960). Family organization and crisis: Maintenance of integration in families with a severely retarded child. *Monographs of the Society for Research in Child Development*, **25**(1, Serial No. 75).

Farber, B. (1968). *Mental retardation: Its social context and social consequences*. Boston: Houghton Mifflin.

Farber, B. (1970). Notes on sociological knowledge about families with mentally retarded children. In M. Schreiber (Ed.), *Social work and mental retardation*. New York: John Day.

Farber, B., & Rowitz, L. (1986). Families with a mentally retarded child. In N. R. Ellis & N. W. Bray (Eds.), *International review of research in mental retardation XIV*. Orlando, FL: Academic.

Farran, D. (1990). Effects of intervention with disadvantaged and disabled children: A decade review. In S. Meisels & J. Shonkoff (Eds.), *Handbook of early childhood intervention*. New York: Cambridge University Press.

Farran, D., Metzger, J., & Sparling, J. (1986). Immediate and continuing adaptations in parents of handicapped children: A model and an illustration. In J. J. Gallagher & P. M. Vietze (Eds.), *Families of handicapped persons*. Baltimore: Paul H. Brookes.

Farwell, J., Lee, Y., Hirtz, D., Sulzbacher, S., Ellenberg, J., & Nelson, K. (1990). Phenobarbital for febrile seizures: Effects on intelligence and on seizure recurrence. *New England Journal of Medicine*, **322**, 364–369.

Finn, R. (1970). A note on estimating the reliability of categorical data. *Educational and Psychological Measurement*, **30**, 71–76.

Freund, L. (1990). Maternal regulation of children's problem-solving behavior and its impact on children's performance. *Child Development*, **61**, 113–126.

Frey, K., Fewell, R., & Vadasy, P. (1989). Parental adjustment and changes in child outcome among families of young handicapped children. *Topics in Early Childhood Special Education*, **8**, 38–57.

Frey, K., Greenberg, M., & Fewell, R. (1989). Stress and coping among parents of handicapped children: A multidimensional approach. *American Journal on Mental Retardation*, **94**, 240–249.

Friedrich, W. (1979). Predictors of the coping behaviors of mothers of handicapped children. *Journal of Consulting and Clinical Psychology*, **47**, 1140–1141.

Friedrich, W., & Friedrich, N. (1981). Psychological assets of parents of handicapped and nonhandicapped children. *American Journal of Mental Deficiency*, **85**, 551–553.

Friedrich, W., Wilturner, L., & Cohen, D. (1985). Coping resources and parenting mentally retarded children. *American Journal of Mental Deficiency*, **90**, 130–139.

Garbarino, J. (1983). Social support networks: RX for the helping professions. In J. Whittaker & J. Garbarino (Eds.), *Social support networks*. New York: Aldine.

Garmezy, N., & Rutter, M. (1983). *Stress, coping and development in children*. New York: McGraw-Hill.

Garwood, S. (1982). Piaget and play: Translating theory into practice. *Topics in Early Childhood Special Education,* **2,** 1–13.

Garwood, S., Fewell, R., & Neisworth, J. (1988). Public Law 94–142: You can get there from here! *Topics in Early Childhood Special Education,* **8,** 1–11.

Gath, A. (1973). The school-age siblings of mongol children. *British Journal of Psychiatry,* **123,** 161–167.

Goldberg, S., Marcovitch, S., MacGregor, D., & Lojkasek, M. (1986). Family responses to developmentally delayed preschoolers: Etiology and the father's role. *American Journal of Mental Deficiency,* **90,** 610–617.

Goldberg, S., Morris, P., Simmons, R., Fowler, R., & Levison, H. (1990). Chronic illness in infancy and parenting stress: A comparison of three groups of parents. *Journal of Pediatric Psychology,* **15,** 347–358.

Golden, M., & Birns, B. (1976). Social class and infant intelligence. In M. Lewis (Ed.), *Origins of intelligence.* New York: Plenum.

Goldman, B., & Johnson-Martin, N. (1987). *Understanding babies' cues: A comparison of parents of normally developing and handicapped infants.* Paper presented at the biennial meeting of the Society for Research in Child Development, Baltimore.

Gottfried, A. (1984). Home environment and early cognitive development: Integration, meta-analyses, and conclusions. In A. Gottfried (Ed.), *Home environment and early cognitive development.* Orlando, FL: Academic.

Gottlieb, G. (1991). Experiential canalization of behavioral development: Theory. *Developmental Psychology,* **27,** 4–13.

Gowen, J., Johnson-Martin, N., Goldman, B., & Appelbaum, M. (1989). Feelings of depression and parenting competence of mothers of handicapped and non-handicapped infants: A longitudinal study. *American Journal on Mental Retardation,* **94,** 259–271.

Grossman, F. (1972). *Brothers and sisters of retarded children: An exploratory study.* Syracuse, NY: Syracuse University Press.

Grossman, H. (1983). *Classification in mental retardation.* Washington, DC: American Association on Mental Deficiency.

Gunn, P., & Berry, P. (1985). The temperament of Down's syndrome toddlers and their siblings. *Journal of Child Psychology and Psychiatry,* **26,** 973–979.

Guralnick, M. (1989). Recent developments in early intervention efficacy research: Implications for family involvement in P.L. 99–457. *Topics in Early Childhood Special Education,* **9,** 1–17.

Harrison, P. (1987). Research with adaptive behavior scales. *Journal of Special Education,* **21,** 37–68.

Hauser-Cram, P., & Krauss, M. (1991). Measuring change in children and families. *Journal of Early Intervention,* **15,** 288–297.

Hauser-Cram, P., Upshur, C., Krauss, M., & Shonkoff, J. (1988). *Implications of PL 99–457 for early intervention services for infants and toddlers with disabilities* (Social Policy Report). Washington, DC: Society for Research in Child Development.

Hayden, A., & Haring, N. (1977). The acceleration and maintenance of development gains in Down's syndrome school-age children. In P. Miller (Ed.), *Research to practice in mental retardation: Vol. 1. Care and intervention.* Baltimore: University Park Press.

Hill, P., & McCune-Nicolich, L. (1981). Pretend play and patterns of cognition in Down's syndrome children. *Child Development,* **52,** 611–617.

Hill, R. (1949). *Families under stress.* New York: Harper & Row.

Holroyd, J. (1974). The questionnaire on resources and stress: An instrument to measure family response to a handicapped member. *Journal of Community Psychology,* **2,** 92–94.

Holroyd, J., & McArthur, D. (1976). Mental retardation and stress on the parents: A contrast between Down's syndrome and childhood autism. *American Journal of Mental Deficiency*, **80**, 431–436.

Holt, K. (1958). The home care of the severely mentally retarded. *Pediatrics*, **22**, 744–755.

Hunt, J. (1961). *Intelligence and experience*. New York: Ronald.

Infant Health and Development Program. (1990). Enhancing the outcomes of low-birth-weight, premature infants. *Journal of the American Medical Association*, **263**, 3035–3042.

Jones, O. (1977). Mother-child communication with prelinguistic Down's syndrome and normal infants. In H. Schaffer (Ed.), *Studies in mother-infant interaction*. New York: Academic.

Jones, O. (1980). Prelinguistic communication skills in Down's syndrome infants. In T. Field, S. Goldberg, D. Stern, & A. Sostek (Eds.), *High risk infants and children: Interactions with adults and peers*. New York: Academic.

Kazak, A. (1987). Families with disabled children: Stress and social networks in three samples. *Journal of Abnormal Psychology*, **15**, 137–146.

Koeske, G. F., & Koeske, R. D. (1990). The buffering effect of social support on parental stress. *American Journal of Orthopsychiatry*, **60**, 440–451.

Kogan, K., Wimberger, H., & Bobbitt, R. (1969). Analysis of mother-child interaction in young mental retardates. *Child Development*, **40**, 799–812.

Krakow, J., & Kopp, C. (1982). Sustained attention in young Down syndrome children. *Topics in Early Childhood Special Education*, **2**, 32–42.

Krakow, J., & Kopp, C. (1983). The effects of developmental delay on sustained attention in young children. *Child Development*, **54**, 1143–1155.

Krauss, M. W. (1986). Patterns and trends in public services to families with a mentally retarded member. In J. J. Gallagher & P. M. Vietze (Eds.), *Families of handicapped persons*. Baltimore: Paul H. Brookes.

Krauss, M. W. (in press). Child-related and parenting stress: Similarities and differences between mothers and fathers of children with disabilities. *American Journal on Mental Retardation*.

Krauss, M. W., & Hauser-Cram, P. (1992). Policy and program developments for infants and toddlers with disabilities. In L. Rowitz (Ed.), *Mental retardation in the year 2000*. New York: Springer.

Krauss, M. W., & Jacobs, F. (1990). Family assessment: Purposes and techniques. In S. Meisels & J. Shonkoff (Eds.), *Handbook of early childhood intervention*. New York: Cambridge University Press.

Krauss, M. W., Upshur, C., Shonkoff, J., & Hauser-Cram, P. (in press). The impact of parent groups on mothers of infants with disabilities. *Journal of Early Intervention*.

Kreppner, K. (1989). Linking infant development–in–context research to the investigation of life-span family development. In K. Kreppner & R. Lerner (Eds.), *Family systems and life-span development*. Hillsdale, NJ: Erlbaum.

Lamb, M. (1986). The changing roles of fathers. In M. Lamb (Ed.), *The father's role: Applied perspectives*. New York: Wiley.

Landesman, S., Jaccard, J., & Gunderson, V. (1991). The family environment: The combined influence of family behavior, goals, strategies, resources, and individual experiences. In M. Lewis & S. Feinman (Eds.), *Social influences on development*. New York: Plenum.

Lazar, I., Darlington, R., Murray, H., Royce, J., & Snipper, A. (1982). Lasting effects of early education: A report from the Consortium for Longitudinal Studies. *Monographs of the Society for Research in Child Development*, **47**(2–3, Serial No. 195).

Levitt, M., Weber, R., & Clark, M. (1986). Social network relationships as sources of maternal support and well-being. *Developmental Psychology*, **22**, 310–316.

Lord, F. (1956). The measurement of growth. *Educational and Psychological Measurement,* **47,** 421–437.

Ludlow, J., & Allen, L. (1979). The effect of early intervention and pre-school stimulus on the development of the Down syndrome child. *Journal of Mental Deficiency Research,* **23,** 29–44.

MacTurk, R., Hunter, F., McCarthy, M., Vietze, P., & McQuiston, S. (1985). Social mastery motivation in Down syndrome and nondelayed infants. *Topics in Early Childhood Special Education,* **4,** 93–109.

Mahoney, G. (1983). A developmental analysis of communication between mothers and infants with Down syndrome. *Topics in Early Childhood Special Education,* **3,** 63–76.

Marshall, N., Hegrenes, J., & Goldstein, S. (1973). Verbal interactions: Mothers and their retarded children vs. mothers and their nonretarded children. *American Journal of Mental Deficiency,* **77,** 415–419.

Maurer, H., & Sherrod, K. (1987). Context of directives given to young children with Down syndrome and nonretarded children: Development over two years. *American Journal of Mental Deficiency,* **91,** 579–590.

McAllister, R., Butler, E., & Lei, T. (1973). Patterns of social interaction among families of behaviorally retarded children. *Journal of Marriage and the Family,* **35,** 93–100.

McBride, B. (1990). The effects of a parent/education/play group program on father involvement in child rearing. *Family Relations,* **39,** 250–256.

McCall, R. (1979). The development of intellectual functioning in infancy and the prediction of later I.Q. In J. Osofsky (Ed.), *Handbook of infant development.* New York: Wiley.

McCall, R. (1981). Nature-nurture and the two realms of development: A proposed integration with respect to mental development. *Child Development,* **52,** 1–12.

McCall, R. (1987). Developmental function, individual differences, and the plasticity of intelligence. In J. Gallagher & C. Ramey (Eds.), *The malleability of children.* Baltimore: Paul H. Brookes.

McCarthy, D. (1972). *McCarthy scales of children's abilities.* New York: Psychological Corp.

McCormick, M., Stemmler, M., & Athreya, B. (1986). The impact of childhood rheumatic diseases on the family. *Arthritis and Rheumatism,* **29,** 872–879.

McCubbin, H., & Patterson, J. (1983). The family stress process: The double ABCX model of adjustment and adaptation. In H. I. McCubbin, M. B. Sussman, & J. M. Patterson (Eds.), *Social stress and the family: Advances and developments in family stress theory and research.* New York: Haworth.

McCune, L., Kalmanson, B., Fleck, M. B., Glazewski, G., & Sillari, J. (1990). An interdisciplinary model of infant assessment. In S. Meisels & J. Shonkoff (Eds.), *Handbook of early childhood intervention.* New York: Cambridge University Press.

McKinney, B., & Peterson, R. (1987). Predictors of stress in parents of developmentally disabled children. *Journal of Pediatric Psychology,* **12,** 133–150.

McLinden-Mott, S., & Braeger, T. (1988). The impact on family scale: An adaptation for families of children with handicaps. *Journal of the Division for Early Childhood,* **12,** 217–223.

Meisels, S. (1985). The efficacy of early intervention: Why are we still asking this question? *Topics in Early Childhood Special Education,* **5,** 1–8.

Meisels, S. (1989). Meeting the mandate of Public Law 99–457: Early childhood intervention in the nineties. *American Journal of Orthopsychiatry,* **59,** 451–460.

Melito, R. (1985). Adaptation in family systems: A developmental perspective. *Family Process,* **24,** 89–100.

Minde, K., Shosenberg, N., Marton, P., Thompson, J., Ripley, J., & Burns, S. (1980). Self-help groups in a premature nursery: A controlled evaluation. *Pediatrics,* **96,** 933–940.

Minuchin, S. (1974). *Families and family therapy*. Cambridge, MA: Harvard University Press.

Moos, R., & Moos, B. (1976). A typology of family social environments. *Family Process,* **15,** 357–370.

Naglieri, J. (1981). Extrapolated developmental indices for the Bayley Scales of Infant Development. *American Journal of Mental Deficiency,* **85,** 548–550.

Noh, S., Dumas, J., Wolf, L., & Fisman, S. (1989). Delineating sources of stress in parents of exceptional children. *Family Relations,* **38,** 456–461.

Olson, C. L. (1976). On choosing a test statistic in multivariate analysis of variance. *Psychological Bulletin,* **83,** 579–586.

Olson, D., Bell, R., & Portner, J. (1982). *Family adaptability and cohesion evaluation scales (FACES II)*. St. Paul, MN: Family Social Science.

Olson, D., Russell, C., & Sprenkle, D. (1983). Circumplex model of marital and family systems: 6. Theoretical update. *Family Process,* **22,** 69–83.

Olson, S., Bates, J., & Bayles, K. (1984). Mother-infant interaction and the development of individual differences in children's cognitive competence. *Developmental Psychology,* **20,** 166–179.

Osofsky, J., & Connors, K. (1979). Mother-infant interaction: An integrative view of a complex system. In J. Osofsky (Ed.), *Handbook of infant development*. New York: Wiley.

Pearlin, L., & Schooler, C. (1978). The structure of coping. *Journal of Health and Social Behavior,* **19,** 2–21.

Piaget, J. (1952). *The origins of intelligence in children*. New York: International Universities Press.

Piper, M., Gosselin, C., Gendron, M., & Mazer, B. (1986). Developmental profile of Down's syndrome infants receiving early intervention. *Child: Care, Health, and Development,* **12,** 183–194.

Piper, M., & Pless, I. (1980). Early intervention for infants with Down syndrome: A controlled trial. *Pediatrics,* **65,** 463–468.

Provence, S., & Lipton, R. (1962). *Infants in institutions*. New York: International Universities Press.

Ramey, C., Yeates, K., & Short, E. (1984). The plasticity of intellectual development: Insights from preventive intervention. *Child Development,* **55,** 1913–1925.

Rauh, V., Achenbach, T., Nurcombe, B., Howell, C., & Teti, D. (1988). Minimizing adverse effects of low birth weight: Four-year results from an early intervention program. *Child Development,* **59,** 544–553.

Redding, R., Harmon, R., & Morgan, G. (1990). Relationships between maternal depression and infants' mastery behaviors. *Infant Behavior and Development,* **13,** 391–395.

Resnick, G. (1985). Enhancing parental competencies for high risk mothers: An evaluation of prevention effects. *Child Abuse and Neglect,* **9,** 479–489.

Riguet, B., Taylor, N., Benaroya, S., & Kline, L. (1981). Symbolic play in autistic, Down's and normal children of equivalent mental age. *Journal of Autism and Developmental Disorders,* **11,** 439–448.

Rogoff, B., Malkin, C., & Gilbride, K. (1984). Interaction with babies as guidance in development. In B. Rogoff & J. Wertsch (Eds.), *Children's learning in the "zone of proximal development."* San Francisco: Jossey-Bass.

Rogosa, D., & Willett, J. (1983). Demonstrating the reliability of the difference score in the measurement of change. *Journal of Educational Measurement,* **20,** 335–343.

Rosenberg, S., Robinson, C., Finkler, D., & Rose, J. (1987). An empirical comparison of formulas evaluating early intervention program impact on development. *Exceptional Children,* **54,** 213–219.

Rubin, K., Fein, G., & Vandenberg, B. (1983). Play. In E. M. Hetherington (Ed.), P. H.

Mussen (Series Ed.), *Handbook of child psychology: Vol. 4. Socialization, personality, and social development*. New York: Wiley.

Rutter, M. (1987). Continuities and discontinuities from infancy. In J. Osofsky (Ed.), *Handbook of infant development* (2d ed.). New York: Wiley.

Rynders, J., & Horrobin, J. (1980). Educational provisions for young children with Down's syndrome. In J. Gottlieb (Ed.), *Educating mentally retarded persons in the mainstream*. Baltimore: University Park Press.

Sameroff, A., & Chandler, M. (1975). Reproductive risk and the continuum of caretaking casualty. In F. Horowitz (Ed.), *Review of child development research* (Vol. 4). Chicago: University of Chicago Press.

Sameroff, A., Seifer, R., Barocas, B., Zax, M., & Greenspan, S. (1987). IQ scores of four-year-old children: Social-environmental risk factors. *Pediatrics, 79,* 343–350.

Scarr-Salapatek, S. (1976). An evolutionary perspective on infant intelligence: Species, patterns, and individual variations. In M. Lewis (Ed.), *Origins of intelligence*. New York: Plenum.

Schnell, R. (1984). Psychomotor development. In S. Peuschel (Ed.), *The young child with Down syndrome*. New York: Human Sciences.

Seltzer, M., & Ryff, C. (in press). Parenting across the lifespan: The normative and non-normative case. In D. Featherman, R. Lerner, & M. Perlmutter (Eds.), *Life-span development and behavior* (Vol. 12). Hillsdale, NJ: Erlbaum.

Sharav, T., Collins, R., & Shlomo, L. (1985). Effect of maternal education on prognosis of development in children with Down syndrome. *Pediatrics, 76,* 387–391.

Sharav, T., & Shlomo, L. (1986). Stimulation of infants with Down syndrome: Long-term effects. *Mental Retardation, 24,* 81–86.

Shonkoff, J., & Hauser-Cram, P. (1987). Early intervention for disabled infants and their families: A quantitative analysis. *Pediatrics, 80,* 650–658.

Shonkoff, J., Hauser-Cram, P., Krauss, M., & Upshur, C. (1988). Early intervention efficacy research: What have we learned and where do we go from here? *Topics in Early Childhood Special Education, 8,* 81–93.

Shonkoff, J., Hauser-Cram, P., Krauss, M., & Upshur, C. (1990). *The early intervention collaborative study: Final report of phase I*. Springfield, VA: U.S. Department of Commerce, National Technical Information Service.

Shonkoff, J., Jarman, F., & Kohlenberg, T. (1987). Family transitions, crises, and adaptations. *Current Problems in Pediatrics, 17,* 503–553.

Shonkoff, J., & Meisels, S. (1990). Early childhood intervention: The evolution of a concept. In S. Meisels & J. Shonkoff (Eds.), *Handbook of early childhood intervention*. New York: Cambridge University Press.

Simeonsson, R., Cooper, D., & Scheiner, A. (1982). A review and analysis of the effectiveness of early intervention programs. *Pediatrics, 69,* 635–641.

Singer, L., & Farkas, K. (1989). The impact of infant disability on maternal perception of stress. *Family Relations, 38,* 444–449.

Slate, N. (1983). Nonbiased assessment of adaptive behavior: Comparison of three instruments. *Exceptional Children, 50,* 67–70.

Slaughter, D. T. (1983). Early intervention and its effects on maternal and child development. *Monographs of the Society for Research in Child Development, 48*(4, Serial No. 202).

Smith, B., & Strain, P. (1988). Early childhood special education in the next decade: Implementing and expanding P.L. 99–457. *Topics in Early Childhood Special Education, 8,* 37–47.

Sparrow, S., Balla, D., & Cicchetti, D. (1984). *Vineland adaptive behavior scales: Expanded form manual*. Circle Pines, MN: American Guidance Service.

149

Spitz, R. (1945). Hospitalism: An inquiry into the genesis of psychiatric conditions in early childhood. In R. Eissler (Ed.), *Psychoanalytic study of the child.* New Haven, CT: Yale University Press.

Stein, R., & Jessop, D. (1982). A noncategorical approach to chronic childhood illness. *Public Health Reports,* **97,** 354–362.

Stein, R., & Jessop, D. (1984). Relationship between health status and psychological adjustment among children with chronic conditions. *Pediatrics,* **73,** 169–174.

Stein, R., & Reissman, C. (1980). The development of an Impact-on-Family Scale: Preliminary findings. *Medical Care,* **18,** 465–472.

Stern, D. (1974). Mother and infant at play. In M. Lewis & L. A. Rosenblum (Eds.), *The effect of the infant on its caregiver.* New York: Wiley.

Stoneman, Z., & Brody, G. (1981). Two's company, three makes a difference: An examination of mothers' and fathers' speech to their young children. *Child Development,* **52,** 705–707.

Stoneman, Z., Brody, G., & Abbott, D. (1983). In-home observations of young Down syndrome children with their mothers and fathers. *American Journal of Mental Deficiency,* **87,** 591–600.

Strain, P., & Smith, B. (1986). A counter-interpretation of early intervention effects: A response to Casto and Mastropieri. *Exceptional Children,* **53,** 260–265.

Suelzle, M., & Keenan, V. (1981). Changes in family support networks over the life cycle of mentally retarded persons. *American Journal of Mental Deficiency,* **3,** 267–274.

Tamis-LeMonda, C., & Bornstein, M. (1989). Habituation and maternal encouragement of attention in infancy as predictors of toddler language, play, and representational competence. *Child Development,* **60,** 738–751.

Terdal, L., Jackson, R., & Garner, A. (1976). Mother-child interactions: A comparison between normal and developmentally delayed groups. In E. J. Marsh, L. A. Hammerlynck, & L. C. Handy (Eds.), *Behavior modification for families.* New York: Brunner/Mazel.

Tew, B., & Laurence, K. (1975). Some sources of stress found in mothers of spina bifida children. *British Journal of Preventive and Social Medicine,* **29,** 27–30.

Turnbull, A., Summers, J., & Brotherson, M. (1986). Family life cycle: Theoretical and empirical implications and future directions for families with mentally retarded members. In J. J. Gallagher & P. M. Vietze (Eds.), *Families of handicapped persons: Research, programs, and policy issues.* Baltimore: Paul H. Brookes.

Upshur, C. (1992). Mothers' and fathers' ratings of the benefits of early intervention services. *Journal of Early Intervention,* **15,** 345–357.

Vietze, P., Abernathy, S., Ashe, M., & Faulstich, G. (1978). Contingency interaction between mothers and their developmentally delayed infants. In G. P. Sackett (Ed.), *Observing behavior* (Vol. 1). Baltimore: University Park Press.

Vygotsky, L. (1978). *Mind in society: The development of higher psychological processes.* Cambridge, MA: Harvard University Press.

Vygotsky, L. (1986). *Thought and language.* Cambridge, MA: MIT Press.

Waddington, C. (1957). *The strategy of the genes.* London: Allen.

Walsh, F. (Ed.). (1980). *Normal family processes.* New York: Guilford.

Waters, E., & Sroufe, A. (1983). Social competence as a developmental construct. *Developmental Review,* **3,** 79–97.

Watson, R., & Midlarsky, E. (1979). Reactions of mothers with mentally retarded children: A social perspective. *Psychological Reports,* **45,** 309–310.

Weisz, J., Yeates, K., & Zigler, E. (1982). Piagetian evidence and the developmental-difference controversy. In E. Zigler & D. Balla (Eds.), *Mental retardation: The developmental-difference controversy.* Hillsdale, NJ: Erlbaum.

Werner, E., & Smith, R. (1982). *Vulnerable but invincible—a study of resilient children.* New York: McGraw-Hill.

White, K., Bush, D., & Casto, G. (1985). Learning from reviews of early intervention. *Journal of Special Education,* **19,** 417–428.

White, K., Mastropieri, M., & Casto, G. (1984). An analysis of special education early childhood projects approved by the Joint Dissemination Review Panel. *Journal of the Division of Early Childhood,* **9,** 11–26.

White, R. (1959). Motivation reconsidered: The concept of competence. *Psychological Review,* **66,** 297–333.

Wikler, L., Wasow, M., & Hatfield, E. (1981). Chronic sorrow revisited: Parent vs. professional depiction of the adjustment of parents of mentally retarded children. *American Journal of Orthopsychiatry,* **51,** 63–70.

Willett, J. (1988). Questions and answers in the measurement of change. In E. R. Rothkopf (Ed.), *Review of research in education* (Vol. **15**). Washington, DC: American Educational Research Association.

Wolery, M. (1983). Proportional change index: An alternative for comparing child change data. *Exceptional Children,* **50,** 167–170.

Woodhead, M. (1988). When psychology informs public policy: The case of early childhood intervention. *American Psychologist,* **43,** 443–454.

Woods, P., Corney, M., & Pryce, G. (1984). Developmental progress of preschool Down's syndrome children receiving a home-advisory service: An interim report. *Child: Care, Health, and Development,* **10,** 287–299.

Wortman, C., & Conway, T. (1985). The role of social support in adaptation and recovery from physical illness. In S. Cohen & S. L. Syme (Eds.), *Social support and health.* Orlando, FL: Academic.

Zigler, E., & Balla, D. (Eds.). (1982). *Mental retardation: The developmental-difference controversy.* Hillsdale, NJ: Erlbaum.

Zigler, E., & Berman, W. (1983). Discerning the future of early childhood intervention. *American Psychologist,* **38,** 894–906.

Zigler, E., & Trickett, P. (1978). IQ, social competence, and evaluation of early childhood intervention programs. *American Psychologist,* **33,** 789–798.

Zimmerman, D., & Williams, R. (1982). Gain scores in research can be highly reliable. *Journal of Educational Measurement,* **19,** 149–154.

# ACKNOWLEDGMENTS

The first phase of the Early Intervention Collaborative Study was supported by grant MCJ-250533 from the Maternal and Child Health Bureau (Title V, Social Security Act), Health Resources and Services Administration, U.S. Department of Health and Human Services, and by a grant from the Jessie B. Cox Charitable Trust, Boston.

We would like to thank the children, families, and early intervention service providers in Massachusetts and New Hampshire who made this project possible. We are deeply grateful for the generous contribution of their time and for their belief in the importance of this investigation.

The broad scope of the study and the successful completion of its first phase reflect the combined efforts of the following individuals:

Helene Chaika Fausold (project coordinator); Kathy Antaki, Dot Marsden, and Ann Steele (research coordinators); Marji Erickson and Gary Resnick (data managers); Seny Bynum, Paul Carmichael, Caroline Fish, Joanne Giuttari, Elaine LeClair, Norma Lee, Patricia McLean, Mary Muse, Ann Odessey, Deborah Pease, Patricia Place, Martha Pott, Naomi Schiffman, Karen Stiles, Elaine Dyer Tarquinio, Ann Taylor, and Michael Thomasgard (research assistants); Eileen Chick, Joanne Delaney, Sandra Duguay, Diane Garcia, Virginia Gow, Deborah Masri, Gladys Rivera, Debra Roy, and Brenda Trombley (administrative and secretarial staff); Karen Adams, Chris Luikey, Kathy Noone, and Ruth Osuch (data coding staff); and Mark Appelbaum, Richard Light, Terrence Tivnan, and Deborah Klein Walker (technical advisers).

*Professional Advisory Board.*—Betsy Anderson (Federation for Children with Special Needs), Allen Crocker (Boston Children's Hospital), Louis Freedman (Massachusetts Department of Public Health), Sharon Goldsmith (Massachusetts Department of Education), F. Kristin Hoeveler (Early Intervention Network of New Hampshire), Margo Kaplan-Sanoff (Wheelock College), Karl Kastorf (Massachusetts Department of Public Health), Susan McBride (Wheelock College), Lorraine Sanik (Massachusetts Early Intervention Consortium), Elizabeth Schaefer (Massachusetts Department of Education), Eunice Shishmanian (Massachusetts Interagency Coordinating Council), and Carole Thomson (Massachusetts Department of Education).

*Parent Advisory Board.*—Frank Galligan, Realer Hamilton, Phyllis Hannon, Maura Kellem, Judith Leccese, Glen Rosenberg, Penny Tannenbaum, and Linda Wells.

*Participating Early Intervention Programs.*—Ann Sullivan Center (Tewksbury, MA), Brockton Early Childhood Intervention (Brockton, MA), Cape Cod Child Development Program, Inc. (Hyannis, MA), Concord Area Early Intervention Program (Concord, MA), Developmental Services Unit (Fitchburg, MA), Early Intervention and Family Support Program (Worcester, MA), Early Intervention Program (Nashua, NH), First Program (Weymouth, MA), Harbor Area Early Intervention Program (East Boston, MA), Infant/Toddler Developmental Program of the United Cerebral Palsy Association of the North Shore, Inc. (Lynn, MA), Middlesex Child Development Center (Framingham, MA), Mystic Valley Early Intervention Program (Winchester, MA), New England Memorial Hospital (Stoneham, MA), Parent-Infant Development Program (Concord, NH), Pediatric Development Center (Pittsfield, MA), Pioneer Developmental Center, Inc. (Chicopee, MA), Preschool Unit Early Intervention Program (Cambridge, MA), Program for Children with Special Developmental Needs of the Newton Guidance Clinic (Newton, MA), the REACH Program (Northampton, MA), the Richie McFarland Children's Center (Stratham, NH), RISE Program (Keene, NH), SNARC Early Intervention Program (Medfield, MA), South Central Early Intervention Program (Southbridge, MA), Step One Early Intervention Program of the South Shore Mental Health Center (Quincy, MA), Taunton Area Early Intervention Program (Taunton, MA), Valley Child Development Center (Milford, MA), Valley Infant Development Service (Springfield, MA), Vinfen Corporation (Brighton, MA), Waltham Hospital Early Intervention Program (Waltham, MA), West Ros Park Early Intervention Program (Roslindale, MA), and WISE Program (Gardner, MA).

Finally, the staff would like to express appreciation to the Starr Center for Mental Retardation, Heller School, Brandeis University, for administrative support, to Boston College for assistance with graphics, and to the Eliot Pearson Department of Child Study at Tufts University and the Early Intervention and Family Support Program at the University of Massachusetts Medical Center for assistance in pilot testing of child and family measures. A special note of appreciation is extended to Gontran Lamberty, Vince Hutchins, Woodie Kessel, Merle McPherson, and the Research Review Committee from the Maternal and Child Health Bureau, Department of Health and Human Services, and to Ala Reid and Mary Phillips from the Jessie B. Cox Charitable Trust, for their ongoing support.

## SYSTEMS, DEVELOPMENT, AND EARLY INTERVENTION

*Arnold J. Sameroff*

If I were asked to identify the most important advance in developmental research in the last quarter century, my answer would be the study of behavior in context. In the cross-cultural literature, there has always been a clear recognition that context is a major factor in social, emotional, and even cognitive differences among children. But what has changed, more recently, is the recognition that within cultures there are microenvironments that have profound effects on the life course of children. Some of these microenvironments can be classified as subcultures where the customs, values, and beliefs of one group can be differentiated from those of other groups, as in comparisons among Hispanic, Asian, and Euro-Americans (Dornbusch, Ritter, Leiderman, & Roberts, 1987); other microenvironments are classified by the number of risk and protective factors that impinge on children and their families, as in comparisons between high- and low-risk families (Sameroff, Seifer, Baldwin, & Baldwin, 1993); and other microenvironments are distinguished by the specific social institutions with which families are involved, as in demonstrations that specific schools within the same community have different effects on their students (Rutter, Maugham, Mortimer, & Ouston, 1979).

A further advance in the definition of context has been the differentiation of families as microenvironments for child development. Where there was an earlier singular emphasis on the role of maternal practices as determinants of child outcome, not only have other family members been added as research targets (e.g., fathers and grandparents; Parke, 1981), but the family is now considered as an interacting system with holistic properties that impinge on the behavior of its members. Still more recent has been the emphasis on the differential effect of families on distinct children in the same family, further expanding the definition of the proximal microsystem for each member of the family (Plomin & Daniels, 1987).

In parallel with the expanded study of context has been the expanded study of process in developmental research. Where earlier investigators sought the secret of development in prior individual differences among children or in social addresses in the environment, current work is directed at how individuals with differing characteristics interact with different contexts to produce different outcomes (Bronfenbrenner, 1979).

As with all major advances, there are dialectically produced antitheses that undercut their progress. As the importance of context became clearer and clearer, it became more and more intransigent to study. When context was defined as maternal practice, it was relatively easy to bring a mother and child into the laboratory and get the mother to vary her behavior in order to study the effects on the child. With context now defined as the micro-, meso-, exo-, and macrosphere of all social institutions from the most proximal to the most distal, it is impossible to use traditional research models. In investigations of the role of nurture, children cannot be assigned to families, cultures, or societies, and, in investigations of nature, intelligence, personality, and disability cannot be assigned to children. It is a testament to the motivation of behavioral scientists that, despite this growth in complexity, they continue to wrestle with these issues.

These remarks provide the context for a commentary on this provocative *Monograph*. The authors have examined the interfaces among children, families, and social institutions with a high level of complexity. They have studied what happens to developmentally delayed and disabled children and their families when they involve themselves in early intervention programs. Their findings relate to major questions about development, the nature-nurture question, the effects of family practice, and the intended and unintended effects of involvement with social institutions.

I would like to organize my remarks around three topics raised by the reading of this *Monograph*. The first is the light that it sheds on the study of social systems, that is, individuals in the context of institutions; the second is the light that it sheds on the study of development through the use of disabled populations as natural experiments in human growth; and the third is the ability of intervention programs to manipulate development, for better or worse.

## Social Systems

The authors stay away from linear models of effects on the child by proposing that characteristics of families and their social support networks mediate between intervention programs and child progress in adaptive behavior. The authors discuss the effects of social policy on programs, of programs on families, and of programs and families on children. What their data offer in addition is the ability to examine reciprocal effects as well, the influence of children on families and of children and families on early intervention programs.

The authors clearly recognize that, by studying children in their natural environments, it will be difficult to go beyond descriptions of their findings. While correlations and regressions entice one to make causal interpretations, the inability to control which children with which disabilities are born into which families and placed in which programs forces one to look at both directions of effects in any analysis. The lack of random assignment further raises the question of whether an unstudied third factor may be producing the correlations between any two of the examined variables.

To begin with the influence of social policy on programs, there is a striking effect of Public Law 99-457 in that all the 29 early intervention programs shared a common philosophy characterized by an integrated family and child orientation with individualized goals for the family as well as the child. This is in marked contrast to what would have been the case in the past, when local custom and finances fostered a variety of philosophies. But within this top-down effect there was substantial opportunity for variation in bottom-up interpretation of the federal mandate such that the variability of programs was one of the important points of this study. Children with the same type or level of disability got very different amounts of service, even within a single program. Whether these differences in treatment were related more to program than to child needs is an important unanswered question.

Program effects on children is of central concern to a study of early intervention, and here we are faced with another strength and limitation of the study. The strength was the importance placed on the longitudinal study of the sample in order to examine individual change in families and children. The limitation was that 12 months makes for a very short longitudinal study, especially in the arena of early development. One of the points emphasized by the authors, and one to which I shall return, is that what goes on during the first 12 months of development may be under very different control than what happens during ensuing years. What does happen is that the vast majority of the children improve in all domains of functioning. However, and this is a very provocative "however," almost none of these changes are related to program variables. Where the trend of programs is to become multifaceted and multidisciplinary, the finding was that more child progress was associated with having a unidisciplinary treatment. But even this effect disappeared when severity of impairment was controlled. In other words, the less severe the disability, the more the children progressed. Children with less severe impairments received more unidisciplinary treatment than those with more severe impairments. With what conclusion is the reader left? A simple one is that intervention for these children is irrelevant. A counterargument is that a no-treatment control group would have produced far less developmental progress than any program. Unfortunately, we will never know because there was no no-treatment group in the study—nor is there ever likely to be in our social context. Legal and ethical considerations mandate that every disabled child be placed in an early intervention program.

A more complex conclusion is that, although early intervention programs may not be strongly affecting child development, their family orientation is strengthening the mediators of later child development, the parents, and their involvement with support systems. So what are the effects of programs on parents? Parental stress was reduced when services were delivered through a single discipline but not when they were delivered through multiple ones. Parental social networks increased in size where services were received in a group format rather than only in an individualized one. However, when the group format involved family group meetings, the mothers reported increased strain, an undesired finding. Confounding this was the finding that parents who participated in group activities had children who were making less progress during the year. One can see the complexity of interpretation needed for these data and the long list of unanswerable questions.

As a beginning, one can turn the arrows around and examine the effects of children and parents on programs or, more specifically, on program utilization. It is easier to make a case that parents of children who are not making good progress are more likely to involve themselves in more program components than to infer that being involved with more programs slows down the child's progress. I have already mentioned the finding that severity of child disability usually elicited multidisciplinary rather than unidisciplinary treatment. Furthermore, the developmental status of the children had an important effect. The older the child, the more interdisciplinary involvement. It is not surprising that, as children advance in cognitive and linguistic abilities, additional therapies can be added to motor therapies.

Another child effect is the type of disorder. An expected outcome is that different child diagnoses should elicit different treatments. An uncontrollable feature of disabled infants is that different disabilities become identifiable at different ages, and, consequently, entrance into early intervention programs is at different ages. Down syndrome is identified at birth, motor impairments are found during the first year of life, and developmental delays are not usually noted until the second year. Would age be confounded with diagnosis in the treatment of these children? The answer is not clear. The youngest and oldest groups, the Down syndrome and the developmentally delayed, respectively, received more similar treatment than the group that is between those two in age, the motor-impaired children. The strongest main effect was produced by the severity of disorder. The more severely disabled infants received more home visits, received more center-based child group treatment, and had mothers who were more likely to participate in parent groups. However, there was an interaction in that the severely disabled children and parents in the motor-impaired group, which had the highest proportion, were less likely to participate in center-based and group activities. What is the explanation for these child effects? What is there about families of motor-impaired infants that leads them to seek or get different patterns of services than other children with similar ages or severity of handicap? We find here both the strength and the weakness of naturalistic approaches. Descriptive studies reveal for us a wider range of phenomena than can be examined in a laboratory or a controlled demonstration program, but not their explanation.

This *Monograph* illuminates the kinds of interactions and transactions within a complex system of disabled children, families, and social programs that will require further investigation, especially the problems inherent in such naturalistic approaches that even a more extended longitudinal investigation may not be able to answer.

### Development

The study of context requires that analyses of development not be restricted to the child but be extended to the family and social institutions of which the child is a part. I have already noted the development of early intervention services in reaction to changes in public law. This *Monograph* did not take such changes as its focus, but it clearly documents the state of such services at this point in time.

When we turn to family and child development, we must again ask bidirectional questions. Do data on normative child and family development influence our understanding of family development with atypical children, and do data on family functioning with atypical children influence our understanding of more typical children and their families?

The analyses of data in the *Monograph* do not use normative studies of family development as a source of hypotheses. A major phase in the development of families is the birth of the first child and the consequent changes in distribution of family time, financial resources, and emotional resources. It is a time of increased stress, emotional distancing between spouses, and decreased marital satisfaction for husbands that does not dissipate for more than a year (Cowan & Cowan, 1990). It would have been interesting to examine the effects of the disabled child on the family in light of these normative life-cycle data. One would hypothesize that families for whom the study child was a firstborn, about a third of the sample, would have reacted differently than families for whom the child was a later born.

With regard to lessons for normative family development, there is a compelling finding of the *Monograph* that strongly warrants description. It is that, for most families, the birth of a disabled child may not have produced major changes. The stable level of family adaptation shown by a preponderance of families was striking to the authors. This conclusion is tempered somewhat by the lack of information on the family's reaction to the initial diagnosis of the child, which most certainly would have produced emotional distress. What appears to happen is that parents are committed to rearing their children and that this commitment is not negated by the birth of a child with some mild problems. On the other hand, children with severe disabilities did significantly increase parenting stress and adverse family effects.

In contrast to many studies of intervention programs, the sample of families in this *Monograph* is fairly well off, fairly well educated, with mostly intact marriages, and not living in inner-city environments. It is an important sample to study because it allows the separation of the effects of rearing a disabled child from the effects of rearing a disabled child in an overburdened family. The funding of many early intervention demonstration and research programs requires that the sample be composed of multiproblem families. In those cases, it is difficult to find successful program effects where interventions are geared to changing single aspects of chaotic lives. In many such cases, the successful rearing of any child, disabled or not, would be a major problem. Thus, it is impossible to separate the stressful effects of having a disabled child from the stressful effects of life in general.

The relatively advantaged families in the current study had good home environments for the children and expressed feelings of competence at being able to rear their children. However, at a more proximal level, mother-infant interactions were initially characterized by difficulties in the behavior of both partners, and, even though the infants became better responders during the year of the study, the mothers did not show comparable improvements. Questions about future family development remain unanswered by the data presented here. Will the parents progress to better interaction patterns in keeping with better general levels of social adaptation, or will the low levels of interactional competence spread to other areas of family functioning? An additional question is how family progress will interact with the type and severity of child disability. The most stressed fathers and mothers were in families with a motor-impaired child.

With respect to the core concern of our discipline, child development, the authors are struck with their finding that there is little program influence on the growth of the children in the sample. Uncorrelated with intervention efforts, these infants progressed through the early stages of development on a fairly predictable timetable, except for the most severely disabled. Following McCall (1981), the investigators conclude that early development is under strong biological control and less influenced by environmental variation than development after the first 2 years of life. It is true that cultural and social status differences in the IQ and language scores of normative populations do not appear until the second year of life (Sameroff & Seifer, 1983; Wilson, 1985). But does this mean that younger infants are impervious to experience? I think not. I believe that developmental models should retain as much consistency as possible in the face of the multiple factors and levels of organization that must be considered in the study of human growth. From this parsimonious perspective, if there is little variance in infant development, then there must be little variance in infant experience. Universal sequences of development are not the result of maturational, preordained factors. They are the result of organisms developing in contexts where experiences are highly buffered. In embryonic stages of human life, experience, albeit biological experience, plays a crucial role in the sequencing of every physical change; no gene turns on or off without the effect of some contextual biological experience. The marvelous thing about ontogeny is that it takes place in a highly insulated uterine environment that is buffered from the typical variations experienced by the mother. Despite this buffering, there are atypical experiences that can have major deviating effects on the fetus. Examples would include the action of drugs such as Thalidomide, excessive consumption of alcohol, and the effects of radiation. These teratogens, mostly too new to have allowed the human species adequate time to evolve effective compensating mechanisms, offer testimony to the effects of experience in even the most tightly regulated developmental system.

Early postnatal development has a similar uniformity of relevant experience. The key conceptual requirement here is to determine what experience is relevant for each phase of infant growth. The key capacities of young infants are centered in their perceptual and motor skills. The relevant experiences are perceptual and motor encounters. To the extent that all infants experience sounds, sights, tastes, smells, and a concrete three-dimensional world, they will have uniform experiences that should facilitate their progress. This universality is true for almost all human cultures. Developmental deviations occur only when such universality of experience is not forthcoming because of either limitations in the infant or limitations in context. On the contextual side are cultures where infant experience is systematically limited, as in the Guatemalan Indian villages described by Kagan and Klein (1973). Infants were swaddled on cradle boards for the first 2 years of life and showed marked delay of motor skills on developmental tests. (Parenthetically, when they were released from the cradle boards, they soon caught up to peers in other less-restrictive cultures.) On the infant side are cases where perceptual or motor abilities are limited, either centrally, in the case of brain damage, or peripherally, in the case of some forms of blindness or deafness. In these instances, development may be permanently arrested unless or until adequate prosthetic devices or treatments are provided.

The limitation of the report in the current *Monograph* is that we do not know what will happen to these children. We do not know if "sleeper" effects of early intervention will appear during later periods of development or if variations in parenting skills will begin to show up as variations in child adaptive behavior. The lessons of longitudinal research with other populations, both normal and biologically "at risk," are that we can expect to see the effects of social variation when the infants are more competent to experience such variation.

## Intervention

An overview of programs for early intervention has to deal with two related but distinctly different questions. The first question is why we have early intervention programs. The second is whether they are effective in changing child behavior and outcomes. The first question requires a cultural answer, the second a scientific one.

Early intervention programs exist because there is a need for them. Children are born with a variety of atypical behaviors that have been associated with current or later social and cognitive dysfunctions. In addition, the care of many of these children requires skills that are not within the capacity of the average parent. Whether programs are effective or not, there will still be a need for them as a social institution. The best of them may be using state-of-the-art programming. Whether state of the art is good enough is a different question. The social need for intervention programs regardless of effectiveness is not unique to education. Before bypass surgery, cardiac surgeons did another procedure in which they opened the chest and sprinkled talcum powder on the heart. That the procedure was not a very helpful one was not a significant reason to stop doing the surgery. Surgeons stopped doing the talcum procedure only when a new procedure came along. They will continue doing bypass surgery until another new procedure comes along. Whether cardiac surgery is valid or not, surgeons must perform it because members of society have heart problems.

Early interventionists will continue to do early intervention as long as there are children who need treatment. Scientists cannot alter these programs by arguing that their activities are ineffective. The only way that these programs will change is if there is a clear demonstration that a new procedure produces better results than the current one. The results of many evaluations of the effects of early intervention with disabled children do not strongly support the effects of current efforts (Castro & Mastropieri, 1986). This *Monograph* does not take a stand on this issue. The study assessed most modes of treatment being offered and found only weak support for program success. The authors do not confront this issue in their conclusions. Instead, they take a different tack in stating that early intervention is a complex, multidimensional enterprise whose components have differential effects. They recommend that programs have flexible service models to address the needs of children and families. Unfortunately, their data do not point to which components will be most successful for which needs.

Intervention with infants has progressed through a number of phases in recent history as hard lessons were learned about program efficacy or the lack thereof (Guralnick & Bennett, 1987). Many benefits of programs were accompanied by unexpected iatrogenic effects where children and families showed evidence of increased suffering. On the child side, behavior modification programs facilitated learning and interaction with the environment but may have hindered self-esteem by placing the child in the position of never achieving complete success. No matter how far the child advanced in the program, there was always another step in the shaping process. With regard to parents, training them in program components augmented their skills in facilitating child progress but created interactional problems when they saw their roles as teachers rather than as parents (Wright, Granger, & Sameroff, 1984). Parent groups that offered mothers and sometimes fathers the opportunity to share worries and emotional reactions were interpreted as intrusive by some parents, increasing rather than decreasing their stress. My conclusion from all this is similar to that of the authors of this *Monograph*. Different families have different needs and capacities to benefit from intervention programs.

A false sense of progress is found in most early intervention programs in that infant development does go on in spite of disabilities, poor parenting, and ineffective treatments. The findings of this *Monograph* are important in emphasizing the powerful thrust of early development. The data from the *Monograph* do not reveal what went on in the therapy and intervention groups. It is not clear whether individual or family procedures were good or bad or whether therapists were good or bad. It is not clear whether current program components bode well or ill for the future of these families. On the other hand, a real sense of progress can be found in reports such as this *Monograph* where attempts are made to describe what happens to children and families in real situations that may have profound importance for their development. I am sure that we will find the answers to many of these questions in the next report of this important longitudinal study.

## References

Bronfenbrenner, U. (1979). *The ecology of human development: Experiments by nature and design.* Cambridge, MA: Harvard University Press.
Castro, G., & Mastropieri, M. A. (1986). The efficacy of early intervention programs: A meta-analysis. *Exceptional Children, 52,* 417–424.
Cowan, P. A., & Cowan, C. P. (1990). Becoming a family: Research and intervention. In I. Sigel & E. Brody (Eds.), *Family Research* (Vol. 1). Hillsdale, NJ: Erlbaum.
Dornbusch, S. M., Ritter, P. L., Leiderman, P. H., & Roberts, D. F. (1987). The relation of parenting style to adolescent school performance. *Child Development, 58,* 1244–1255.
Guralnick, M. J., & Bennett, F. C. (1987). Early intervention for at-risk and handicapped children: Current and future perspectives. In M. J. Guralnick & F. C. Bennett (Eds.), *The effectiveness of early intervention for at-risk and handicapped children.* San Diego: Academic.
Kagan, J., & Klein, R. (1973). Cross-cultural perspectives on early development. *American Psychologist, 28,* 947–961.
McCall, R. (1981). Nature-nurture and the two realms of development: A proposed integration with respect to mental development. *Child Development, 52,* 1–12.
Parke, R. D. (1981). *Fathers.* Cambridge, MA: Harvard University Press.
Plomin, R., & Daniels, D. (1987). Why are children in the same family so different from each other? *Behavioral and Brain Sciences, 10,* 1–16.
Rutter, M., Maughan, B., Mortimore, P., & Ouston, J. (1979). *Fifteen thousand hours: Secondary schools and their effects on children.* London: Open Books.
Sameroff, A. J., & Seifer, R. (1983). Familial risk and child competence. *Child Development, 54,* 1254–1268.
Sameroff, A. J., Seifer, R., Baldwin, A., & Baldwin, C. (in press). Stability of intelligence from preschool to adolescence: The influence of social and family risk factors. *Child Development, 63,* 234–265.
Wilson, R. S. (1985). Risk and resilience in early mental development. *Developmental Psychology, 21,* 795–805.
Wright, J. S., Granger, R. D., & Sameroff, A. J. (1984). Developmental implications of parental acceptance of a handicapped child. In J. Blacher (Ed.), *Severely handicapped children and their families: Research in review.* New York: Academic.

**Jack P. Shonkoff** (M.D. 1972, New York University School of Medicine) is professor of pediatrics and chief of the Division of Developmental and Behavioral Pediatrics at the University of Massachusetts Medical School. His professional interests focus on atypical development in infancy, family adaptation to childhood disability, and the effect of early intervention services on developmentally vulnerable children and their parents. He has received fellowships from the W. K. Kellogg Foundation and the National Center for Clinical Infant Programs, has served as a consultant and panel member for the Committee on Child Development Research and Public Policy of the National Academy of Sciences, and is a member of the Board of Directors of the National Center for Clinical Infant Programs. He is associate editor of the *Infant Mental Health Journal,* serves on the editorial boards of several scholarly journals, and is the editor (with Samuel Meisels) of the *Handbook of Early Childhood Intervention* (1990).

**Penny Hauser-Cram** (Ed.D. 1983, Harvard Graduate School of Education) is assistant professor of education at Boston College and an associate in pediatrics at the University of Massachusetts Medical School. Her work has concentrated on the investigation of the effectiveness of educational and support programs for young children and their families. Her current interests focus on the development of competence in children with typical and atypical development. She is the editor (with F. Martin) of *Essays on Educational Research: Methodology, Testing, and Application* (1983) and the author (with D. Pierson, D. Walker, and T. Tivnan) of *Early Education in the Public Schools: Lessons from a Comprehensive Birth to Kindergarten Program* (1991).

**Marty Wyngaarden Krauss** (Ph.D. 1981, Brandeis University) is associate professor of social welfare at the Heller School at Brandeis University and director of social science research at the Eunice Kennedy Shriver Center for Mental Retardation. She is also an associate in pediatrics at the University of Massachusetts Medical School. Krauss's research focuses on the development of community-based services for persons with mental retardation and on the effects of mental retardation on families throughout the life span. She is the editor (with Matthew Janicki and Marsha Seltzer) of *Community Residences for Persons with Developmental Disabilities: Here to Stay* (1988) and author (with Marsha Seltzer) of *Aging and Mental Retardation* (1987). She is also the editor (with Sharon Landesman Ramey and Rune Simeonsson) of a special issue on research on families for the *American Journal on Mental Retardation* (1989). She was a 1990 recipient of the Future Leaders in Mental Retardation Award from the Joseph P. Kennedy, Jr., Foundation.

**Carole Christofk Upshur** (Ed.D. 1975, Harvard Graduate School of Education) is an associate professor in the College of Public and Community Service at the University of Massachusetts at Boston and an associate in pediatrics at the University of Massachusetts Medical School. Her work has focused most recently on the planning and evaluation of services for young children with disabilities and their families and encompasses policy analysis and evaluation research on a range of issues affecting families and children at risk. Among her publications are "Early Intervention as Preventive Intervention," in *Handbook of Early Childhood Intervention*, ed. S. Meisels and J. Shonkoff (1990); "Measuring Parent Outcomes in Family Program Evaluation," in *Evaluating Family Programs*, ed. H. Weiss and F. Jacobs (1988); "Caretaking Burden and Social Support: A Comparison of Mothers of Children with and without Disabilities" (with M. Erickson), *American Journal on Mental Retardation* (1989); and "Respite Care for the Retarded and Other Disabled Populations: Program Models and Family Needs," *Mental Retardation* (1982).

**Arnold J. Sameroff** (Ph.D. 1965, Yale University) is a research scientist at the Center for Human Growth and Development and professor of psychology at the University of Michigan at Ann Arbor. He is the editor (with R. N. Emde) of *Relationship Disturbances in Early Infancy: A Development Approach* (1989); the coeditor (with F. S. Kessel and M. H. Bornstein) of *Contemporary Constructions of the Child: Essays in Honor of William Kessen* (1991); the author (with R. Seifer and M. Zax) of *Early Development of Children at Risk for Emotional Disorder* (*Monographs of the Society for Research in Child Development*, Serial No. 199, 1982), and the editor of *Organization and Stability of Newborn Behavior: A Commentary on the Brazelton Neonatal Behavioral Assessment Scale* (*Monographs of the Society for Research in Child Development*, Serial No. 177, 1978). His interests are in developing models of human growth integrating biological capacities and environmental constraints in the areas of development disabilities and developmental psychopathology.

The *Monographs* series is intended as an outlet for major reports of developmental research that generate authoritative new findings and use these to foster a fresh and/or better-integrated perspective on some conceptually significant issue or controversy. Submissions from programmatic research projects are particularly welcome; these may consist of individually or group-authored reports of findings from some single large-scale investigation or of a sequence of experiments centering on some particular question. Multiauthored sets of independent studies that center on the same underlying question can also be appropriate; a critical requirement in such instances is that the various authors address common issues and that the contribution arising from the set as a whole be both unique and substantial. In essence, irrespective of how it may be framed, any work that contributes significant data and/or extends developmental thinking will be taken under editorial consideration.

Submissions should contain a minimum of 80 manuscript pages (including tables and references); the upper limit of 150–175 pages is much more flexible (please submit four copies; a copy of every submission and associated correspondence is deposited eventually in the archives of the SRCD). Neither membership in the Society for Research in Child Development nor affiliation with the academic discipline of psychology are relevant; the significance of the work in extending developmental theory and in contributing new empirical information is by far the most crucial consideration. Because the aim of the series is not only to advance knowledge on specialized topics but also to enhance cross-fertilization among disciplines or subfields, it is important that the links between the specific issues under study and larger questions relating to developmental processes emerge as clearly to the general reader as to specialists on the given topic.

Potential authors who may be unsure whether the manuscript they are planning would make an appropriate submission are invited to draft an outline of what they propose and send it to the Editor for assessment.

This mechanism, as well as a more detailed description of all editorial policies, evaluation processes, and format requirements, is given in the "Guidelines for the Preparation of *Monographs* Submissions," which can be obtained by writing to Wanda C. Bronson, Institute of Human Development, 1203 Tolman Hall, University of California, Berkeley, CA 94720.